INSIDE TRACK

My Professional Life in Amateur Track and Field

≡

CARL LEWIS

with Jeffrey Marx

A FIRESIDE BOOK
Published by Simon & Schuster
New York   London   Toronto   Sydney   Tokyo   Singapore

F

FIRESIDE
Simon & Schuster Building
Rockefeller Center
1230 Avenue of the Americas
New York, New York 10020

Copyright © 1990, 1992 by Carl Lewis and Jeffrey Marx

First Fireside Edition 1992

FIRESIDE and colophon are registered trademarks
of Simon & Schuster Inc.

Designed by Irving Perkins Associates
Manufactured in the United States of America

1 3 5 7 9 10 8 6 4 2

1 3 5 7 9 10 8 6 4 2 Pbk.

Library of Congress Cataloging in Publication Data

Lewis, Carl, date.
Inside track: my professional life in amateur track and field /
Carl Lewis; with Jeffrey Marx.
p.   cm.
"A Fireside book."
Originally published: New York: Simon & Schuster, © 1990.
Includes index.
1. Lewis, Carl, date.   2. Track and field athletes—United
States—Biography.   I. Marx, Jeffrey, date.   II. Title.
GV697.L48A3   1992
796.42′092—dc20
[B]   92-750
                                                        CIP
ISBN 0-671-68937-1
ISBN 0-671-78024-7 Pbk.

There have been wonderful times and tragedies. This book is dedicated to three people who have shared both with me: Dalton "Chip" Benson, Andre Ramey, and my father, William McKinley Lewis. Dad, I'll be all right, and I'll always love you, too.

—CARL LEWIS

These pages are written for Mom, Dad, Jim, and Wendy. They are also written for the heroes who save lives through organ donation and transplantation.

—JEFFREY MARX

ACKNOWLEDGMENTS

We start by thanking three families: the Lewises, the Marxes, and the Santa Monica Track Club. They are the people closest to us, which makes it all the more amazing that they have managed to put up with us. The Lewises: Evelyn "Girl" Lewis, Carol Lewis, Mack Lewis, Cleve and Fran Lewis, aunts, uncles, cousins. The Marxes: Peggy Marx, Richard Marx, Jim Marx, Wendy Marx, and everybody else, with Deedee and Pop leading the way. The Santa Monica Track Club: Joe Douglas, David Greifinger, Rose Warne, and SMTC members past and present.

We have also received incredible support from: Deborah Barefield and family, Janice Warne, Tom and Kay Tellez, the University of Houston track and field staff, Roy and Mary Cullen, the Willingboro (N.J.) High School athletic department and the Willingboro Track Club, Thomas Mayfield, James "Al" Garner, Narada and Anukampa Walden, Sri Chinmoy and his disciples, Sam and Sharon Mings, Bob and Sharon Carey, Lay Witnesses for Christ, Willie Gault, Timothy S. B. Danson, Ruth, Vrandle and Maggie and Bandit, David Protess, John and Lee Carroll, Michael and Becky York, Virginia Anderson, Harry Merritt, Bob Houlihan, Jr., Sandy Padwe, Paula Ellis and the Knight-Ridder Washington Bureau, Frank Deford, Rob Fleder, Harold Sanco and Franklin Blackstone III (Hank and Frarold), Tom Connolly, Eric Mogentale, Lisa Ann Collins, Rena Vicini, John and Jane Miller, Toni and Renate Linhart and the Baltimore (yes, Baltimore) Colts, Mike Woodrow, Jim Spano, Gary McLain, and, of course, The Boys (Rusty Gorman, Greg Katz, Mitch Loveman, Peter Ripka).

Sterling Lord and Flip Brophy are the only literary agents who could have put together this team. Our thanks to Sterling and Flip.

Carl Cannon is a great reporter/editor and an even better friend. Thank you, Carl.

Bob Bender took what we gave him and made it into a book. Thank you, Bob.

—Carl Lewis and Jeffrey Marx
Washington, D.C.
March 1990

CONTENTS

ONE

≡

Showdown

September 24, 1988
Seoul, South Korea

MY THOUGHTS before a big race are usually pretty simple. I tell myself: Get out of the blocks, run your race, stay relaxed. If you run your race, you'll win. Just run your race. Channel your energy. Focus.

But this time was different. It was hard to focus when I saw Ben Johnson on the track before the finals of the Olympic 100-meter sprint. This was minutes before a gun would be fired to start the biggest race of our lives. I was walking around behind the starting blocks, stretching my arms and legs, and I approached Ben to shake his hand and wish him luck. I always shake hands with my opponents. This one was a quick shake. We are not friends.

Ben, in his red Adidas wear and gold necklace, hardly looked at me. Quietly, I said, "Good luck," and as I looked at him, I noticed that his eyes were very yellow. A sign of steroid use. Ben looked like a weight lifter, and I was used to that by now, but those yellow eyes . . . I couldn't stop thinking about those yellow eyes. That bastard did it again, I said to myself. I had known from people close to Ben and from other people on the track circuit that, in the past, he had taken steroids to make himself stronger and faster, to gain an illegal advantage. Now, I figured he was on something again. My focus was drifting. I kept reminding myself, just run your race, just run your race. But I was not focusing properly. Ben looked like his attitude was: I don't know what we're waiting for. I'm going to win. It's man against boys.

Four years earlier, at the Olympics in Los Angeles, I didn't know much about Ben and didn't really care about him. He was just another sprinter, a Canadian who claimed he could beat me, but nobody paid much attention to him back then. I won the gold medal, running 100 meters in 9.99 seconds. Ben took the bronze. It was the beginning of a rivalry that would become as fierce and bitter as any in the world of track and field. But the rivalry would take a while to develop.

I beat Ben the first seven times I faced him in the 100, including the '84 Games. Then he beat me in five of six races from August 1985 to August 1987. That's when we arrived in Rome for the World Championships, and that's when the rivalry really got going.

Ben broke the world record for the 100, tearing down the track in 9.83 seconds, an absolutely incredible time. It was a full tenth of a second better than the previous world mark, set by my American teammate, Calvin Smith. My second-place 9.93 tied me with Calvin for the American record, but nobody in Rome wanted to talk about that. Everybody was too busy talking about the new force in sprinting, Ben Johnson. I didn't appreciate the way Ben handled his victory. He did everything he could to tell the world how great he was, that nobody could beat him anymore, and that pissed me off.

A year later, the month before going to Seoul, I broke Ben's streak at a race in Zurich. Ben was third, behind me and Calvin Smith. But still, he was boasting about the world record. "Who's going to break it?" he asked. "Me? Yeah. Sure." But nobody else, not according to Ben. He was too big, too powerful, too fast. He could not be beaten.

Ben was twenty-six, I was twenty-seven. Heading to Seoul, I was still up on Ben, nine to six, in career head-to-head 100-meter races. I was entered in three other events: the 200-meter sprint, the 4 × 100 relay, and the long jump. The same events, along with the 100, I had won in 1984. The same four events Jesse Owens had won at the 1936 Olympics in Berlin. But the 100 is the most glamorous race in the Olympics, the race that determines the world's fastest human. This is the one everyone would remember, Carl against Ben, the big showdown of the 1988 Games.

I finished my handshakes and pulled off my sweats. The letters on my uniform screamed USA, and I felt that Americans were now behind me more than ever before. In the past, I had been criticized for acting like an individual who happened to be part of a team, *from* the United States, but not *of* the United States team. Now, I was Carl Lewis *of* the United States team . . . and the guy I had to beat was representing Canada. This was not just personal. I was representing my nation against the best athletes from other nations. It was everything the Olympics are supposed to be.

An official pinned a number, 1102, on my uniform. The crowd was buzzing. The fans—seventy thousand in Olympic Stadium—were terrible, the worst I had ever heard, because they would not shut up. They had talked all the way through the preliminary heats, and now they were talking again. They didn't cheer when they should have, and they were loud when they should have been quiet.

The one man I most wanted to be in the crowd was missing. My father, William, had died just more than a year earlier. I had buried with him the 100-meter gold medal from 1984. The medal would be his forever. Now I wanted a new one—for myself and for my father. I did not want to let him down.

Forget the fans, I said to myself. Just run your race. I had to tell myself over and over: Focus, run your race.

Seconds before getting in the blocks, I lost my focus again, thinking about all the pressure, the thousands of people in the stadium and billions watching on television. I wondered if I wanted to do this anymore. Luckily, these thoughts didn't last long, maybe ten seconds, but the gun was less than a minute away. Something clicked, and I was able to snap out of it. Just run your race. Focus.

It was time to get in the blocks. I was assigned to lane 3. Ben was in lane 6, next to his Canadian teammate, Desai Williams. Two other Americans, Calvin Smith and Dennis Mitchell, had made the finals, along with sprinters from Brazil, Jamaica, and Great Britain. Once you're in the blocks, you can't do anything but blow out of there and run. That's when I get nervous, in the blocks. I'm used to saying, "Oh, I'm cool, I'll get in the blocks, listen for the gun—no big deal."

But I really get anxious in the blocks. That is the moment of truth. All the training is done, all the head games have been played. Now, all you can do is run the best you can . . . the best you can run on this given day, as the old cliché goes.

Runners take your mark. Set. There are so many things to think about when the starter calls you to the "set" position. Am I in the right position? Can I hear the gun? Will I accelerate the way I should? Am I ready? The hundred is a split-second thing. You win or lose by split seconds. If I make a mistake in the start I will know it in the first step. And by five meters I know whether I'm going to run a fabulous race, a medium race, or a lousy race. Now, I just wanted to hear the gun and have a great start, a perfect start.

The gun was fired. I didn't see Ben coming out of the blocks. But knowing the way he gets out, I knew he would be in front. That was fine. I got out well, too, and knew I would catch Ben in the second half of the race. *Just run your race.* The 100-meter dash lasts only about ten seconds, but it seems like ten years. So much is happening—strategy, thinking, small adjustments—that the race seems slow. Fifty or sixty meters down the track I glanced to my right and saw Ben in front, maybe by five feet. He was mine. He needed a bigger lead than that.

Ben and I run different races. He gets out of the blocks faster than anybody, then tries to hold on. I'm a slower starter but I'm more consistent down the track. Everybody decelerates toward the end of a 100-meter race; it is impossible to keep accelerating. Maybe you can do it in a 50-meter or a 60-meter race, but not the 100. Ben tends to decelerate more than other sprinters because he uses so much energy out of the blocks. Then again, who knows what was going on in that body? Or what was in it? Anyway, when I win it is because I run smoother than anybody else and do not decelerate as much as my opponents do.

But about eighty meters down the track—with the finish line flying toward us—I looked at Ben again, and he was not coming back any. He still had those five feet on me. Ben had pretty much the same lead all the way through, and I knew I couldn't get him. Damn, I thought, Ben did it again. The bastard got away with it again. It's over, Dad. God, I wanted to win it for Dad. But that was impossible now. It wouldn't happen.

Before reaching the finish line, Ben shot his right arm into the air, pointed his index finger, triumphantly signaling that he was number one, and turned his head to look over his left shoulder at me. I looked at him, too, and I couldn't believe what was happening. I was so pissed. Ben crossed the line with a time of 9.79 seconds. He had again lowered the world record, running even faster than he had in Rome. I was second with a 9.92. It was my best time ever—except for a wind-aided 9.78 at the U.S. Olympic trials—but not good enough to win. The 9.92 was a new American record. But not good enough to win. That was the big thing.

I wanted to stand tall. I couldn't accept or acknowledge Ben's victory. He was a cheater. But I had to show Ben and everyone else some class—for myself and for my father. I didn't have the medal to replace the one I had given him, and that hurt. But I could still give something to my father by acting the way he had always wanted me to act, with class and dignity.

Whatever Ben was doing, whatever he was taking, whatever he was getting away with, he had pulled it off again. I was not the least bit happy, but I would find a way to congratulate him. Ben went to the edge of the track and stood like a heavyweight champion in front of all the photographers. I followed him, not out of respect, but simply because it was the right thing to do. I reached with my right arm and grabbed Ben by his right elbow. No reaction. He was reaching for something—a Canadian flag, I think—with his other arm. Ben was ignoring me. I put my left hand on his left shoulder to spin him around. He still didn't want any part of this. But he was stuck.

I knew what I should have said: Congratulations. But I didn't say anything because, if I opened my mouth, I didn't know what would come out. A four-letter word probably would have been in there. It was another quick shake, like the one before the race, and Ben turned away.

On my way out, someone from NBC grabbed me for a live interview. I didn't mind talking but I wasn't going to stay for long. I was not in the mood, still surprised at the race, wondering exactly what Ben had been doing. Plus, the Korean security people were out of control. As soon as a race was done they would grab us and shove us off the track. They were incredibly rude and pushy.

I told the interviewer, "I gave it my best shot."

Could you feel Ben at all?

"He caught a flyer." In other words, a great start. "Because he was way out again, just like Rome. I think I could have run better. I just ran the best I could, and I was pleased with my race."

End of interview. Of course, I was pissed, upset, disappointed, but I did not want to tell the world what I was really thinking. I just wanted to get out of there. Just wanted to be alone with my thoughts.

Ben, I can't believe you got away with it again. Dad, I can't believe I let you down.

TWO

≡

"The Runt"

LONG BEFORE he taught me anything, my father was quite an athlete himself, willing to try new things in order to grow, even if that meant leaving his family behind in Chicago. In the late 1940s, William McKinley Lewis, Jr., left Chicago to play football and compete as a sprinter for Tuskegee Institute in Tuskegee, Alabama, near Birmingham. Bill Lewis was the first member of his family to leave Chicago and the first to attend college. He was tall and handsome and alone.

Evelyn Lawler was the daughter of a pipe-shop worker in Gadsden, Alabama. Her father, Fred, was born in Alabama in 1897 and would live there all of his seventy-two years, always in charge when his seven children helped during cotton-picking season, but never during school hours. Fred Lawler did not let his children miss school. Fred was always in a hurry, and so was Evelyn. She played basketball and ran track in high school, and it was her talent in track that helped her become the first of her family to attend college. She got a scholarship to Tuskegee to long-jump, high-jump, sprint, and study to be a physical education teacher.

Bill Lewis and Evelyn Lawler met at Tuskegee, fell in love, and got married soon after Evelyn graduated. Bill would get his degree a year later.

Evelyn was the track star of the couple, making the national team

that competed in the first Pan American Games, held in Buenos
Aires, Argentina, in 1951. She placed sixth in the 80-meter hurdles
and was considered a favorite to make the 1952 U.S. Olympic team.
That was her dream. Her nightmare was an injury that kept her from
qualifying. Evelyn pulled muscles in her leg and could not run in the
U.S. trials.

But Bill and Evelyn Lewis were prepared for more than running
and jumping. They took teaching jobs in Montgomery, Alabama, and
started a family. Mack was their first child, born in 1954. Cleveland
came the next year, and I became son number three in 1961. Two
years after that, the Lewises had their only daughter, Carol. She must
have been born with her mouth open because she has been talking
ever since.

I don't remember much about Alabama, although I would later
hear a lot about it from my parents. The big events of the time
centered around the civil rights movement, and my parents were
right in the middle of it. My mother and father marched with the
Reverend Martin Luther King, Jr., and he baptized Mack and Cleve.
A young cousin of mine was in on a messy confrontation between
marchers and the police, who had the help of vicious dogs and powerful fire hoses. My mother remembers watching people being
knocked down, then washed up and down the street by those fire
hoses. "This was a tough time, a time of sacrifice," my mother would
later tell me. "But if we wanted to make things better, we had to
sacrifice first."

Some of the sacrifices were devastating. One of my father's closest
friends was a man named Chris McNair. His little girl, Denise, was
one of four girls killed in a bombing of the 16th Street Baptist Church
in Birmingham on September 15, 1963. Young, innocent girls killed
in a church.

With four children of her own in the house and more and more
horror stories surrounding her, Evelyn Lewis kept talking to her
sisters, Freddie and Sue, about New Jersey, where they were living.
In New Jersey, the civil rights movement was in the newspapers, not
in the streets, and better teaching opportunities existed for Bill and
Evelyn. In late 1963, my parents moved us to Willingboro, New
Jersey, a quiet, middle-class suburb of Philadelphia. We settled in a
four-bedroom house with a large backyard. We were another middle-
class American family, going to church, playing Little League, getting

to know the neighbors, talking and laughing around the dinner table.

There was one thing that definitely made us different, though. In 1969, my parents started building a tradition in track and field. Few people in Willingboro cared about the sport before the Lewises showed up. My mother, teaching at Willingboro High, could not talk the principal into a track program for girls. On her own, she coached a few promising girls a year, but that was it. My father, teaching social studies at the other high school in town, John F. Kennedy High, coached boys in sprinting, but there was no girls' track there either.

My mother wanted young girls to have the same opportunities she had in sports, so she and my father established the Willingboro Track Club. It started with a dozen or so girls, the youngest of them nine-year-olds, with two practices a week at Kennedy High. Before long, some boys wanted in, and they were accepted.

Taking me and Carol to the track saved baby-sitting money, so we naturally became interested in track and field. The long-jump pit was our baby-sitter. Sometimes Carol and I tried to imitate the drills everyone else was doing, but most of the time we just played in the sand, building castles in the pit, then smashing them while our parents were busy with their athletes. At first, playing in the sand was a lot more fun for me than paying attention to what Mom and Dad were doing.

It was Carol, even though she was younger, who noticed first that running and jumping *into* the sand could be fun too. When she was six years old, Carol started competing in any event she wanted to try, and she was amazingly good, bigger than most boys her age and much more talented than most, including me. I started to learn what I could about track, but I was a very slow starter, too small, too shy, and too overshadowed by Carol for anyone to notice me.

In 1971, my parents started sending teams to novice meets in Philadelphia. The club held dances and raffles to raise money, and my parents kicked in some of their own so that nobody would be left out. The meets in Philadelphia were named after Jesse Owens, who, my father told us, was the best track athlete ever. My father told us that Owens had won four gold medals in the 1936 Olympics. We did not really know what that meant, but my father spoke so highly of Owens that we were impressed. Before leaving Chicago, young Bill Lewis had seen Owens every now and then when the track star was working as a district manager for a dry-cleaning chain. When Owens stopped at a local store, Bill and the other neighborhood kids would gather around and bombard him with questions. In his dress clothes for work, Owens would demonstrate his sprinter's start. The kids of Chicago loved it.

At my first Jesse Owens meet, my father introduced me to Owens, who was fifty-seven then, and took a picture of my cousin and me with him. Owens did not recognize my father, of course, but once he was reminded of the dry-cleaning store in Chicago, he recalled the good old days there. It was a very brief meeting and I was just one of hundreds of kids who met Owens at the meet. I did not win anything that day. But I do remember one thing Owens said to me: "Have fun." He wanted us to know that having fun was the most important thing we could do.

Back at home, Carol and I held our own track meets. We took a pile of sand my father bought for a patio and turned it into a long-jump pit, spending the better part of an afternoon leaping into it. We used tables and chairs as hurdles, competing against each other for hours and hours when nobody else was around, and Carol usually won. She would celebrate, parading around the house with one of our mother's medals or trophies as if she had just won the biggest meet in the world.

A bunch of neighborhood kids—all boys, except Carol—would come over to the house for our "meets." At first, Carol and I shared some of our mother's awards with the other kids. But that didn't last long. When my mother noticed her medals were disappearing, she went from house to house, collecting them. Then she considered giving us a whipping. Her favorite threat was, "I'm going to beat you within an inch of your life." Or she would say, "Wait till your Dad gets home." But by the time Dad got home, Mom's medals would be back in the attic, and we never would get that whipping.

Carol was the ultimate tomboy, no long dress, ponytail, and pocketbook for her. She was big for her age and full of the competitive spirit she saw in Mack and Cleve. Mack was doing very well in track by now and Cleve was the best soccer player in the area. I was small for my age, the runt of the family, the nonathlete, and my father wondered if that was the way it would always be. He figured that little Carl must have gotten the nonathletic genes in the family.

In the backyard, we would imitate a television announcer talking about the world-record sprinting time before we raced. Trying to talk in a deep voice, one of us would say something like, "The record is 9.95 seconds. Carl or Carol could beat it here at the Championship of America. The pressure is building. They're at the starting line . . ." Then Carol would crush me, as usual.

When I learned about the world long-jumping record held by a man named Bob Beamon, I went to the front yard with a measuring tape. I marked off 29 feet, 2½ inches, the distance Beamon had jumped at the 1968 Olympics, and I went into my announcer voice. *Here it is, folks, Carl Lewis is one jump away from the world record. All he has to do is jump this far.* It was just another day in our little fantasy world. I was not aware then of what an incredible jump Beamon had made. I knew it was long, but everything was long to me then. After marking off the Beamon jump, the first thought I had was, Wow, that's longer than a Cadillac.

One day, after another meet and another loss, I came home and complained to my family that I was tired of losing. The only thing I could do was keep trying. I pinned pictures and articles about track and field on a bulletin board in my room, and I started setting goals, writing them down and tacking them onto the board. The goals were simple, nothing too grand, but they gave me something to shoot for, a time in the 100-yard dash or a distance in the long jump.

Not many people my age participated in the long jump then, so I usually had the long-jump area to myself at practices. I liked an event that allowed me to run and jump at the same time. I still was not any good, but the more I jumped, the more I enjoyed it. There would be no more building and busting of castles in the sand. Now I was too busy for that.

In 1972, clear across the country in California, a high school mathematics teacher named Joe Douglas looked back on his own career as a runner, drew on his experiences as a coach in Texas and California, and formed a track club to develop world-class athletes. The purpose was simple: Create an environment to provide coaching, managing, an entire support system to help athletes succeed internationally. There were plenty of track programs for youngsters and college athletes, and a few clubs for all-stars beyond the college level. But Douglas wanted to fill what he considered to be a huge void. He wanted to provide training and travel for postgraduate athletes not quite good enough to be recruited by existing clubs but full of potential and desire that could eventually carry them to the Olympics and beyond.

Of course, I knew nothing about Douglas at the time, and my parents didn't either. Years would pass before I would meet him and learn about what he started in 1972.

At the time, he was thirty-six years old, teaching at Westchester High in Los Angeles. Douglas had spent his childhood in a tiny town called Archer City, Texas, won a number of local meets, and gained a scholarship to Texas Christian University. He later competed nationally as a half-miler for the Los Angeles Track Club, then one of the biggest clubs on the West Coast. But the LA club lost sponsors, and folded in the mid-1960s. Douglas was disappointed, not ready to accept that his club was doomed. He appealed to the city of Santa Monica for money to keep a club alive, and there was some help from local officials. Before long, though, the coach of the club quit, and the athletes were on their own. Douglas, no longer competing, started coaching at Westchester.

In 1972, he placed an advertisement in a national track magazine, seeking athletes for what would be called the Santa Monica Track Club. Douglas knew more about middle-distance and long-distance running than he did about sprints, and he considered sprinters to be the least stable of all track athletes. So the new club would focus on middle- and long-distance running. It would be a community club, meaning anybody interested in running could join. And some of the members—doctors and businessmen more interested in jogging in their neighborhood than competing in the Olympics—helped pay for the best athletes to compete at invitational meets. The club started small, but Douglas thought big.

Finally, I won a local Jesse Owens meet in Philadelphia, placing first in a 1973 long-jump competition for twelve-year-olds. Once again Owens had come to town for the meet named after him. He wandered by, saw how much smaller I was than the other kids my age, and told them, "You should learn a lesson from this smaller guy. He was determined and he really tried hard." For once, I felt good about what I was doing. I had qualified to go with other members of the Willingboro club to a national Jesse Owens meet in San Francisco. It was the first time Carol and I went to a meet that far from home without our parents. Of course, Carol dominated, taking first place in her events. I was just another kid who ran, jumped, and went home empty-handed.

When Carol was thirteen, she entered her first pentathlon, a competition that includes five track-and-field events. She won, breaking the national record for a girl her age. And it was not even a big deal to her. In fact, she never competed in another pentathlon. I was fifteen, and hardly ever winning anything.

Being the loser in the family was so frustrating. Carol was very successful. Mack was all-state in track, the county record-holder in the 220-yard sprint. Cleve was an all-American in soccer. I was the runt. My father was very supportive of us all, but he always talked about Cleve being the best at this or that. People were waiting to see what Mack's little brother could do, what Cleve's little brother could do, and I couldn't do much. Every family seems to have someone who is not talented, and I thought I was the one for our family.

My parents always treated us like young adults, not kids, even when we were real little. They did that because they wanted us to be individuals, to learn how to take care of ourselves, to achieve things on our own. Back when I was about to enter first grade, my mother took me to the school the day before classes started. She wanted to show me where to go. Then that was it. I would be on my own. The first day of classes, other kids cried while their parents pushed them through the halls. I just went where I had to go, and waited for everybody else to settle down.

Each summer, we would go to Alabama to see relatives and friends. At the airport, my parents would let us buy our own tickets (with their money, of course). They wanted us to approach the ticket counter and speak up for ourselves. Back then, it was just fun to do new things. My parents were not the type to hover over their children. They gave us a lot of space. And now I realize that doing things like buying our own tickets helped us to grow, to become individuals. Buying tickets by myself taught me something about traveling, and something about being independent. Both would be valuable lessons.

When I saw my older brothers doing what they wanted to do— shopping, going out to eat, leaving to see a movie—I also wanted to do things on my own. First, I would need to make a few dollars. So

I got a newspaper route, delivering the *Burlington County Times* in Willingboro when I was in junior high school. My parents had told me that my only jobs were school and sports, and that I should do those as well as I could. So the decision to deliver papers was entirely mine. I enjoyed riding my bicycle up and down the local streets, running up and down the sidewalks, jumping over bushes and steps, tossing rolled-up papers as close to the front door as possible. It was always a challenge to see how quickly I could get done. On Fridays, I was supposed to collect delivery money from customers. On Saturdays, I had to deliver the payments to the newspaper office. I never liked collecting on Friday. It was a school day, and I did not want to spend so much time ringing doorbells. So I came up with a plan. If I had a checking account, I could pay the newspaper office by check on Saturday, but they would not be able to cash my check until Monday. Meanwhile, I could collect my money on Sunday evening (when most people are home), then deposit it Monday morning. I was not yet old enough to drive, but I had a creative way of doing things—and a checking account before most of my friends even knew where the bank was.

My second job, when I was sixteen, was cooking hamburgers at McDonald's. But that didn't last long. I hated flipping burgers, and I was embarrassed when friends came in to order. The worst was one night, just before closing, when the place was empty and I was watching the clock. All of a sudden, people started streaming in. The high school basketball game had just let out. All the guys on the track team dogged me, ordering as much as they could, and laughing the whole time, because they knew I had to work like crazy to fix their burgers. That night was it for me. No more McDonald's. I would have to find another way to make it in this world.

By this time, my parents were coaching at rival high schools, kissing and hugging each other before their teams competed, then coming out fighting. They enjoyed teasing each other about the competition. They were very serious about their teams, and pretty tough on their athletes.

But they were toughest on me, much tougher than they ever were on Mack, Cleve, or Carol. Mack and Cleve were now old enough to be left alone. And Carol was talented enough that she did not have to be pushed all the time. With her talent, Carol trained only when she felt like it. At times, I resented the way my parents worked me. They would urge me to do drills right after a meet, when I could have been resting or doing something with my friends. And I always had to do extra drills. If Carol was on the track for one hour, I would have to be there for two.

Back then, I was never sure why I was being pushed. But now I think I have a pretty good idea. My parents knew how much it hurt me to be the worst in the family, knew how much I wanted to succeed, and they spotted some talent in me before anyone else did, myself included. They thought that if they pushed me, they could help me develop that talent.

THREE

≡

Getting Good, Getting Recruited

SOPHOMORE YEAR of high school, I finally started growing. And once I started, it seemed like I wasn't going to stop. I grew between two and three inches in just a few months, and my legs had trouble adjusting. My knees were killing me, and for a while I even had to walk with crutches to ease the pain. But the growth was good. Finally, I was not a runt anymore. I was the size of most of my classmates. If my wobbly knees would catch up with the rest of me, I figured, the added height would help me run faster and jump better.

At the end of the year, I long-jumped a little better than 22 feet, and I was thrilled. For years, the school record at Kennedy High had been 22 feet, 2 inches. Only a few high schoolers in the whole county had ever jumped beyond 22 feet, and the record was 22 feet, 8 inches. I had never competed much in the triple jump, but I decided to try that at one meet, and ended up breaking the state record for a sophomore. My confidence was building, but then there was a major setback.

I was running a hurdle relay with three older, more experienced teammates. It was a shuttle relay. The first man runs the 120-yard hurdles, and when he crosses the finish line, the second man starts back over the hurdles in the opposite direction, and so on, through four legs. I was the youngest, and the slowest, so I would run the last leg. My teammates thought they could get enough of a lead that even I couldn't blow it. Part of the plan worked. They got the lead. When it was my turn to run, we were ahead by four hurdles. But I blew it. We were running on the grass infield, not the track, and I was wearing the wrong spikes for grass. They were too short. I started slipping, and once I started slipping, I got scared. I lost, and I felt the lowest I had ever felt after a race. We were supposed to have the best relay team in South Jersey, and I had just lost the race for us. I couldn't believe I had run so badly, and couldn't believe I had let down my teammates. They couldn't either.

There was a little tent at the track, and I went in there to find a quiet place to be alone. My father found me there, asked what had happened, and I told him that I had slipped. I had been wearing a new pair of spikes, and they were not right for the grass. My father never liked excuses. He left the tent. Then came my relay teammates, and I didn't even have a chance to explain anything to them. They were too busy attacking me.

"There's no way we should have lost, Carl. We had it, man. Anyone could have held that lead. There's no way you're going to run with us again. You had your chance."

They went on and on, and I had to sit there and take it. They were older, and they were right. I had definitely messed up. They were so vicious about it, and I was so hurt. When my teammates left the tent, I sat there alone, crying.

That night I made two decisions. One, I was going to transfer to the other high school in town. All year I had thought about switching to Willingboro High. It was closer to home, so most of my neighborhood friends went there, and I wanted to be with them. The way I was treated after the relay convinced me that I should transfer. Two, I was not going to be humiliated on the track again. I was either going to quit or I was going to dedicate myself to working harder than I had been. I told myself, If you're not willing to work hard and make the sacrifices you'll have to make, then quit—just get out of it. But I was not going to quit. Just the opposite. I was going to commit myself to being more competitive than ever.

Junior year—my first year at Willingboro High—I put a "25" on my jacket. It was a symbol. I wanted to long-jump 25 feet before leaving high school. A lot of people laughed at me, telling me I was crazy to think I could jump that far. But my parents had taught me to set goals, and I was not going to change my goals based on what other people thought of them.

Willingboro was a lot more fun than Kennedy. I was in school with most of my friends, including Thomas Mayfield, my best friend, neighbor, and—now—teammate. We had a great time practicing and competing together, and being around friends helped me focus on becoming a better athlete. My confidence got a nice boost when I was named anchor man on the relay team, and before long I was South Jersey champ in the 100. Butch Woolfolk, who would go on to play football at the University of Michigan and in the National Football League, drilled me in the 100 at the state meet. But I did well enough in the long jump to qualify for the junior nationals. Other than the Jesse Owens meets for youngsters, this was the first time I made it to a big meet outside New Jersey. It was at Indiana University.

Carol, only fourteen years old, also went, and at the nationals she beat all the older girls to win the long jump. She was incredible. Michelle Glover, Carol's best friend from home, also qualified for the junior national team, as a sprinter. I would have to place first or second in the long jump to make the national team, along with Carol and Michelle. Members of that team would go to the Soviet Union for a meet. I jumped 24 feet, 9 inches, and was in second place until the last round. (We jump six times; only the best jump counts.) My final jump was a foul, and I finished third. Not bad for my first junior nationals, but I was disappointed that I would not be able to travel with Carol and Michelle. In the end, my slip from second to third also cost Carol and Michelle the trip to the Soviet Union. My parents would not let them go without me, so they stayed home. I felt terrible about that.

But I wouldn't be keeping Carol and Michelle home for long. My time in the 100-yard dash kept getting better. First 9.7 seconds, then 9.6, and the times kept coming down. At the national age-group meet in Memphis, I ran the 100 in 9.3 seconds. In a year, my time had dropped from 10.6 to 9.3.

My jumps were also getting a lot better. I made that goal of 25 feet—several times—so nobody was laughing anymore about the number on my school jacket. At the Eastern States schoolboy track-and-field championships, I jumped 25 feet, 3¼ inches. The next day's newspapers started to compare my performance with the jumps of a great athlete I would hear a lot about in the years to come. The winning jump was only one-quarter of an inch behind Bob Beamon's meet record, the papers said. But that was just the beginning for me. At the meet in Memphis, I jumped 25 feet, 9 inches.

Everything was happening so fast. I had always set goals, but I had never imagined that I could improve so much in just a year. I was sixteen, and all of a sudden I was one of the best high school track athletes in the country. I couldn't believe it. Now Carol and Michelle and I could go to the same meets and have a great time together.

During a meet at Franklin Field in Philadelphia, I saw Jesse Owens again. By now, I knew a lot more about him than I had when I shook his hand and posed for pictures at the age of twelve. I had read a book about Jesse, and I had a lot more appreciation for what he had accomplished. I was old enough to understand a little bit about the pressures he had faced in 1936, when he represented the United States in a cruel region dominated by Nazis. I was old enough to understand something about the prejudice he faced in his own nation, even as an Olympic hero. And I had heard that he had struggled financially for years.

This time, at Franklin Field, Jesse knew more about me, too. Now he knew of me as a successful high school jumper, not just another little kid running around in one of his age-group meets. He had read somewhere that I had started out by competing in his meets, and we talked a little about my development to that point. This was a lot more exciting than the other times I had seen Jesse because now it was like we knew each other.

But it was not until the beginning of my senior year, when the college recruiters started coming after me, that I fully appreciated what I was accomplishing.

Track and field has little in common with major American sports like football and basketball. But on the high school level, there is at least one similarity. If you are very good, you get recruited. And getting heavily recruited by colleges means hearing a lot of things you're not supposed to hear, like offers of money and gifts, all in violation of the rules that govern college sports. High school and college stars are supposed to be the purest of amateurs. But they aren't. We know that athletes in the so-called revenue-producing sports—football and basketball—are enticed by money, cars, free trips, anything a wealthy booster or outlaw coach can pass "under the table." We hear about those things all the time.

But most people don't think that they happen in a "minor" sport like track. Well, they do—in a big way. Some coaches offer money. Some promise to arrange deals for payments from meet promoters, especially in Europe, where appearance fees are paid in cash. Then there are the routine offers of "gifts" like free trips to meets, airline tickets for parents to visit school, shoes and athletic equipment. It didn't take me long to learn that the major shoe companies and the coaches working for them are some of the biggest, most blatant rules-breakers in our sport.

A guy named Russ Rogers, coaching at Fairleigh Dickinson University in New Jersey, talked more than any other coach about money, trips, shoes, and "taking care of me." He even said he would be able to get me a car if I came to his school. That was the only time I heard that from a coach, and I was surprised.

At the time, Russ was the only black head coach I knew of at a decent school. I respected him because of that. But the more I talked to him, the more I realized he was more like an agent than a coach. His whole recruiting pitch was money, money, money.

Russ was connected with Puma, and he said he could get me a shoe contract. I would be paid just to wear Puma, and I would receive all the free shoes and athletic gear I needed. Russ was very open about this. He discussed it with my parents, even though they knew that a deal like this would be against the rules. He told my parents that they also would get whatever they wanted from Puma. In fact, as if to prove himself, he came to our house with a duffel bag full of Puma stuff. Everyone in the family started sporting Puma gear.

At the same time I was getting these things from Puma, I was also getting shoes and clothes from Adidas. That was arranged by a coach named Billy Maxwell, who was recruiting me for the University of Tennessee. Billy told me he knew an Adidas representative named John Pennel, and that he could arrange with John to have a package of Adidas stuff sent to my home. Once I got the package, all I had to do for more shoes or equipment was call John. He was a former Olympic pole vaulter and a very nice guy. John had been working for Adidas since 1975, and it was easy for him to get me whatever I wanted. Later, I was introduced to another Adidas rep who handled distribution in New Jersey, and I was told to call him whenever I needed anything. I did that several times, and also visited an Adidas outlet in North Jersey to get what I needed.

Having all this stuff available to me was fun. I figured, why not keep Puma and Adidas going as long as possible? Russ Rogers and Billy Maxwell didn't seem to care. So I would keep collecting from both companies. One time, Puma paid for me to go to a track meet in California, the 1979 national championships, and I didn't even wear my Pumas there. I wore Adidas, because I liked them better. I usually wore Pumas for my regular high school meets and Adidas for big, special meets.

Nobody from the shoe companies ever took the time to notice. They had so much money to throw around the track circuit, they didn't seem to care where it ended up. And they certainly didn't care about the rules of the National Collegiate Athletic Association (NCAA). The most important thing for the shoe companies is visibility. The best advertisement they can have is a top athlete wearing their products, so the companies try early to grab the young athletes with the most potential. That way, the companies hope to develop loyalty before an athlete gets really big.

There was one other thing the people from Adidas offered: They wanted to send me to Europe for meets the summer after I graduated from high school. Talking about Europe was also a big thing with Russ Rogers. He said he would take me there each summer, beginning with the summer between high school and college. All my expenses would be covered. And, as long as I performed well enough, he would collect appearance fees for me. That is where the real money is in track and field, appearance fees from European promoters. A lot of them don't know about NCAA rules for athletes at American schools, and those who do know, don't care. They think it is silly to place restrictions on the money an athlete can earn—especially an American athlete, a product of the great land of free enterprise.

While he was recruiting me, Russ kept telling me that I was all set to go to Europe with him. But once I chose another school, he dumped me. My family was upset about that at the time, but now the whole thing seems kind of funny. I was all packed and ready to go, waiting to hear from Russ. But he never called when he was supposed to. When I finally tracked him down, the day I was scheduled to leave, Russ told me he didn't have a ticket for me. I unpacked my bags and realized it would be difficult to believe in Russ anymore.

The most unusual of the recruiting offers had come from Jumbo Elliott, the Villanova coach. Jumbo had been at Villanova since the 1930s. He was a living legend when he came to see me, and by the time he died in 1981, he was one of the biggest names in the history of American track and field. He had coached his teams to eight NCAA track and cross-country titles. Twenty-eight of his athletes had made the Olympics, including five runners who won gold medals. He had been named track-and-field "Coach of the Century" by the Intercollegiate Association of Amateur Athletes of America. Elliott was the track version of football's Bear Bryant or basketball's John Wooden. Jumbo was also wealthy, having made a fortune selling construction equipment.

If I had gone to Villanova, my family could have made a lot of money, too, because Jumbo offered to set them up in business. He was involved with a chain of sporting goods stores called Athletic Attic, and Jumbo told my parents he would "help them" get a franchise. They did not have enough money to open a store on their own. But several times during his recruiting pitches, Jumbo said he would "help" with financing. They never got into the details of where the money would come from, or how much would be needed. But my family was interested, especially my brothers. One day, Jumbo took Mack to look at an Athletic Attic store. The message was clear: "If Carl comes to Villanova, your family will be the proud owner of a profitable business."

My parents tried to stay out of my decision-making. They were pretty good about that. But Mack and Cleve were in my face. They wanted that store. Ultimately, though, the decision would be mine. This was a tough spot for a high school senior. Should I take Villanova and the store? Or should I keep searching for the school that offered the best program, the best overall situation to develop as an athlete and an individual?

One of the toughest things about recruiting was having to say no to people who were very nice to me. But the phone was ringing ten times a night, and I was getting tired of talking to coaches. My parents urged me to start narrowing down the list of choices. If you believed everything each coach said, then each had the best school, the best track program, the best location, the best way of helping young people become great citizens—all the things that athletes and their parents want to hear. But now it was time to start saying no.

I cut the list down to my final choices: Tennessee, Villanova, Houston, Kansas, UCLA, and Indiana. Then I told everyone I would make my decision on Easter Sunday.

The week leading up to that was crazy. Everybody called in their last-minute pitches, on a daily basis. My parents were leaning toward Villanova, not because of the store, but because it is near Philadelphia and they would have liked me to stay somewhere close to home.

The night before Easter, I went to sleep thinking it was going to be Tennessee. I told Cleve that I was leaning that way, but I didn't tell anybody else. Sunday morning, my mother woke me up, asked me what I had decided, and I blurted out "Houston." I'm not sure what changed my mind, but that's what I felt.

Tom Tellez, the Houston coach, had impressed me more than any other coach with his knowledge of our sport. He had started coaching in Germany while serving in the army during the late 1950s. Then Tellez spent a lot of time in California, coaching high school and junior college teams before moving to UCLA. In 1977, Tellez became the head coach at Houston. Technically, he seemed to be light-years ahead of all the other coaches.

He had not offered money or a car or a shoe contract, but he didn't need to. I had decided to choose the best program, not the biggest dollar signs. Tennessee was a close second. But I kept coming back to something one of the Tennessee athletes had told me: For better coaching, go to Houston. I figured if one of Tennessee's own would tell me that, then Houston must be the place to go.

Easter Sunday, I told everyone I was going to Houston. My father was kind of upset that I had not picked Villanova. But he stressed that the decision was mine. Billy Maxwell cried when I told him Tennessee was out. But at least he knew when to stop recruiting. Not Villanova's coaches. They kept calling, saying I could still go to Villanova if I changed my mind. And they kept talking badly about Houston. "You'll hate the weather. Tom Tellez is not proven as a coach." Stuff like that. That's when I lost all respect for Villanova. They should have known when to stop. They should have remembered that I was a high school student, not a businessman they needed to bully to close a deal.

One of the best experiences of high school came the day of my senior prom. That afternoon I was entered in the Martin Luther King Games in Philadelphia, competing against the sprinter I had always idolized, Steve Williams. In 1976, he was the world's number one sprinter, but he was hurt in the U.S. Olympic trials and didn't make the Olympic team. Still, Williams, from New York, had made plenty of headlines while competing for San Diego State and after leaving school. In our old backyard track meets, I had always pretended that I was Williams, or pretended that I was beating him in a race. But this was the first time I actually lined up against him.

A lot of great sprinters—college athletes and graduates—were entered in the King Games. But there had been a couple of openings in the 100-meter dash, and I was one of two high school sprinters invited to fill them. It was great just to be in the same race with all the big-timers, but I certainly didn't expect to beat any of them.

Houston McTear, a sprinting star from Florida, won the race. He had qualified for the 1976 U.S. Olympic team that Williams missed, but McTear also had to sit out the actual Games. He had pulled a leg muscle.

I finished behind McTear and three others, which was fine with me. Then I realized that I had finished ahead of Williams. Incredible. I was going to be late for the prom, but this was definitely worth it. A high school kid beating Steve Williams! After being the best sprinter in the world, he should have retired before losing to a high school student.

On the way to the prom, I had two thoughts—that is, two thoughts related to track. First, I realized that I could be a world-class athlete. I had beaten Steve Williams, so why not? Second, I told myself, there's no way I'm going to run past my prime. If I reach the top of my sport, I'm not going to lose to a high school kid.

By now, I was getting pretty good at accepting awards. Reach with your left hand, shake with your right, and smile for the cameras. The only problem was when I had to speak. The worst was when I was introduced at a banquet as the state Long Jumper of the Year. The other award winners had said a few words, and I was expected to stand behind a podium and do the same.

But I had nothing to say. I had always been shy, and now I was a wreck. Ten seconds behind that podium seemed like two hours. A few hundred people in the audience seemed like a few million. Every set of eyes was focused on me. And my throat was one big lump. I never felt this nervous when I was competing. But this was different. I was totally uncomfortable. I was frozen.

Finally, I got out a "thank you." But even that was a struggle. I could not wait to get out of the place, and I was determined that something like that would never happen again. After all those years of being shy, I didn't expect to be Mr. Perfection as a public speaker, but I didn't want to be totally helpless, either. Whatever it would take, I would work on being better in public. I never wanted to be so uncomfortable again.

FOUR

≡

At Houston

THE NIGHT I arrived in Houston, I went out with a group of guys from the track team. The next day, I went in to see Coach Tellez. "The guys on the team are great," I told him. "Everyone has been really nice. The place is great, and we're gonna have a great year. I can't wait to get started." All the things a normal freshman would say. Then I threw in something I doubt Coach T had ever heard before, especially from a kid who had not yet been in his first college meet, and did not even know where the classrooms were. "I want to be a millionaire," I said, "and I don't ever want a real job."

At the time, in 1979, top track athletes made decent money, but nothing near what the superstars in other sports earned. Still, I had no idea what the limits were. And I didn't want to know. I was more interested in possibilities than limits.

Coach T kind of ignored what I said about being a millionaire. He heard only what he wanted to hear, focusing on what I had said about my teammates and how excited I was to get started. "I'm glad you're here," he said. "We're going to work hard, we'll have a lot of fun and everything will work out just fine."

Right away, I learned what Coach T meant by working hard. He wanted to change my form completely in the long jump. My whole life I had been a "hang" jumper. I would run as fast as I could to the board, plant my right foot, and jump, swinging my body and arms forward, then hanging with little motion and falling into the sand. Coach T wanted me to go to what is known as a double-hitch kick. He wanted me to run off the board better than I had been doing, then "run" through the air, pumping my arms and legs in a cycling motion.

The double-hitch would be easier on my body, especially my right knee—the knee I jump off—which had been giving me a lot of trouble. I had patella tendinitis, which causes swelling and pain; running off the board instead of planting on it would reduce the stress. That was not the only reason Coach T wanted me to learn the double-hitch. He thought that once I got used to it, I would be able to jump farther than I did by hanging. But getting used to the new technique was very difficult. Changing a jumper's form that dramatically is like entirely changing the way a baseball player hits, or the way a golfer swings. It takes lots of practice, and even if the new form is working in practice, you tend to revert to your old ways once you get in a competition.

Two or three days a week, I worked in practice on nothing but my jump. I had always considered myself a jumper first, sprinter second, and Coach T agreed. "You can run, too," he said. "But you're a jumper. We're going to get you jumping the right way." Changing to the double-hitch was somewhat frustrating, but I had total confidence in Coach T. He was the reason I had chosen Houston, and it would not make sense to doubt him now. Coach T said, "Give me a year to make this work," and I would do that, listening to all his suggestions and following his instructions the best I could.

The first major test would be the NCAA indoor championships. For a while, I wondered if I would even make it to the meet. To begin with, I had an extremely painful boil on my thigh. Then our flight from Houston to Detroit was diverted to Columbus, Ohio, because of snow in Michigan. We had to make a long, late-night bus ride to Detroit, and on the way I had one of the biggest scares of my life. The entire right side of my body became paralyzed. I must have aggravated a nerve or something while I was sleeping on the bus. One of my teammates gave me a massage, cracked my back a few times, and I was okay by the time of the meet. I was relieved just to be able to compete, but I had no idea how I would do.

When I jumped 26 feet, 4½ inches, the best I had ever jumped indoors, I didn't think anybody could beat me. And nobody did. In my first NCAA meet, with my new double-hitch jump, I had my first national collegiate title. Jason Grimes of Tennessee was second with a jump of 25 feet, 10¾ inches. That was kind of funny, the runner-up being from Tennessee, because Tennessee had recruited me so much. Fairleigh Dickinson had its moment in the spotlight, too, with one of Russ Rogers's long-distance runners, Solomon Chebor, winning the 3-mile run. Jumbo Elliott's Villanova squad had been one of the favorites to win the team title, but injuries and illness kept some of the Villanova athletes out of the meet. The championship went to one of our in-state rivals, Texas-El Paso.

Three months later, at the NCAA outdoor championships, I won the long jump again, with a new personal best, 27 feet, 4¾ inches. I did not compete in any individual sprints, just a relay, because I did not think I was ready for more than one individual event per meet at the national level. But the week before the NCAAs, I had run the 100 in an invitational meet and beaten James Sanford, the world's top-ranked sprinter in 1979. For the first time, I heard a comparison that I would hear for years. My performances were compared to those of Jesse Owens.

"The comparisons seem inevitable," Neil Amdur wrote in the *New York Times*. "Both could sprint and jump with equal ability and world-class credentials. Both seemed blessed with strong characters. Now that Carl Lewis has won his first National Collegiate outdoor long-jump title as a freshman . . . the 18-year-old moves a step closer to being linked to the career of the late Jesse Owens."

It was definitely too early to even think about comparing me to Jesse Owens. But being asked about this was a thrill. Jesse was such a big figure in track, in the Olympics, and in my early years, when I went to his meets for youngsters. He was an inspiration for me, and for many other people. Being compared to him was very flattering, but also a bit embarrassing. I was not trying to be Jesse Owens. I was just a freshman trying to adjust to college, trying to improve my long-jumping by listening to Coach Tellez and practicing the double-hitch kick he was teaching me.

After the NCAA outdoors, I went to the U.S. Olympic trials in Eugene, Oregon. The United States was boycotting the 1980 Olympic

Games in Moscow because of the Soviet invasion of Afghanistan, but I still wanted to make the team. Being an Olympian would be a great honor, something I had always wanted, and it would mean I could travel with the national team to some big international meets. I wanted to make the team in the long jump, which I did, and the 100, which I just missed, finishing fourth. Still, that was good enough to be part of the sprint relay team, so I was pleased. Carol also made the team, as a long jumper.

The biggest track meets are like conventions for all sorts of people in our sport, and conventions are always good for making business contacts. At the trials, Coach Tellez introduced me to one of his old coaching friends, Joe Douglas, whose Santa Monica Track Club was getting ready for its annual summer trip to Europe. Coach T asked Joe to take me with him as part of the club, and I was excited about the possibility. But Joe said he would have to think about it. Each year, he took his best athletes, mainly long-distance runners, on the international circuit, and from what I had heard, the Santa Monica members were treated pretty well. The club did not have a big name or anything, but it was growing, and I would be thrilled to be associated with *any* club.

But Joe did not like to coach sprinters, or even travel with them. He found them to be too high-strung, much more uptight than his long-distance runners, and hard to deal with, too demanding, and in many cases, spoiled. Coach T convinced Joe that he would be able to work with me, that he would actually enjoy working with me—even though I was a sprinter—and I was invited.

I would make one trip with the Olympic team for a few meets, and I would travel with Santa Monica for about half a dozen meets. For the first time, I would receive appearance fees, just like the other top athletes did. Being in college made no difference to me or the other college stars on the international circuit—even though we were breaking college rules by accepting appearance money. Someone paid for our travel—in my case, Adidas—and we collected as much as we could from meet promoters who wanted to put together the best fields possible, no matter what that cost them. With track being so big in Europe, most of the promoters would make back their money, and then some. It was not unusual for the biggest meets to draw thirty thousand or forty thousand fans, just like a football or baseball game in the States, so money was not a problem for meet promoters and sponsors.

My name did not mean much in Europe then, so I was paid on the low end of the scale, three hundred or four hundred dollars per event, depending on the meet. Joe would collect the money for me, in cash, so there was no way the NCAA or anybody at Houston would know. Besides, almost everybody took money even though they were not allowed to. It was no big deal. I roomed with Stanley Floyd, a great sprinter from Auburn who was competing as an individual, not with a club, and he was making considerably more money than I was. But Stanley was hilarious with his cash. He was always afraid he was going to lose it or somebody was going to steal it, so he kept his money hidden in his shoes—even when he was wearing them. By the end of the summer, he had grown a few inches.

Now that I'd made the Olympic team and done well in Europe, my position with the shoe companies was even better. Freshman year, just before Christmas, Adidas had given me five thousand dollars to wear their stuff exclusively. I had bought a stereo and put some of the money away. Then I got a bonus from Adidas for making the Olympic team, and I was ready to think about a new car.

With the help of Bill Yeoman, who was coaching the Houston football team, I got exactly what I wanted, a burgundy Trans Am. Bill and I had become friendly; we would always talk when we saw each other at the athletic offices or the stadium. He told me he had a friend who could help with a loan for the car, and he did. Bill also talked to someone at the dealership for me, and the sticker price suddenly went down. Bill had to be one of the nicest coaches in the world, in any sport.

At the beginning of sophomore year, Adidas offered me the biggest deal I had heard. John Pennel wanted to give me a base payment of eight thousand dollars a year to sign a four-year contract through the 1984 Olympics. There would also be bonuses based on performances.

But at the same time, a former sprinter named Bill Collins, now working for the Tiger shoe company, said he could get me fifteen thousand dollars a year for signing with Tiger. I told Pennel this, but he would not raise his offer. He said his hands were tied. Adidas had chosen James Sanford as its top sprinter and had projected Larry

Myricks to be the world's best long jumper through 1984. Myricks, from Mississippi, had already been on two Olympic teams, and had been favored to win a medal, but hadn't done so. In 1976, he broke a bone in his right ankle while warming up for the final round of jumps at the Games in Montreal. The ankle took a year and a half to heal. Then, in 1980, having won the World Cup a year earlier, Myricks was favored to win the gold in Moscow, but missed his opportunity because of the American boycott.

Sanford and Myricks would get the big offers from Adidas, Pennel told me. He also said he doubted that Collins would come through with the amount of money he was talking about. The Adidas offer to me was eight thousand dollars a year, Pennel said for the last time. I could take it or leave it.

Right then, I told Pennel that Adidas was mistaken about Myricks. He was not going to be the best jumper through '84. He was not going to be the best jumper period, starting now. I was sick of hearing about Myricks, and I was going to start beating him.

Pennel listened. We had always liked each other, but he stuck with the company line. There was nothing he could do. I turned down Adidas. But the Tiger deal didn't come through. Pennel had been right about Collins and Tiger. They talked a better deal than they were willing to make. I had done the best I could, being totally inexperienced at negotiating something like this, but now I had no contract at all. I was still getting shoes and equipment from Adidas, but I wanted a contract.

The only thing left to do was go to a different company. By now, a former athlete, Don Coleman, my roommate two years earlier at the Pan American Games, was working for Nike. I respected and trusted Don like he was a big brother, and he got along real well with my family, so I decided to give him a call. I asked if Nike would give me a contract, and what I could make for signing, and Don said five thousand dollars for a year—even less than Adidas had offered. But I accepted right away, and as soon as we were done talking, Don shipped me a bunch of Nike shoes and clothes.

Nike would pay for four trips to meets during the year, and, de-pending on my performances, I could also earn some bonus money. First in the World Cup would be worth five thousand dollars. A world record, five thousand dollars. American records would be worth less, but still would pay well: twenty-five hundred dollars for an outdoor record, seven hundred and fifty for an indoor mark. Not bad for a college student. And first place in the NCAA championships would get me a bonus of five hundred dollars. I was a little surprised that Nike would put all this in writing—documenting rules violations—but the company did, in a memo written by Don Coleman in January 1981.

At the time, I was sharing an off-campus apartment with Mack, who was back in school, and Cleve, who was working as a financial consultant. All along I had been telling them I was going to start making fifteen thousand dollars a year. We had all been fired up about that, so I was a little disappointed with my first attempt at playing deal-maker. Still, I had to keep everything in perspective. I didn't know any other college sophomores who were making five thousand dollars for wearing free shoes.

At the Southwest Conference championships, I put together the best indoor jump of my career—and it turned out to be the best indoor jump of anybody's career, a world-record 27 feet, 10¼ inches. The previous record, 27 feet, 6 inches, had been set by Myricks the year before. I would have liked to see the reactions of the Adidas people when they saw that I had broken their "number one" jumper's record. They could not have been too happy, and apparently Myricks wasn't either. Through the grapevine, I heard that there were rumors going around about me, saying that I was probably on steroids. How else could I have improved my jump so dramatically? How else could I be better than Myricks? At first, I didn't care much about these rumors. They were totally false, and anybody who knew me would know that. But the more I thought about it, the angrier I got. I was convinced that Myricks was helping to spread these rumors about me. The Adidas situation had already given me great inspiration to beat Myricks, but now I wanted to make sure that Larry would have to make a major adjustment in his attitude. He would have to get used to being second best.

After more than a year of practice, I was finally comfortable with the double-hitch jump, and I was able to focus more on sprinting. That showed when I won the 60-yard dash at the same Southwest Conference meet. My time, 6.06 seconds, was the third best indoors, just behind the world record of 6.04 seconds. My European tour roommate, Stanley Floyd, had set the record two weeks earlier—running with no money in his shoes. The competition against Stanley was a lot of fun because now we were teammates and friends. He had transferred from Auburn to Houston.

At the NCAA indoors, I won the long-jump title again, going 27 feet, 10 inches, just a quarter-inch short of the record I had set three weeks earlier. But everyone had expected me to win the jump. I knew I had to do that to have a good indoor season. What I really wanted, though, was my first sprint title. That would elevate my season from good to great, and that's the way it ended up. I won the 60-yard dash, my fourth NCAA individual title after three victories in the long jump.

But the real fun would start in the spring when we could go back outdoors. There is a lot more room to jump outside, which makes for better performances, and the 100-meter dash is an outdoor event. Indoor tracks are not long enough to run it.

To make a serious move in my sport, I would need a good spring. In college track and field, that is a prerequisite course for Introduction to European Money. Good results during the college season mean good appearance fees on the summer circuit. To an outsider, that might sound crass. After all, I was breaking the NCAA rules and I *knew* I was breaking rules by taking money. Why did I do it?

As far as I was concerned, any college athlete who had been to Europe and been exposed to the opportunities for track athletes would be crazy not to think about the money. After all, the whole idea of a summer job is to put some money away for the school year.

The 1981 NCAA outdoor championships in Baton Rouge, Louisiana, would be a family affair. Mom, Dad, and Carol came from Willingboro, Mack and Cleve from Houston. Carol was finishing high school, being heavily recruited, and would soon choose Houston, as I had. They had all heard the buildup, and they were excited. With victories in the long jump and the 100 I could become the first athlete since Jesse Owens in 1936 to win a track event and a field event the same year in the NCAA outdoor championships. The reporters would have a lot of fun with a story like this. It was one way to get the attention of their editors, who usually did not bother to follow track and field too closely.

The NCAA meet lasts five days, but for me it would happen all at once. The long-jump final and the 100 semifinals and final were all the same day. First I jumped—indoors because of heavy rain—and won with a mark of 27 feet, ¾ inch. An hour and a half later, back outdoors, I won my 100 semifinal race. And less than an hour after that, I was back on the track for the final. I won with a wind-aided time of 9.99 seconds, beating Jeff Phillips of Tennessee (10.00) and Mel Lattany of Georgia (10.06). After crossing the finish line, I held my arms high and enjoyed the victory. I jogged a little, thinking about what I had accomplished, knowing that I would soon be asked to talk about it, talk about it, and talk about it some more.

All the things that matter in competition—the preparation, anticipation, concentration, execution—all those things had come together for me, and now I was feeling the joy of achievement. It is *the* greatest feeling for a world-class athlete, a feeling that makes you forget about pressure and pain and shoe contracts and appearance fees and everything else. But how would I ever be able to express that feeling to someone on the outside?

The way it turned out, I didn't have to try. The only thing reporters wanted to hear about was the Jesse Owens comparison. That was the story that would guarantee them good play in their newspapers. So I listened to Jesse-question after Jesse-question, and I told them the truth. I said what a thrill it was to do something similar to what a hero of mine had done. "That's why the 100 win meant something special to me. It was the biggest thrill of my life. Jesse Owens was such a big figure in my life as well as in track and field. A person like him will live on forever. To put me in the same category is to flatter me. He's an inspiration."

It didn't take long for the European track promoters to find out about the NCAA meet. Joe Douglas called me in Baton Rouge to tell me he was already hearing from people who wanted me in their meets, and the first firm offer was in. Enrico Dionisi, who was organizing a meet in Florence, Italy, had offered two thousand dollars, five times what I had ever gotten for a single meet. But I would have to be there in two days. I was tired and wanted to rest after all the excitement of the NCAAs. But two thousand dollars? I returned to Houston, unpacked my bags, packed again, and got on a plane for Europe.

It turned out that the best thing about Florence was not the money, but my room assignment. I was paired with Steve Williams, my childhood idol. I couldn't believe it. Here I was, a college kid just finishing my sophomore year, and I was in the same room with my idol, the guy I used to pretend to be in my backyard track meets in Willingboro, the same person I was shocked to beat in that race the day of the high school prom. For two days I asked Steve about every race he had ever been in—or, at least, it must have seemed that way to him—and he patiently answered all my questions. Hearing his stories made the trip worthwhile. I never would have admitted this to the meet promoter, but I probably would have gone to Italy for nothing if I had known who my roommate was going to be.

The 1981 U.S. national championships—for all Americans, not just college athletes—were next on the schedule, in Sacramento, California. I had been to the U.S. nationals before, but now I wanted to prove that the NCAA double was not a fluke and that I could win against older, more experienced athletes, the best in our country. Larry Myricks, who had beaten me in all but one of our nine meetings up to now, would be waiting for me in the long jump, and a bunch of great sprinters—including James Sanford, Mel Lattany, and Stanley Floyd—would be in the blocks for the 100. Winners in the nationals would qualify to compete in the World Cup in Rome, and I really wanted to go to that one. For the best chance of winning the 100 and the jump, my plan was simple: I wanted to jump as little as possible and still win. That way, I would be rested for the 100 final, which was the same day.

On my first jump, I went 28 feet, 3½ inches. It was the second-longest legal jump in history. (There had been longer wind-aided jumps, but when the wind is blowing more than two meters per second, the jump cannot be considered for the record books.) I figured I was done jumping for the day. Myricks would need a miracle to beat that, and I would jump again only if he took the lead. On his first jump, Myricks landed with his right hand caught under his shoe, spiking himself, and he came up with a handful of blood and sand. He went for medical help and I went to run the 100.

I trailed the first half of the race, as I often do, but caught everyone the second half and won by a full meter. I shot my arms skyward, and the Santa Monica emblem on my chest showed clearly for all the photographers. With the college season over, I was competing for the club again. My time was 10.13 seconds. Stanley Floyd was second in

10.21 and Lattany was third. Sanford finished fourth. Lattany, Floyd, and I would go to the World Cup for the 100, and Sanford would join us as a member of the 4 × 100 relay team.

After some quick interviews, I returned to the long-jump pit to make sure I didn't have to jump again. By then, Myricks had fouled twice and was preparing for his last jump. He got off his best jump of the day, 27 feet, 8¾ inches, which was the fifth-best legal jump in history, but not good enough to win. "It was the greatest long-jump competition ever," I said, not really knowing if it was, but thrilled with the result.

A reporter asked if I had ever considered jumping again, just for distance, once Myricks was done and I had won the event. "No," I answered. "The only objective here was to win. Even if I'd gone 29–1 on my first jump, I couldn't think of records." I had followed the plan that made the most sense: Jump as little as possible and win. People who followed track and field would soon be used to that strategy of mine, and most agreed that it was a wise way to conserve energy and avoid injury.

Media coverage of the nationals was like a repeat of everything we saw and heard two weeks before at the NCAAs. Once again, it was time for the Jesse Owens story. Carl Lewis is the first person since Jesse to win the long jump and the 100 at the nationals. Jesse did it forty-five years ago. How does it feel to match that, Carl? It felt great, and I fed the reporters the stock answers. "Jesse was a hero. . . . He had a big impact on me. . . . I'm flattered, thank you very much." All of what had become the usual stuff. I would have liked to say, "It's time for a new question." But I understood why everyone was following the same angle. It made for good stories—even though reporters missed what would have been a much better one.

I don't have any idea what went on with things like shoe contracts in Jesse's day, but if a reporter had been paying attention to the shoe companies, his story would have been a lot more explosive than "Carl matches Jesse." I had not forgotten what John Pennel told me less than a year earlier about Adidas. The company had decided that Myricks was the jumper of the future and Sanford was going to be the top sprinter. Sorry, Carl, but we can't offer you what we're paying those guys.

Well, look what happened at the nationals. The mighty Adidas athletes had been beaten by a college kid wearing Nikes. The people from Nike certainly noticed because I was rooming with Don Coleman, the Nike rep. He was paying for everything, and we definitely ran up some bills. Don never minded spending money on a winner. Nike had plenty to spend, and part of Don's job was to keep the Nike athletes happy—even if that included breaking a whole bunch of NCAA rules.

The double double—two wins at the NCAAs, two at the nationals— had the Nike people all excited. They wanted to give me a contract through the 1984 Olympics. I was too naive to know how to handle something like this—national champion, yes, but businessman, no. Plus, everything was happening so fast. Joe Douglas was handling my meet appearances, but not my other business. My family knew a lot about track, but little about big contracts. So I turned to Don Coleman. I thought of Don as a friend before I thought of him as a Nike rep. I figured I could trust him, and I went to him for advice. What will Nike offer? How much should I ask? All the basics.

Don told me what I should ask for: a four-year deal through the 1984 Olympics and into 1985, a series of base payments ranging from forty to sixty-five thousand dollars a year, and a whole bunch of possible bonuses. Base pay for the four years would total two hundred thousand dollars. I would be considered a "consultant" to the company, making public appearances for Nike and always wearing Nike shoes and clothes during meets and appearances. The only time I would be excused from wearing Nike would be if I had to wear a school uniform or the uniform of another team that was not using Nike. As a student, I needed that exception, and Nike understood.

This all sounded great to someone whose current shoe deal was worth only five thousand dollars a year. I asked for the figures Don had suggested, and Nike agreed. A contract would be made, and Nike sent its director of promotions, John de la Forest, to sign me. He met me at home in Willingboro, and, with my parents watching proudly, we signed at the dining room table. I would return to school a wealthy man.

Just as there had been in my first Nike deal, there were bonuses in the new contract, only they were much bigger this time. Now a world record would be worth up to seventeen thousand, five hundred dollars, depending on when and where I got it. Being ranked number one or two in the world in the 100 would pay ten thousand dollars. Same for being one or two in the long jump. And if I were ranked one or two in the 100 *and* the long jump, I would get an extra twenty-five thousand dollars. There was more.

A gold medal in the Olympics would be worth forty thousand dollars. Silver would pay fifteen thousand and bronze would be worth an extra ten thousand. Medals would also be worth money in the NCAA Championships, Pan American Games, World Cup, World Championships, and the U.S. national championships.

But this time there were some clauses that brought new pressure. Nike's payments would be cut in half if I wasn't ranked in the top five in the world in at least one event or if, for any reason, I didn't compete in the 1984 Olympics. If track had not been a business for me up to this point, it certainly was now. The thrill of competing and performing well was still most important. That was number one, without a doubt. But the people who make money from athletes had turned track into more of a business than a sport long before I showed up. Now I was learning how to play by their rules, and those were the rules of business—supply and demand, free trade, you're worth whatever someone is willing to pay you, all that stuff. The way Nike taught me business, I didn't need to study economics in my classes.

The Italy meet set a precedent for the rest of the summer. My standard appearance fee would be two thousand dollars. But even that couldn't keep me from wanting to be home. The European schedule can be exhausting, traveling from country to country every few days, never having time to adjust to a new hotel or time zone or language or anything before it is time to board a bus or a plane again. There is not much time for sightseeing, and even if there were, that would take too much energy. The track circuit is not a summer vacation. The whole idea is to rest when you can: Sit in your hotel room, watch television, read a magazine, play cards, whatever. Otherwise, you won't be ready to compete once you get to the stadium.

After a couple of weeks, all I could think about was going home. I had a few more meets scheduled, but didn't want to compete anymore, so I decided to fake an injury. Clyde Duncan, the Houston assistant coach, and Cleve were with me in Oslo, Norway, and before the 100-meter race I told them I would go down with a fake injury, make it look like I pulled a hamstring or something—anything to get home. They thought I was crazy but I assured them that I was going to do it. I wasn't kidding. I wanted to go home, and an injury was the only way I could pull out of meets.

At the end of the 100 (which I won) I fell on the track, and the place went nuts. Meet officials hurried over, trainers flew at me, and I stayed down, holding the back of my leg, groaning. Clyde came rushing down from the stands as if he didn't know what was going on. My act was so convincing that even he was scared.

"You alright, Carl? You alright?"

Of course I was, but this wasn't the time to say that. Clyde would have to worry a little longer. I was helped off the track, and faked a limp the rest of the night. I would have to go home to get my leg better, I told everyone. Maybe I will be able to train in Houston and try to come back for some meets later in the summer. I had to continue limping in the airport, and even when I got up to use the bathroom on the plane, because there was another athlete on the flight back to the States. I couldn't blow the act.

Later in the summer, I did return to Europe, and during the first meet, in Zurich, Switzerland, I got a little something in return for my fake injury. I strained a hamstring, for real this time, while I was long-jumping. On my sixth jump, I felt a cramp behind my right thigh while I was in the air, tried to land on my left foot, but couldn't. I landed on the right, and pulled the hamstring pretty badly. I figured, that's what I get for faking in Oslo.

The next meet was one of the biggest of the year, in Berlin. A doctor there treated me, and the meet promoters pressured me to compete, saying they couldn't disappoint the fans. But I couldn't do it. The leg was far from ready. I went to Brussels, where I would try to run, but again, after five more days of therapy, I still couldn't compete.

The last meet before returning to school would be the World Cup in Rome, where I was entered in three events, the long jump and the 100 one day, then a leg of the 4 × 100 relay the next day. On my second jump, I went 26 feet, 9 inches, not great, but maybe good enough to win, and I passed on my third jump so I could prepare for the 100, which I was favored to win. Halfway through the race, my leg pulled again, and I grabbed my right thigh, slowing down. I finished dead last in 10.96 seconds, way behind Allan Wells of Great Britain, the Olympic 100-meter champion, who won in 10.20. I skipped the rest of my jumps, but still won that competition. I would have to skip the relay too. On the way to a local hospital for treatment, I figured this was probably the only time I had ever finished first and last the same day.

I could live with losing a race, especially given the circumstances, but I did not appreciate what Allan Wells said to me afterwards: "See, Carl, I told you, you can't do the 100 and jump the same day. Takes too much out of you."

People like Wells inspired me to keep doing what I was doing. I *could* do both events in the same meet, same day, and people telling me I couldn't would make me work that much harder. Back in Willingboro, when I was the runt of the family, a lot of people told me things I couldn't do. Now I was doing them.

Back at school for fall semester of my junior year, I started thinking that this would be my last year competing for Houston. I wanted one more good year, but what would be left after that? I already had six individual NCAA titles, a bunch of records, and enough of an income that people might start wondering what was going on. At some point, someone would figure out that Nike was paying me big money, and that would be the end of my eligibility. I didn't want that to happen because the school would get bad publicity for something I had done on my own. In fact, one of the Nike reps told me that someone from the Houston athletic department had called the company to make sure I didn't have a contract. Someone at Nike lied.

I trained with the team for indoor season, and everything was fine until final exams, when I skipped a history test. I had not studied enough, and rather than fail the test when everyone else was taking it, I figured I would take an incomplete and try to arrange for a makeup test after Christmas break. I thought the plan was working until Coach T called.

"You failed history," he told me. "That'll make you ineligible."

"What are you talking about? I took the test and everything. What's the problem?"

My response was a little weak, I guess, and Coach T knew me well enough to figure he might not be getting the whole story. The teacher did not have a test from me, and that was the bottom line. No test, no grade. No grade, no eligibility.

We called the teacher, who said that I could have a makeup test. If I passed, I would pass the course. If I failed, I failed. At this point, Coach T called the athletic director, Cedric Dempsey, to let him know that everything was under control. Carl was going to get a makeup test. But Dempsey said not to do it that way. The athletic department had to make all the arrangements through proper channels.

I kept calling Dempsey to see if any progress was being made, but he kept saying, "Wait, wait. We don't know anything yet." I jumped at a meet in New Jersey and again set the indoor record with a jump of 28 feet, 1 inch. Not knowing what was going to happen, I wore a USA uniform, not my Houston gear.

Then I went to a meet in California, and stuck with the national uniform. Reporters started asking what had happened to the Houston uniform. Are you done with school? They didn't have to wonder much longer. Just after I competed in California, I found out that there would be no makeup test. I was academically ineligible for the rest of the year. I could stay in school but couldn't compete until my senior year, and then only if I finished certain classes.

Dempsey thought I had been competing in too many meets and that was why I had failed a class. From then on, Dempsey told Coach T and me in a meeting, he wanted to cut down on the number of invitational meets I could enter. That was his condition for taking me back.

My reply was that I wasn't sure that I *was* coming back.

Dempsey was stunned. He wasn't expecting to hear something like that. After a long struggle, he had just secured the 1983 NCAA meet for the Houston campus. He was all excited about that, and was counting on me to stay around and score points for the home team.

But I knew right then that I wouldn't come back. I loved the program, Coach T, the camaraderie of the team. But if I waited around, then followed Dempsey's schedule, my athletic progress would be stifled. I wanted to continue to grow. I needed to grow.

School had been great, with the exception of that history class. I was not the best student on campus, but I was certainly far from the worst, keeping up with most of my work, which was not easy given the demands of track. I had especially enjoyed my speech classes, and I had learned to be a lot more comfortable in front of a crowd than I had been years before when I froze in front of the audience at a high school banquet.

I was through with competing for Houston. I would compete for Santa Monica and myself. But I decided to stay in school. My parents had taught me that there is a lot more to life than running and jumping, and I didn't want to rule out anything I could learn in the classroom.

FIVE

≡

A Religious Heart without Boundaries

GENERALLY, I stay in my room the night before a meet. I don't really want to see anyone. I just want to relax by myself. But June 3, 1981, was different. The date is easy to remember because it was one of those few days in my life, as in any of our lives, that can be identified as a turning point. It was the day I was exposed to a group of Christian athletes called Lay Witnesses for Christ.

This was my sophomore year, the night before I was to compete in the NCAA meet in Baton Rouge. Willie Gault, who was competing for Tennessee, came to my room and said he wanted me to meet somebody. Willie and I had been friends for a few years, having spent time together at track meets and talking about a lot of things that had nothing to do with track. Willie was a football star (playing wide receiver for Tennessee), a track star, and one of the nicest, brightest people I had met in sports. He would later star in the National Football League for the Chicago Bears and the Los Angeles Raiders. Willie really didn't say much about the person he wanted me to meet. I didn't know who or what he was talking about. But we went to a meeting room in the hotel. A lot of other athletes were there, and people were talking in little groups. I knew this had something to do with religion, but I did not know what.

A gentleman introduced himself—his name was Sam Mings—and

his group, Lay Witnesses for Christ. It was the first time I had heard of either. Sam, a former track athlete, said he had formed Lay Witnesses in 1976. The idea then was to carry the gospel to what Sam called "society's down-and-outers," young and old alike. But after a meeting at the University of Tennessee, Sam changed his focus to athletes. He was at Tennessee speaking on behalf of the Fellowship of Christian Athletes, and he saw thirty-eight people saved in one night. One of them was Willie Gault.

Willie suggested to Sam that he come to the meet in Baton Rouge. So Sam rented a hotel room, bought some soft drinks, and hung signs saying Chapel Services. Sam told us, "We want to open our doors to anyone who wants to seek the Lord and pray to receive Christ. A lot of athletes need or want help with their lives. We can reach a lot of athletes here."

Sam talked about the love of Jesus for man. He talked about how Jesus had come to earth, had lived a sinless life, died on the cross, and rose again. Sam talked about the satisfaction of having a personal relationship with Jesus. A few other people spoke, we prayed, and Sam said, "If you'd like to be more involved, if you feel like you want to accept the Lord in your life, well, then come back tomorrow. We'll have a meeting at ten in the morning and six in the evening."

I was raised a Lutheran in New Jersey, and we went to church quite frequently. But I don't know how committed I was. I always believed in God, always believed in the Lord and His power. I felt His presence. But I was not tuned in the way I could have been.

Sam seemed to be somebody you could really open up to and become close to very quickly. For one thing, he knew a lot about track, and that helped him relate to us. More important, though, he didn't really preach when he discussed religion. He just spoke. And he was open-minded. If you wanted to come back, great. If not, fine, we still love you. His approach was low-key, his manner was calm, and his voice was soothing. I was very comfortable in this setting, especially because I was around so many people I knew from track.

The next day I won the long jump. Then I went back to hear Sam again. This time, Sam asked some of the toughest questions I had ever been asked. "Have you invited Jesus Christ into your life? Has He changed your life? If you were to die today, are you sure that you would go to heaven?"

This was the first time I had ever been confronted with such difficult questions, and I felt like I might be missing something in my life. I looked at Sam as someone who could provide a great opportunity to grow spiritually, and the situation was just right. With my entire family in Baton Rouge for the meet, I could discuss my thoughts with the people closest to me. After I shared with them what had happened in the meetings, my brothers Mack and Cleve went with me to the next meeting, and we prayed together to receive Christ. My mother, father, and sister were next, each meeting Sam and making new commitments to the Lord. I think our involvement with Lay Witnesses was the final link to bringing our family as close together as it could be.

Lay Witnesses is not all that different from the Fellowship of Christian Athletes. Both are nonprofit groups committed to the Lord. But I think the fellowship focuses more on college campuses. We've been able to bring in world-class athletes on a much broader scale.

We advertise before we speak in public. We have to do that to let people know who we are and where we are speaking. But we don't preach in the streets or anything. That is one of the things I like about Lay Witnesses. We don't ram our religion down your throat. We are not trying to convert people. We are just trying to reach them. Then they can do what they feel is right.

I do not sing about religion every time I am interviewed. If I am asked about my talent, I say, "I feel it is a God-given talent and I feel very fortunate about that. But I also feel it has taken a lot of hard work." I do not thank the Lord in every interview after every victory because I believe religion is much more personal than that. Sometimes it is expressed publicly. But most of the time it is personal.

At least, that is the way it *should* be. Some athletes obviously disagree. How often do we see a baseball player grabbing a microphone to thank the Lord for every hit in a baseball game? "Well, it was a pretty good fastball. I'm just thankful that the Lord wanted me to hit it over the fence." We hear a basketball player thanking the Lord for every free throw he sinks. "I might have been nervous on the line, but deep in my heart I knew the Lord did not create me to shoot bricks." Then there is the boxer who praises the Lord after a championship bout. "Thank you, Lord, for letting me punish my opponent's face more severely than he punished mine." That is not being a witness for Christ. That is being a show-off.

There is nothing wrong with thanking the Lord when appropriate.

But this God-squad mentality can get pretty obnoxious. I am all for reading and citing Scriptures. But I want to be a responsible Christian, not an obnoxious one.

Worship means the most when it is intensely personal. That is what makes religion work for me. And it must be one other thing: open-minded. A closed mind blocks the growth of spiritual feelings. There should be no limits on spiritual feelings.

A couple of years after meeting Sam Mings, my open-mindedness was put to a great test. By then I was a director of Lay Witnesses, working closely with Sam, Willie Gault, and Reggie White, another football star from Tennessee, planning events for the organization. So I was a little surprised when a close friend of mine, Narada Michael Walden, wanted me to meet a man named Sri Chinmoy, who is an Indian spiritual teacher.

Narada is a very talented and successful musician who has won all sorts of awards, including a Grammy and an Emmy. I met him in 1983 after a track meet in San Jose, California. I had several of Narada's albums so I recognized him when I saw him walking outside the stadium. He was with his wife, Anukampa, and I stopped them to introduce myself. It turned out that Narada had been a fan of mine just as I had been a fan of his, so we talked for a few minutes, said we would keep in touch, and later became friends.

Now Narada was encouraging me to meet Sri Chinmoy. A little Hinduism for someone who was still coming to terms with his Christian beliefs? A lot of Christians would probably scream, "What are you talking about? Get out of here!" But I did what was natural for me. I was willing to listen and learn.

Narada said he knew about my Christianity. He knew about my participation in Lay Witnesses and did not want to change any of that. But he said that Sri Chinmoy could enhance my relationship with the Lord. Sri Chinmoy was born in India in 1931, and he spent most of his childhood in an ashram, or spiritual community. As a youngster, he loved sports, playing soccer and volleyball and becoming a sprint and decathlon champion in his community. As he grew older and more devoted to his religious beliefs, Sri Chinmoy started promoting athletics—in his words—"as an adjunct to spiritual fitness." In 1964, Sri Chinmoy came to the United States, and over the years he has built quite a following. He leads meditation sessions for diplomats at the United Nations, and he is very well respected by all sorts of different people—rich and poor, famous and ordinary, men and women, young and old. "Next time you're going to be in New York," Narada said to me, "let me know and we'll go see Sri Chinmoy."

A few months later, Narada and Anukampa met me in New York and we went to Queens, where Sri Chinmoy lives. It is also the home of his center for spiritual growth and peace. Sri Chinmoy believes that meditation is a key to inner peace and detachment from the cares of the modern world. "When we have this kind of peace," he says, "it is a solid rock within us. The earthly turmoils—fear, doubt, worries—will all be shattered, for inside is solid peace."

Sri Chinmoy also says that we can all benefit spiritually by stretching our physical limits. One believer, a man named Ashrita Furman, has gained a lot of publicity for stretching his limits. To honor Sri Chinmoy's fiftieth birthday, Furman set a world record by giving his spiritual teacher a fifty-hour standing ovation. If that sounds unusual, it should not—not for Furman. Seeking spiritual benefits, Furman had already set records in juggling, underwater pogo-sticking, and somersaulting. He performed ten straight miles of somersaulting.

And I thought long jumping was tough. I was not going to take a pogo stick in a swimming pool. But I was open to finding out more about Sri Chinmoy, or "Guru," as his followers call him. Sri Chinmoy does not run a cult or anything. I wouldn't want anyone to get the wrong idea. But in deference to the tremendous spirit and powerful teachings of the man, calling Sri Chinmoy "Guru" is certainly appropriate.

When I met him, he was wearing a jogging suit. He said he was a fan of mine and that Jesse Owens had been his childhood idol. We were at a public high school in Queens. A bunch of Sri Chinmoy followers were there for a day of athletics and a picnic. A few people pulled out banners they had made to greet me, including one that said "The Greatest," and there was almost nothing mentioned about religion. It was just a nice day, a time for sports and food and friends. Everyone was so friendly that it was like I was meeting a whole group of relatives I somehow had not met before.

The next day, there were some sports competitions, a lot of music, and some spiritual talk. But it wasn't like anyone was beating down the door for religion. At the end of the day, though, Sri Chinmoy told me he would like to talk to me. Privately. I thought, Whoa, wait a minute, here comes the big whammy. I asked if Narada could come with me, and he did. We went into a little office Sri Chinmoy uses, and the first thing I saw was a picture of Jesus on the wall.

"Obviously, you know what I am," Sri Chinmoy said. "I am of the Indian faith. But I'm going to tell you something. I'm a big believer in Jesus. For me to say that Jesus is not the way is wrong, because Jesus is a wonderful way. But Jesus is not the only way. We have open beliefs. If I see Jesus, I am inspired. If I see Krishna, I am inspired. If I see Buddha, I am inspired. I am inspired by religion. I am not intimidated by anything. I do not shy away from anything.

"The most important thing about religion is inspiration, no matter where that inspiration comes from. It isn't always just looking at Jesus, a picture of Jesus, or praying to someone or meditating. If you see a flower that is beautiful, that can be a spiritual experience. A lot of it is personal. A lot of it is your own feelings and your relationships."

He just went on and on. But he continually reinforced my feelings for the Lord whom I believed in. Sri Chinmoy said he would never infringe on that feeling. But he said he wanted us to become friends. Then he could always motivate me to pray.

I'm not going to say this whole thing did not seem a little strange. It did. At first, Sri Chinmoy had just wanted to meet me. But the second day, he told Narada that my soul had come to him. Strange, I thought. I felt whole. I did not know my soul had been anywhere.

Anyway, my soul supposedly let Sri Chinmoy know that he had inspired me, which was true. He had. My soul also conveyed to him that I could love Jesus more than I already did. I could love anything. I could be inspired by religion.

Actually, I think what happened was, my athletic abilities had inspired Sri Chinmoy long before I met him. Then when we met he saw that I was open to spirituality or religion or whatever. And he just figured, hey, let's go with it. We talked about his beliefs. I told him I would like to keep in touch. And that was that.

Weeks later, Sri Chinmoy called Narada. Sri Chinmoy had felt my soul again and this time my soul let him know that I wanted a name. Sri Chinmoy gives Sanskrit names to his followers. Narada was not always Narada. He was just Michael Walden. Narada, which means "the ultimate drummer," is a spiritual name given to him by Sri Chinmoy, and it is a perfect name because Narada is a great drummer. Sri Chinmoy said he was not sure if I was ready for a name, so he wanted to talk to me about this.

After a while, Sri Chinmoy decided I was ready and he asked me if I wanted a name. He assured me that getting a name doesn't mean that life as I know it ends and I have to start running around in Indian get-ups. A name just means that I am receptive to the spiritual inspiration of Sri Chinmoy. I would not have to use the name in public—I could if I wanted to—but he and his followers would know me by my new name.

It was given to me during a ceremony Sri Chinmoy conducted in the auditorium of a school in Queens. More than one hundred people participated, most of them disciples who had been through similar ceremonies to receive names of their own. There was music and singing and praying. When Sri Chinmoy finished singing, he called me up to the stage, where he stood, smiling, as he often does. He was wearing a shiny silk outfit and socks. We were all wearing socks without shoes. Sri Chinmoy and his followers usually leave their shoes at the door. I was dressed simply, white athletic socks, jeans, and a sweater, and I sat on a metal folding chair. Sri Chinmoy placed a flower between my hands, and I pressed them together in front of me, closing my eyes in prayer, just as he did. The flower was to symbolize the birth of a new name. Sri Chinmoy touched my hands, and he said something like "Shoot-a-hota." He said it quietly a few times. Then he said it out loud so everyone could hear. "Shoot-a-hota. Shoot-a-hota." I just sat there, having no idea what was going on. Finally, Sri Chinmoy stopped and said, "I guess this isn't getting through." He whispered, "That's your name. Say it." So I said it.

It is spelled Sudhahota, and it means "unparalleled sacrificer of immortality." Pretty heavy stuff. Sri Chinmoy explained that he had interpreted the name from what he found in my soul. He said, "You always give it your all. A lot of times people do not think what you are doing is the right thing. But it *is* what you think is right. You're always a sacrificer for what you believe in and what you think is right."

It has often seemed since then that Sri Chinmoy was very perceptive. A lot of times I am criticized for the things I say in public. It would be a lot easier for me if I did not say some of the things I believe. But if something is right and people need to know about it, I say it. I learned at a young age the way Dr. Martin Luther King, Jr., stressed the importance of sacrifice. If you live without sacrifice—on a small or big level, in your professional or personal life, at home or in public—then you have missed a very important part of life. I had always believed that. It was amazing, though, that Sri Chinmoy picked up on that. I had never expressed that feeling to him. At least, not in words.

Narada and Anukampa joined us on stage, Narada on my right, Anukampa on my left. They sat on the floor, legs crossed, hands pressed together in front of their chests, in prayer positions.

Later, Sri Chinmoy helped me with another advancement in my spiritual life, teaching me how to meditate. Sometimes I use a mantra to help me concentrate, other times I don't. Either way, I find meditating to be more demanding than praying. In praying, we are often thanking God or asking God to do something, focusing on a specific need or desire. In most cases, that does not take much energy. When I meditate, the goal is to open myself up to God, seeking total concentration on accepting His power and energy, not focusing on any specific need or desire. This can be relaxing, draining, or invigorating, depending on any number of things, most of which would be impossible to understand or explain. I try to meditate several times a week in a quiet, secluded place, usually my home when I am in Houston or my hotel room if I am on the road.

Some people are going to read this and say, "You're crazy. You're with a cult." Some are going to say, "Oh, that's interesting. I'd like to know more." And some people are not going to care one way or the other.

But there are plenty of people who go to church every Sunday only because someone shames them into going, making them feel terribly guilty if they don't attend services. People like this are not comfortable in church but they go anyway. Well, maybe if they met a Sri Chinmoy or someone like him, they would be more inspired to go to church or learn more about religion.

I don't know what Willie Gault will think of all this. I don't know what other Christians—especially my friends with Lay Witnesses— will think about my relationship with Sri Chinmoy. But I don't see any conflict between my Christian beliefs and my spiritual understanding of Sri Chinmoy and his beliefs. Both inspire me.

I don't think my Christian friends will be offended by my association with Sri Chinmoy, because they know I am completely tuned in to Lay Witnesses and my commitment to Jesus. Sri Chinmoy does not take anything away from my Christian beliefs. He strengthens them. Yes, I meditate regularly, practicing techniques learned from a man I call "Guru." But I also read my Bible on a daily basis. When I'm home, it sits by my bed so I can read from it every night, and when I'm on the road, my Bible goes with me.

My involvement with Sri Chinmoy is an extra step forward to spiritual fulfillment, not a step backward from Christianity, and I really enjoy that extra step. I am not saying that other Christians limit themselves by not taking a step like this. That would be entirely out of place for me to say. But the extra step works for me.

Sri Chinmoy does not take away from the Bible and the Bible does not block out someone like Sri Chinmoy. I will always be thankful that Willie Gault introduced me to Lay Witnesses for Christ and I will always be glad that Narada and Sri Chinmoy made me Sudhahota.

SIX

≡

Carl-Bashing

THERE WAS never an official announcement—"Let the hype begin!"—but none was needed. The American media were hungrier than ever for Olympic stories. The U.S. team, at the direction of President Carter, had boycotted the 1980 Games, but in 1984 we were going to compete, and on our own soil, in Los Angeles. Circumstances like these would require the biggest of buildups, some serious hype, starting as early as the beginning of 1983. With the start of the '83 indoor season—two indoor seasons and two outdoor seasons before the Games would begin—reporters already wanted to talk about the summer of 1984.

Could I win four gold medals like Jesse Owens did? Could I break Bob Beamon's record in the long jump? I would offer a simple response—"Everything is fine. Everything is on schedule." And that was enough to make headlines. I would say that the long jump was progressing well and the 29-foot range was my goal. Again, headlines. Sure, the Olympics were my long-term project, I would say in response to questions, but I would also stress that almost anything can happen in a year, especially in sports. It was too early to say a whole lot about the '84 Games. But that would do nothing to slow down the hype.

I could no longer be Carl Lewis. I would have to be Carl Lewis the

Next Jesse Owens. And even as the Jesse comparison grew, there were others. I know that sportswriters sometimes need a comparison to put an accomplishment in perspective, to show how rare or difficult something is, but with the pre-Olympic hype, there was comparison after comparison, and it seemed like nobody would just let me be me. At the 1983 U.S. indoor championships, when I won the 60-yard dash and the long jump, I became the next Barney Ewell. I had never heard of him, but I was told he had been the last guy to win the sprint and the long jump at a national indoor meet. That was in 1945. A few months later, I won the 100, 200, and long jump, a rare triple, at the U.S. outdoor championships, and without even realizing it, I was the next Malcolm Ford. Again, not exactly a household name in the 1980s. He won three golds in 1895 and 1896.

No matter what I did, no matter where I did it, I was going to exist in a world of comparisons, and under a media microscope. The press always needed a story, and any comparison would help. The more comparisons, the more hype, and the more hype, the better exposure a story would get. This is something I would have to accept, even though I didn't always like it. The press was, for the most part, very positive toward me at this point, but that was not enough to make me entirely comfortable around reporters. I didn't like the idea of living under a microscope, in a world of comparisons. In a lot of ways I was still the shy kid in Willingboro, but now I was expected to be so much more than that. I *had* to be so much more than that. So I would lean on my family—which by now included Coach Tellez and Joe Douglas—and I would do the best I could.

Still, I would have to deal with outsiders on my own terms. I would not be able to make good on every request for an interview or appearance that came my way. And when I did talk to reporters, I would answer their questions without saying a whole lot more than I had to. I would try to be polite, but I wasn't interested in being best friends. I had no desire to share my private life with reporters who would want to analyze it, then splash it into print and onto television. As a result, some reporters would later label me "distant" or "arrogant" or "shy" or whatever, but I could live with that, and for now, most of the reporters were writing very positive things about me. Still exaggerating, still searching for comparisons and hype, still focusing way too much on whether I could win four events in the Olympics, but very positive. That was the way it would be until the official introduction of a new event on the international track-and-field circuit.

The new event—Carl Lewis–bashing—hit the circuit in mid-1983. Before then, some jealous athletes had taken shots at me here and there, but they had not gotten much attention. A few reporters had also taken shots, but the positive press had far outweighed any negative stories. Now was the time to make bashing a demonstration sport. If I had been beating you in sprints or the long jump, you could enter the competition by spreading false rumors about me. Bring me down, and you could bring yourself up. And if you were really good at what you were doing, the press would help you achieve your goal. When certain reporters heard what you had to say, they would do some bashing of their own, and that would escalate the whole thing. Then the press would take over. The reporters would no longer need the help of athletes. All by themselves, they would line up to do some Carl-bashing.

There were basically three bashing categories: Carl thinks he's better than everyone else, and he loves to show it. Carl does drugs. Carl is gay.

Pretty strong stuff. None of which would help my image a whole lot. But the competition was on. *Let the hype begin.*

Carl-bashing was introduced at the U.S. national outdoor championships. I won the 100 for the third year in a row, won the long jump without much trouble, and won the 200 in near world-record time. But the Carl-bashers wanted to focus on the end of the 200. With ten meters to go, I was way ahead, knew the race was mine, and I raised my arms in celebration. I wasn't trying to make anybody else look bad, wasn't even *thinking* about anybody else. I was just excited, the way anyone in my situation would have been. I was twenty-one years old, having fun, and the crowd loved it. But this was the beginning of category number one: Carl thinks he's better than everyone else, and he loves to show it.

The reactions: (a) Carl is being too much of a hot dog; (b) raising his arms and slowing down probably cost him a world record. My time was 19.75, an American record. But the world record was 19.72.

Larry Myricks was one of the athletes who spoke out against me, and that was no surprise. When I had raised my arms and looked over my shoulder, he had been in second place. He was sick of losing to

me, and he told reporters, "There's going to be some serious celebrating when Carl gets beat." That was okay because Myricks certainly wasn't going to be the one to beat me. He was too much of a
choke artist.

Edwin Moses, the best hurdler in the world, was another pretty
aggressive Carl-basher. Asked about me during an interview, Edwin
said: "I think he rubs it in too much. I could dog my competitors and
make them feel bad, but I don't. There's a lot of controversy surrounding the guy now, a lot of negative vibrations. Here's a guy who
comes along, runs fast, jumps far and steals the whole show. It bothers me a little, but not enough to affect me. I just think a little
humility is in order. That's what Carl lacks."

Edwin's coach, Gordon Cooper, wasn't thrilled with me, either.
"Do you think Edwin Moses would have hot-dogged it by raising his
hands, smiling and making a fool of himself 20 meters away from a
world record?" he asked. "To Edwin, track is an art form and he can't
stand to see it defiled."

Gordon's choice of words, especially the phrase "art form," would
look kind of funny later in Edwin's career. Edwin started dodging
people to preserve a winning streak, and I would hardly call that
being an artist. But anyway . . .

I had just done what came naturally to me, and I didn't know what
the big deal was. I had not been trying to "dog my competitors" or
"defile" our "art form." I was just being myself. I had been after the
triple and I had achieved it. I hadn't been thinking about a record,
just trying to win a race. Great times and world records would come
with time, but not by worrying about them. They would take care of
themselves. But anything I said didn't really matter at this point.
Criticism would be my new companion, and this was only a preview
of bashings to come. They would get a lot worse. The media bashers
had not even warmed up yet.

Category number two: Carl does drugs. This one had already gone
around back when I was in college. Back then the rumor had not
made it too far, but now it was spreading. The better I performed, the
more I heard about a few other athletes, including Myricks and one
of his teammates, Mel Lattany, saying, "What do you expect? He's on
drugs." The drug talk peaked during the World Championships in
Helsinki, Finland, in August 1983.

This was the first time the World Championships were held, and it turned out to be one of the best meets of my career. In the 100-meter final, I ran 10.07 to win the gold. I won the long jump, going 28 feet, ¾ inch. Then I rested for the 4 × 100-meter relay. I ran with Calvin Smith, Emmit King, and Willie Gault, and we set a world record, 37.86 seconds. Up to then, the best time had been 38.03 seconds, run in 1977 by another American team, including my old idol, Steve Williams.

With all of this positive stuff going on, most of the reporters in Helsinki did not pay much attention to what a few athletes were saying about me and drugs. For one thing, I had the body of a little teenager, not the bulk of a steroid user. Plus, the press box was full of people who still wanted to write mostly positive stuff about me.

The *New York Times* headline said, "Carl Lewis Emerges at Helsinki: He's the Best at All He Does." *Sports Illustrated* put me on its cover with the headline, "The Best in the World . . . Carl Lewis Scores a Stunning Triple at Helsinki." The *Sporting News* said, "Finns Agree: Lewis Is the Greatest." Nice stuff all the way around in the American coverage of the World Championships.

But one Norwegian reporter tried to mess everything up. He had paid too much attention to the drug rumors, and he wrote a completely false story that said I had tested positive for steroids. By the time he wrote it, I was gone. I was in another country for another meet, and I couldn't believe it. The story circulated all over Europe, and some American publications picked it up. People who tried to substantiate the story were told by meet officials that it was preposterous. But that didn't matter much. Once the story was out, it was out, and people who closely followed our sport would remember it for a long time. They would wonder if I had really tested positive or not, and rumors would keep flying.

The next one was even crazier: Carl has been taking gorilla hormones, and as a result, a cyst the size of a golf ball has grown on his chest. Surgery is required, so Carl will not be competing for a while. Some meet promoters in Europe actually called Joe Douglas to ask if this were true. Of course not, Joe told them. Just more Carl-bashing. Carl is fine.

Category number three: Carl is gay. He is closest with men, not women. I have never been one to judge others by their sexual preferences. Everyone makes his or her own choice, and that's fine. But like it or not, a lot of people judge by labels like this, and I did not

At my first Jesse Owens meet, my father introduced me to Owens, who said, "Have fun." He wanted me to know that having fun was the most important thing about competing. Shown here, from left to right, are: me, my cousin Jim, Owens, and another man, whom I don't know. (Lewis family photo)

Yes, I was definitely the runt of the family. It seemed to take *forever* for that to change. (Lewis family photo)

3

4

Running and jumping for Willingboro High School, I was finally good enough to be noticed. I was heavily recruited and signed with the University of Houston. (Dennis McDonald photos)

Here I am at the Penn Relays in April 1981, competing for Houston. There were a lot of exciting meets in the States, but I learned that the business of track is best in Europe. (Dennis McDonald)

The two most important people in my life: my father, William Lewis, and my mother, Evelyn Lawler Lewis. They were both track coaches and loved to travel with me—even if they sometimes had to wait before crossing borders between countries.

6

Here's a photo I particularly like of the entire family. Back row: Mack; my father, Bill; myself; Cleve. Front row: Carol and my mother, Evelyn.

7

University of Houston coach Tom Tellez (*left*) introduced me to Santa Monica Track Club founder Joe Douglas (*right*). Coach T has been my coach and friend for a decade. Joe has been my manager and friend for almost as long.

My sister Carol joined me at Houston, and has traveled with me all over the world, competing herself as a long jumper in the 1984 and 1988 Olympics. (8- DUOMO/Paul J. Sutton; 9- DUOMO/Steven E. Sutton)

8

9

I am sometimes a billboard for Lay Witnesses for Christ. At the same time, I am inspired by my relationship with Sri Chinmoy, an Indian guru. In 1983, Sri Chinmoy conducted a ceremony to give me a new name, Sudhahota. I am sitting between my friends Narada Michael Walden and Anukampa Walden. Sri Chinmoy stands to the side. (10-DUOMO/Paul J. Sutton)

There was plenty of time to celebrate—alone and with teammates—when I won three gold medals at the 1983 World Championships in Helsinki, Finland. But Carl-bashing started to interfere with the fun. (13- DUOMO/Steven E. Sutton)

want to carry a label that didn't fit me. Ironically, the undisputed champion basher for this category was a young woman who had been in bed with me more than enough times to know that I was not gay. She said that she loved me and wanted to marry me, and there was a time when I really enjoyed her company, but that was before I knew what she was really like.

She was a long jumper who competed on the track circuit at the same time I did. We had spent time together when we saw each other at meets. Then she came to Houston and shared an apartment with my sister. She and Carol knew each other from long jumping, and she figured the closer she could get to my family, the closer she could get with me. Not a bad strategy, but then she started getting much too demanding, and she started spreading lies, telling people we were in love, we were engaged, and it was just a matter of time before we would get married. That was one way she tried to keep other girls away from me. Another way was spreading a rumor that I was gay. Carl is gay, so don't even bother.

This one peaked in Helsinki, too. She was telling people she had heard that one of the other male athletes and I had pushed our beds together in a hotel room, and, oh, it was so horrible, she just couldn't stand to hear it. She was very careful about the way she said this. She didn't want it to look like she was *starting* this rumor, just that she had heard it and was troubled by it. Her objective was to make it seem like everybody hated me except her. She really cared for me, and I should stick with her. The rumor spread quickly among the American athletes, and it was just the kind of stuff someone like Myricks wanted to hear, another rumor he could use against me.

At the same time she was putting out the gay rumor, she was also telling other girls on the circuit that she had me. I was hers. And when we got back to Houston, she started making up other stuff about me and my family. She was damaging my reputation, threatening the reputation of some other great athletes, and she was causing a great deal of dissension on the practice track at Houston, where she had been training with us. Some of the other athletes told me what she had been saying and doing, and some of them just stopped talking to me. They didn't know what to think.

Finally, I had to put an end to all this. I got a group of my teammates together in a room in the athletic department building, and I confronted her in front of everybody. I trapped her in a web of lies she had told different people in the room, and I said, "How dare you spread all these lies and hurt all these people?" Without answering, she ran out of the room, and more than a year went by before she was seen by anybody I know.

Unfortunately, even when she disappeared, she left a lot of damage behind. The people at Houston learned from that meeting what had been going on, and we all started getting along just fine again. But what about everybody else on the track circuit, and the reporters who had heard bits and pieces of what had been said? I would always hear whispers about being gay, and that would always remind me of my former girlfriend. She had been around such a short time, but she had started something that I would have to deal with for a long time in terms of my public image. That hurt, and I would have to find ways to deal with it.

In the past, reporters had usually asked me nice questions about competing, my family, my goals, stuff like that. Now they started prying. What are you *really* like? How do you spend your free time? Some athletes think you are gay. How do you respond?

It got ridiculous. I would say, "No, that's not true, I'm not gay, and I have nothing to hide. If I were gay, I would be all uptight about this, I guess. But I know what the deal is. It's really not an issue."

Sometimes when a reporter asked if I was gay, I would answer with a question: "Are *you*?"

"No."

"Well, if I called you that, what would you do?"

"Nothing. I'm not gay, so nothing."

"Thanks. You just answered your own question for me."

Sometimes I would use a different approach: "I guess saying that someone is gay is the easiest, most effective way to attack a male, especially an athlete, who is supposed to be all macho. I should really be upset, right? Well, what am I going to do, raise my voice and kick your ass? Why do I have to do that? I don't have to prove anything to you. You don't seem to like me, so why am I going to waste my time with this?"

The rules for Carl-bashing in the media changed a great deal in 1984. You couldn't just say bad things about me while talking to athletes or other reporters. You had to write them and circulate falsehoods among millions of readers. If you were a writer out to make a name for yourself, you could compete in Carl-bashing by making up almost anything nasty about me. It was best if nobody else had made it up first. That way, you could win twice, in Carl Lewis–bashing and in some journalism contest for people who write the best fiction and pass it along as fact.

The all-time champion of Carl-bashing was a *Sports Illustrated* writer named Gary Smith, who, of all the people I have met in my entire life, remains the one person I respect the least. That is a nice way of putting it. I would rather not think so negatively about another person, but Gary didn't leave me a choice. He treated me unfairly, lied about me, shared some of his lies with millions of readers, and worst of all, apparently didn't care about the damage he was causing. Probably didn't even think about what the damage would be.

Gary does deserve some credit. He wrote one of the best short stories I have ever read. There was only one problem: the person he kept calling Carl Lewis was not me. He was the sloppy creation of a writer who wanted more than anything to write a story that had never before been written. Gary painted the subject of his story as an asshole, and he identified the asshole as Carl Lewis.

When the story came out—in the July 18, 1984, issue of *Sports Illustrated*—I knew from the first sentence that it was trouble. The story started: *He stands at the top of the runway, his warmup-jacket collar flipped up over his neck in the style of someone who wants very much to be different, which he does, and his expression saying Oh, it's up. Breeze must've caught it.*

This was vintage Gary Smith, right from the start. He was going to analyze everything, as if a flipped-up collar is full of symbolism. The whole thing was written to make it look like I had an incredible ego, like I was an arrogant, singular person who doesn't listen to anybody.

Lewis is a child who has climbed a tree and lost himself in the self-absorption of seeing how far out on a limb he can go. The long jump wasn't far enough, so he added the 100-meter dash and conquered that. That wasn't far enough, so he added the 4 × 100 relay and the 200, and lived with the nagging thought that 48 years ago a man had won gold medals in all four of those events. He planned to become a sportscaster after the Olympics, but there were so many other athletes doing that it began to seem common, so he added acting and singing. . . . Four gold medals, a gold record, a golden Oscar— none would be an end in itself for him. Each would merely give the child in the tree a surer grip, more control, to assure him he could move a few more feet out on the limb—out to the frail, lonely end, where the wind whips and only the true original clings.

The whole story, one of the longest ever written about me, was full of this "out on a limb" crap. Who did Gary Smith think he was, Sigmund Freud?

Gary even tried to make a big deal out of my participation in sports as a youngster.

When Carl was 8, playing Pony League, he happened to find himself in centerfield with a fly ball. His father's eyes followed the arc of the ball and then shifted to his son. His son was busy picking daisies. When the ball stopped rolling, Carl picked that, too. He didn't play baseball much longer.

I'm not going to say I was a good baseball player. I was not. But I was eight years old. Give me a break. Being analytical about an eight-year-old playing Little League? I just didn't like baseball. Simple as that. It had nothing to do with wanting to be an individual and not wanting to play a team sport.

He seriously played one team sport—soccer. The field seemed large enough, the movements unregulated enough, for him to join and still be Carl Lewis.

Total opinion. Ridiculous. I wanted to play soccer because one of my brothers, Cleve, was one of the best soccer players around. Everybody in Willingboro knew Cleve because of soccer, and I looked up to Cleve, so playing soccer was automatic. It certainly had nothing to do with the large field or unregulated movements.

He must risk. He must wait sometimes until the last jump to uncork the record beater; he must heighten the Olympic pressure by huckstering; he must weave through interstate traffic, blinking high beams on dawdlers. The easier it comes to the child on the limb, the more he must chance—Look, one foot!—the more he must tickle dozing fate to make sure he controls her. How could he be distinct if each step were predictable?

Again, Sigmund Freud at his best. It would have been amusing, except that so many people were going to judge me based on what was written in this story. Gary Smith could not take facts and leave them alone. Then again, Gary had trouble with the concept of a fact. He apparently did not understand that a fact is supposed to be true.

Gary wrote that I went to the University of Houston, not local track power Villanova, so I could become more independent. Not true. Tom Tellez was the reason I went to Houston. It had nothing to do with getting away from home or being independent.

He would major in radio and TV so he could use track as a springboard to another career.

False. Actually, I started studying business at Houston. I switched to radio and TV after my sophomore year, and that was only because I had a speech teacher who had really impressed me.

Then there was this about driving my car with my friend Thomas Mayfield: *One night the BMW hit a slick patch and went out of control, spinning 360 degrees. In the passenger seat, Mayfield was terrified. Lewis laughed—wasn't that turn of fate under his grip, too? "Don't worry," he said. "I had it all under control."*

Nice little story. But it never happened.

One of the most amazing Freudian passages was in a section on Bob Beamon's world-record jump: *Lewis loathes mystery. The day he sails farther, he must know every element that created the jump, he must know how to duplicate it, he must feel he controlled it—or it won't be a triumph. In the long jump, as in life, Lewis must happen to it—he cannot let it happen to him.*

Again, harping on his fixation that I think I must always be in control, whatever that means.

Gary completely cut out every positive thing he could have said about me.

The worst thing about the story was not the story itself. That would come and go. The worst thing was that a lot of reporters and columnists who knew nothing about me would now base their writing on what they read in the magazine. Without knowing me, they accepted as fact what Gary wrote. This was in a special issue of the most prominent sports magazine in the world just weeks before the Olympics in Los Angeles. So the story would be clipped and saved by reporters from all over the world who needed background for their own coverage of the Games, and it would affect the way they covered me. It would have been one thing if *Sports Illustrated* readers finished the Carl Lewis-is-a-jerk story and then it disappeared. But this would not go away.

SEVEN

≡

The 1984 Olympics

July 28, 1984
Los Angeles

TIME TO forget the distractions and let the Games begin—finally. Well, almost. First we would attend the opening ceremonies.

Athletes from every country would march into the Coliseum. There would be singing, dancing, and speeches, including a short one from President Reagan to declare the official beginning of the Games.

The American athletes would be last to enter the Coliseum, so we waited next door in the Sports Arena. Most athletes stuck with the people in their sports. But I see enough of the track regulars. I wanted to meet the basketball players—Michael Jordan, Patrick Ewing, Wayman Tisdale, Sam Perkins and company.

We were stuck in the arena for two hours, missing a lot of activity in the Coliseum. But I enjoyed talking and joking with the basketball players. This was a great opportunity to become friends with some of the athletes I watched on television and admired the most.

On the way into the Coliseum, I learned they were just like me, always wanting to clown around. Tisdale and Jordan wanted to be the last athletes into the stadium. Anything to be different. So, of course, I joined their little game. Moving toward the field in a tunnel under the stadium, we kept ducking into little rooms along the way, trying to hide from each other. Then, after all that, I don't even remember which one of us entered last, just that we had fun along the way.

One of the most exciting moments of the ceremonies was when the Olympic torch arrived. The big secrets of the day had been: Who will carry the torch on its final leg into the stadium? And who will take it from the final runner to light the flame that would burn throughout the Games?

The final runner was identified as Gina Hemphill, a name that did not mean anything to most spectators. But it did to me. I had met Gina long before this, had heard some things about her family, and would be hearing a lot more. Gina is the granddaughter of Jesse Owens. She was invited to the Games as a reminder of his achievements.

To succeed in Los Angeles, I would have to focus on my present, not Jesse's past. But watching Gina take her lap, it was impossible not to think about all that Jesse had accomplished, the respect he gained, my brief encounters with him when I was younger. The basketball players kept asking who Gina was, and I felt good because I was able to tell them.

The answer to the second big question was Rafer Johnson, the former decathlete. Gina gave the torch to Johnson, who won a gold medal in the 1960 Games, and he carried it up a long flight of stairs to light the Olympic flame.

Another highlight of the day was provided by Edwin Moses, who had been chosen to lead the oath of the athletes. It was a great honor, and Edwin deserved it. But he stood up in front of all those thousands of people and forgot what he was supposed to say. The whole time he was struggling, the words of the oath were displayed on the stadium scoreboard. Either Edwin didn't know that or he was too proud to look up and read. Finally, he got through the oath. But not without a lot of the athletes laughing at him.

For track athletes, the end of the ceremonies means the beginning of a long wait. With my first event—the 100—still a week away, I wanted to stay as relaxed as possible, training each day and watching television coverage of the Games each night. But nothing was going to be that simple. Not with a pack of media wolves starving for stories.

First, reporters with nothing better to do made a big deal out of the fact that I was staying in a rented house, not a dorm in the Olympic

Village at the University of Southern California. The U.S. Olympic Committee, which loves policies, especially if they are outdated and inflexible, demands that every member of the team lives in the village. But that is not the best place for some athletes.

I checked into the village for a day, and found out that I was supposed to share with five other athletes a dorm room designed for two. Walking outside the dorm, I was mobbed by athletes from other countries. I had to keep stopping to sign autographs, pose for pictures, meet some friend of a friend, do all the things that drain energy.

It was a no-win situation. If I stayed in the village and didn't sign autographs or pose for pictures, everyone would say I was being a jerk. If I stayed there and did everything expected of me, the week before the 100 would be spent making others happy, not focusing on what I needed to do.

So staying elsewhere was the most sensible solution. I would stay in Hollywood with my family and a former Houston teammate, Kirk Baptiste, who had qualified for the U.S. team in the 200. Of course, nobody complained about Kirk not staying in the village. That would not be a sensational newspaper story. But take a shot at Carl Lewis, portray him as a spoiled star who would not stay with the other athletes—now, that was great journalism.

Another big complaint was that I would not cooperate with the press. For weeks, Joe Douglas and I had made it clear that we would do only one press conference before my events. That was the way it had to be, we tried to explain, because I did not want to drain my energy on distractions. This was the biggest track meet of my life, and I had never done all four events in such a short period of time. Joe and Coach Tellez wanted me to be overly cautious about distractions, and I agreed.

But once again, the theme was: Carl is a jerk. Not, Carl is being sensible. *Carl is being a jerk.*

Even when we did our big press conference, two days before the 100-meter heats, reporters found ways to take jabs at us.

Joe looked out at about a thousand reporters, photographers, and camera crews from around the world, and said, "I would like to keep this on a positive note."

Then, for almost an hour, I sat with Joe, my parents, and Carol, listening to the usual questions and dishing out the usual answers. Of course, the deal with the Olympic Village was a biggie. What about staying and training outside the village? "It's very distracting there. They encourage all the athletes to stay there as much as they can, and I try to be around. But the main issue is for me to compete well."

There must be a great deal of pressure. How do you handle it? "I try my best. I have a God-given talent. . . . If I run my hardest and do my best, I can't see failure. I compete for the love of the sport, and the people around me, and for the glory of God."

Is it true that you have broken Bob Beamon's record in practice? "Since I don't do a full long jump in practice, that isn't possible. My issue is to do the best I can, compete the best I can. Right now, I'm not thinking of world records."

Someone asked if Beamon's record could be broken at sea level, and I said, "Definitely." But when I was asked about motivation, I said, "First, the gold medal is most important. It's difficult because you only have one shot. You have a lot of chances to break the record, but only one for the medal."

I had been stressing this in interviews for so long. *I don't focus on records.* But reporters would soon forget.

Money was another hot topic.

What about the financial rewards of being a star? "That's handled for me by Joe. . . . The people around me handle that so I can keep my mind on the competition."

Is the discussion of money out of place at the Olympics? "Well, I understand ABC has paid somewhere around $275 million for rights to it. What we're talking about is minuscule in comparison."

Would you rather be a folk hero, like Jesse Owens, or a millionaire? "Money has nothing to do with my goals. . . . My job is to be the best role model, to further track and field, to be respected—rather than to be the rich millionaire."

At the time, I did not think much about it. But Joe once again made a comparison we could have done without. Talking about my potential earnings, Joe was quoted in one newspaper as saying: "Anyone at the apex should do well. We've had offers but we haven't accepted them yet. We think what Carl does will visibly enhance him in the Games. We think he can make as much as Michael Jackson."

Another paper quoted Joe as saying: "I frequently use the Michael

Jackson analogy. I hope that he's worth as much as Michael Jackson. We'll know after the Olympic Games."

Most of the reporters got the Michael Jackson stuff down—in one form or another. And they would later use it to bury us.

Finally, I was asked one of the most ridiculous questions I had heard in a long time.

If you are reincarnated, what do you want to do in your next life? "I'll leave that to whoever is in charge. It's not something I worry about."

One thing I would rule out for my next life—being a reporter.

Nobody at the press conference had given me any indication that anything was wrong. Everybody was perfectly nice.

But the next morning, the big story was that I had been late for the press conference. The first four words in the *New York Times* article were "He arrived fashionably late."

The headline in the *Los Angeles Times* was "Carl Lewis Is Slow Getting There, Then He Quickly Puts Media Away." The LA story started: *Carl Lewis, who hates wasting time unless it's somebody else's, kept about 1,000 of the world's journalists waiting an hour, arriving at 11 o'clock for his scheduled 10 a.m. press conference at the Convention Center Wednesday.*

All those questions and answers in the press conference, and this was the angle—Carl was late—chosen by some of the biggest publications in the country. By this time, it was open season. The reporters must have been getting bonus points from their editors for new ways of making me look spoiled or selfish. After reading Gary Smith's creation in *Sports Illustrated,* the reporters had to write the same sort of garbage, with fresh fiction.

If anybody at the press conference had bothered to ask why I was late, the story would have been ruined. I was not late to be "fashionable" and I was not "Slow Getting There." I was late only because the U.S. Olympic Committee changed the time of the press conference without telling me until an hour before the new starting time.

A few days earlier, Joe Douglas and the USOC had agreed on a press conference to begin at 11:00. But at 9:00 the day of the conference, someone from the committee called Joe at home and told him we had to be there at 10:00 instead of 11:00. The schedule had been changed.

Joe called me immediately, and we made it to the Convention Center as quickly as we could. After all the commotion, the press conference started at 10:30—half an hour earlier than we had planned, but half an hour after the reporters expected us.

For that, I was blasted. At least the *New York Times* used a fact to make its conclusions. The article said I arrived "a half-hour after advertised." The *LA Times*, in an effort to be twice as good, exaggerated a little, saying I was a full hour late.

The negative press bothered me some. But I was not going to let it affect my performances. I tried to forget about the papers and followed the Games by television. I watched a lot of the other events, and especially enjoyed the excitement of the U.S. men winning the team title in gymnastics and the 800-meter relay in swimming. But I was anxious to compete myself.

The 100-meter races were first—two preliminary heats one day, then the semifinal and final the next. When I ran a 10.04 in the second preliminary heat, I knew I was ready. Most of the best sprinters like to cruise through preliminaries without wasting too much energy before the finals. But in the biggest meets, I like to run a fast time in the preliminaries, just to let everyone know what to expect. If I can intimidate some competitors, great.

By the time of the finals, the other sprinters knew it would take something special to beat me. The biggest threats were two other Americans, Ron Brown and Sam Graddy. Ron had beaten me earlier in the year, indoors in San Diego. He had been drafted out of Arizona State to play wide receiver for the Los Angeles Rams. That would have to wait until after the Games. Sam, from the University of Tennessee, had won almost all his races in 1984, including the NCAA 100-meter championship.

On the way to the starting line, I heard someone calling me from the stands. *Carl, Carl.* I hear it all the time, and usually ignore it before a race, but there was a familiar ring this time. It was my high school sprints coach, Patsy Marino.

Back in Willingboro, it had taken a long time for Patsy to understand me, and we had been through more than our share of problems. We had our biggest clash when I was a senior in high school and Patsy was the new coach for sprinters. After practice one day, Patsy told us to cool down by running a mile. And if anybody finishes before you, he told the sprinters, you have to run another mile. Of course, the long-distance runners on the team beat us all. I refused to run another mile, trying to explain that it makes no sense to wear down a sprinter, and Patsy exploded.

"I am the coach," he said, "and if you want to be on this team, you will listen and follow instructions." We listened, but didn't follow. So Patsy turned up the volume. "I AM THE COACH." Fine, but I was not raised to do everything someone with authority tells me to do. I was raised to do what was right, and having sprinters run two miles at the end of practice definitely was not right. Patsy was new to coaching, and did not understand the differences between training for sprinters and long-distance runners. The other sprinters followed me as I walked away from the track, and it took a long time for me and Patsy to respect each other. We never became friends, but we did respect each other.

Toward the end of my senior year, Patsy pulled me aside one day, and said, "I finally understand you. It hasn't been easy. But I understand the way you are, and you're going to make it."

Now, minutes before the biggest race of my life, it was nice to see someone from home. I walked to the stands to say hello, and Patsy said he had come all the way to Los Angeles just to see me compete. "Wouldn't have missed it for the world," Patsy told me. And that really charged me up, knowing that, after all our problems, he cared about me that much.

The gun sounded and we bolted out of the blocks. But we had to come right back and do it again. One of the sprinters I did not know much about, a Canadian named Ben Johnson, had been called for a false start. Trying to gain an early advantage, he had moved too soon.

Sam Graddy got out quickest on the next start, but I felt good. Halfway down the track, I started closing on Sam. By eighty meters, I had the lead, and nobody could touch me the rest of the way. I crossed the finish line about eight feet in front of anybody else, and the event that had worried me the most was over.

My time was 9.99 seconds. Sam won the silver medal with a 10.19. And Ben, in a big surprise, took third in 10.22. After failing to make the finals in the Helsinki World Championships, now Ben was an Olympic medalist. Ron Brown, running with a sore knee, was fourth.

All the hard work, the training, the waiting, the controversy—all of that was worth it now. I looked in the stands for my parents, but couldn't find them. I tried to gather my thoughts, but couldn't. I was overwhelmed with excitement, joy, relief, all the possible good feelings wrapped up in one.

I felt a charge from the crowd that I had never felt before. Or maybe it had nothing to do with the crowd. Maybe this was what it feels like when you reach a goal that has been your constant companion for years.

This would be the most enjoyable victory lap of my life. Fans waved at me, and I waved back. They screamed, and I smiled. A lot of people waved American flags. About a third of the way around the track, I saw a guy waving a huge flag, so I jogged toward him and took it. I waved the flag while I continued the victory lap, then returned it, thanking the guy who owned it. And that was that: just something that happened with all the positive energy running through me.

On the way out of the stadium, I saw Coach Tellez, who had been waiting for me. I figured that he would be as excited as I was, and eager to hear his reaction to the race, I asked him what he thought. His first words were: "Technically, you were bad out of the blocks. You should have broken the world record."

So much for all that positive energy. My bubble was burst—temporarily, at least. But Coach T hugged me, said I ran a great race, and we left on a positive note. Still, there was work to do: improvements to be made later in the 100, and three more events in the Games—three more chances to satisfy Coach Tellez.

The next day, I heard someone (I don't remember who) saying that the whole flag-waving scene must have been planned, staged to look like a spontaneous celebration, but really part of a victory script. I didn't think much about that because it was such a silly comment. But then I heard that this stuff was all over the newspapers. The Associated Press reported that the flag had been given to me by Clyde Duncan, the assistant coach when I was at Houston. The *New York Times* reported that "a source close to the United States Olympic Committee" said that Duncan had been involved. I couldn't believe it.

Some newspapers included one article saying the flag-waving was staged and another saying it was not. It was typical of the way reporters and columnists sent the public so many mixed messages about me. How does a reader know what to believe and what to throw away?

Some of the *LA Times* writers criticized me for waving the flag, but at the same time, the paper ran a story with the headline, "The Flag Run Wasn't Staged." A reporter had interviewed the guy (identified as Paul Tucker, fifty, from New Orleans) who owned the flag. Tucker said he wasn't a "plant," that he had carried the flag into the Coliseum in a bag for his own enjoyment.

Still, it would take some papers weeks to clear up the story. Almost two weeks would pass before the *New York Times* wrote that the flag had been given to me by a stranger. And some papers never wrote about it again, leaving millions of people across the country to believe that the flag-waving was part of an effort at self-promotion. The story was easily believed by reporters and editors who had already formed their opinions of me. They wanted to believe that I would do anything to be different, to be special, to be all that crap that Gary Smith had written about in July. The pattern would continue: Win a gold medal, get blasted in the papers.

The long jump competition took place on a cool Monday evening, August 6. My first jump was 28 feet, ¼ inch. Only one other jumper in the Games, Larry Myricks, had ever jumped 28 feet, and I really didn't think he would be able to do that now. First of all, the wind was swirling and it was cold, terrible conditions for jumping. Second, Myricks consistently chokes in big events.

In the second round of jumps, I fouled. My steps were off, so I had to abort the jump, running through the pit instead of jumping off the board.

I still had leg trouble, a very sore hamstring. I had never fully recovered from the tough U.S. Olympic trials, and this was the first time I had to face that reality. In order to be ready for my final two events, I would have to cut this one short. Unless somebody jumped well enough to take the lead, I would pass on my remaining four jumps.

I passed one jump at a time so the other athletes would have to wonder if I was coming back, and I jogged and stretched to make it look like I would jump again. Why not give the other jumpers something to worry about? I also started drinking water, so I would not have to spend much time in the drug-testing center once the event ended. I would be ready to fill a bottle.

The best Myricks could do was 26 feet, 9¼ inches—the choke of the century, even for him. He should have finished second, but dropped to fourth. Australia's Gary Honey was second and Italy's Giovanni Evangelisti was third. Each jumped 27 feet, ½ inch, but Honey's second-best jump was better than Evangelisti's.

The first crowd reaction was kind of strange. There were boos when it was announced that I had won my second gold medal. Fans are fans, I thought. They will boo you one second and cheer you the next. That's how it is with all sports, and the Olympics are no different.

The Coliseum was sold out, with more than ninety-two thousand people there, and they obviously wanted to see me jump more. They wanted to see me break the world record. But they did not understand what was going on. They were sports fans, not track fans.

Taking another jump in those conditions and on a bad leg would not make sense, especially with two events left. Track fans understand the beating a long jumper takes each time he explodes off the board and lands in the pit. But fans who were there just to see the Olympics, to be able to tell their friends and families that they had been there, would not understand. They were the ones who booed.

It was kind of funny, though, because only minutes later, during the victory ceremony, I received a huge ovation. I don't know why fans boo one second and cheer the next. But I did know the media would dwell on the boos, not the cheers.

All along, I had said that I was going for a win, not a world record. But that was ignored in press coverage the next day.

The *LA Times* said that paying $50 to see what I gave fans in the long jump "was like paying $50 to hear Frank Sinatra sing one song. . . . But Lewis does it his way." The *Pittsburgh Press:* "To some, Lewis' decision was an insult." United Press International: "Has Carl Lewis taken his single-minded pursuit of four gold medals too far? That apparently was the sentiment of many fans who wanted to see him take six shots at Bob Beamon's 'unbreakable' long-jump record."

But some writers understood.

In the *Washington Post*, Robert Fachet wrote: "The crowd's reaction was a commentary on the paying customers' lack of knowledge of what they were seeing. The organizers chose a lottery system of selling tickets, and while the crowds have been enormous, they are largely people watching their first track meet and more interested in waving flags than appreciating performances. The only thing Lewis could have accomplished by taking his last four jumps would have been to hurt himself. There was no chance anyone could pass him, and the swirling wind made it impossible for Lewis to challenge Bob Beamon's record."

Amazingly, even Larry Myricks defended me. "I don't blame him for not jumping anymore," Myricks told reporters. "He's run a lot of races already, and he's got a few more races to go."

It would have been easy to let the reaction to the long jump get me down, especially with all the other stuff that had already happened, and I started to wonder if I had lost my perspective. Maybe I was completely lost, and I was doing things wrong, making bad decisions, acting in ways that I should not have been. With so many of my moves being criticized, with each great performance being followed by a not-so-great reaction, I had to wonder: What was the deal?

But I spent the day after the long jump with the people closest to me—my family, Coach Tellez, Joe Douglas, Sri Chinmoy, and a large gathering of Christians—and everybody kept reassuring me that everything was just fine. I was not doing anything wrong, so I should keep doing what I do best, and should keep doing it my way. As usual, the people closest to me, especially my family, helped me to settle down and block out distractions. With all these positive people surrounding me, I was able to focus again on positive thoughts, not negative media coverage.

First, I had a pleasant, uplifting meeting with Sri Chinmoy. I visited him at a house he had rented, and we meditated, focusing on letting the power of the spiritual world carry me through the rest of the Olympics. Guru told me he was proud of me, and he kept everything extremely positive. "You're doing great," he said. "Spiritually, you're touching a lot of people. Keep your faith, and you will keep going. Two events to go. Just keep your faith."

One other thing I remember Sri Chinmoy talking about: the 200-meter finals. He had been thinking about the race, and he wanted to ask a few questions about some of my competitors. Not questions about athletic ability, questions about character and personality. Then Sri Chinmoy left me with a prediction. I would win the 200, and it would be an American sweep. He said that Kirk Baptiste would place second and Thomas Jefferson would take third. Fine with me. I hoped that Sri Chinmoy would be right, and based on everything I knew about him, I had a feeling he would be.

Hours after visiting with Sri Chinmoy, I was surrounded by many of my friends from Lay Witnesses for Christ. A testimony and prayer session (called "Three Hours with the Stars") had been scheduled at the First Baptist Church in Van Nuys, and this was the night. Several thousand people came to worship God and listen to testimony from about a dozen athletes. When it was my turn to speak, I stressed that the thrills of adulation and Olympic medals paled in comparison to my relationship to Jesus. Track-and-field records come and go, as do all earthly accomplishments, but a relationship to Jesus never ends. "It's the one element that's going to be there today, tomorrow, and every day." When I finished saying that, I heard the biggest applause of the evening, and it meant so much more to me than anything that had happened at the track, or in the newspapers.

Willie Gault, who had introduced me to Lay Witnesses for Christ and was now playing wide receiver for the Chicago Bears, put his arms around me as we stood on a platform and prayed. Sam Mings, the founder of the organization, stood on the other side of me. By now, more than thirty-eight hundred amateur athletes were working with Lay Witnesses for Christ, a direct tribute to Sam's hard work and commitment to the Lord. What a great feeling it was to stand between Willie and Sam. It was the perfect ending to a special day, and a great boost to help me through the second half of the Games.

My leg was still sore for the 200-meter finals, and all I wanted to do was finish the race. But I felt good out of the blocks and ended up with one of the best 200s ever, just by staying relaxed. My time was 19.80 seconds, an Olympic record. I had run only one faster 200, the 19.75 a year before in Indianapolis, and the only faster time in history was Pietro Mennea's 19.72, in 1979 at high altitude in Mexico City.

To make things even better, we had an American sweep, and it was just as Sri Chinmoy had predicted. Kirk Baptiste was second, two meters behind me and two meters ahead of Thomas Jefferson, a senior at Kent State University. The three of us hugged and shared a private moment, kneeling together on the track, saying a little thank-you. We had reached our goal—a sweep!—and we would share a victory lap.

Kirk and I carried small American flags, waving them in celebration. But Thomas was definitely the center of attention, wrapping himself in a large flag, which was a nice touch, a special moment for himself and the fans. Of course, if I had wrapped myself in a flag like that, I would have been ripped in the next morning's newspapers. But Thomas was not a media target. He was free to enjoy himself, free to express his joy, to act spontaneously. And that was the way it should have been. I was happy for him.

In an interview the day of the 200 finals, a Los Angeles doctor made some very strong accusations about top athletes taking performance-enhancing drugs. Dr. Robert Kerr said that more than a dozen athletes who used banned steroids had won medals. The athletes had escaped detection, Kerr said, because they stopped taking the drugs several months before the Games. But Kerr was short on specifics. I don't know if reporters didn't believe him, didn't want to believe him, or what. But the story was buried in the back of sports sections, and there would be little, if any, follow-up. That was a shame. I wanted to know more about what Kerr had to say, and the public deserved to know if athletes were using banned drugs.

The 4 × 100-meter relay was supposed to be a lock for the United States, the easiest win of my four events. And it was. The team was made up of the four top finishers in the 100-meter final at the U.S. trials, and the baton went from Sam Graddy to Ron Brown to Calvin Smith to me. It was as simple as that sounds, and we won by seven meters. Our time of 37.83 seconds was a world record, the only track-and-field world record of the Los Angeles Games.

That was one way to look at the relay—a record. And I was thrilled to be part of an American team that accomplished that. But there was another way to look at the victory. My four events were done, and I had survived. I had been challenged from every direction, criticized for reasons I still failed to understand, but I had survived. There was joy—incredible joy—but more than that, I felt relief. It was over—finally. There would be no more expectations, no more predictions, just four events, four victories. Period. What a relief!

A week and a half since being blasted for arriving late at a press conference, it was once again time to meet with reporters. Now they wanted me to look back, not forward. But most of the questions were similar to those I had been hearing for a year, so the answers should not have caught anyone by surprise. I was asked about the comparisons between Jesse Owens and me—as I had been asked so many times—and I said: "Jesse Owens is still the same man to me he was before. He is a legend. I'm just a person. I still feel like the same Carl Lewis I was six years ago, except I'm a little older and a lot more people come to my press conferences."

Yes, I told the reporters, I had been misunderstood many times the last two weeks, just as I had been so many times before. "Too many people built me up before the Games." But that did nothing to erase the personal satisfaction, the joys of achievement, that I would take away from the Games. This had been the time of my life.

EIGHT

≡

The Feeling That I Feel

WHEN THE Games ended, all the American medal-winners were invited on a cross-country tour. One last victory lap, it was called, one last chance for athletes to wave and fans to cheer. About two hundred athletes, along with a guest for each, would go from Los Angeles to New York for a parade. Then they would go to Disney World, Dallas, and home. The trip was sponsored by the Southland Corporation, which is best known for its 7-Eleven stores. Southland put up more than one million dollars to make the tour possible, and received a lot of positive press for its donation. In public, everything about the tour was very nice. Privately, though, Southland showed another attitude.

When someone from the company first asked me and Joe Douglas about the tour, we told him I was sorry, but I couldn't go. I had already committed to a series of meets in Europe, and would not be able to do both. There was no way to back out of the meets, not after promoters had promised fans and sponsors I was going to compete. Southland was pissed. The company was spending a lot of money, and now one of the top athletes was not going to participate. What would that do to Southland's publicity push?

Other athletes were skipping the tour. Greg Louganis, the great diver, for example. But he had an easy out, an excuse that could be related to his hard-working image. Southland could say that Greg had to prepare for the nationals, which were coming up in his sport. But I was different. When tour organizers heard I was going to Europe, they knew I was going to be well paid for my meets there. That was the way reporters had been writing about me—Carl the money man. So Southland came up with a plan to pressure me into making the American tour.

The guy from the company told me that if I didn't change my mind, he would make a public announcement that would hurt me. He was going to say that Joe and I had asked for a lot of money to make the tour, and the company turned us down. "You know that's not true," we said.

"Doesn't matter," we were told. "Everyone will believe it."

He was probably right. The way reporters had been dogging me, they would certainly want to believe something like this. And their editors would be thrilled with the story. They would never question it. I couldn't believe we were being threatened like this, so dishonestly, but what could I do about it? I was going to Europe, and if the guy from Southland was going through with his threat, I would have to take a few more lumps in the press. What the heck. The media coverage couldn't get much more negative than it had already been.

In the end, I got lucky, if you can call it that. When I got back to Houston, I found that my house had been broken into while I was at the Olympics. Crystal was smashed, and the place was a mess. Silver was stolen, along with video and audio equipment. This was not a pleasant discovery, but at least it gave me an excuse for missing the Southland tour. Before the company had a chance to make an announcement about me, I would call a friend at a television station to make sure the story about the burglary got out.

I called Bob Allen, a sportscaster at Houston's KTRK-TV, where I had been working part-time, and told Bob about the break-in. I was so upset about the situation that I would have to change my travel plans. The Southland tour was off, and my trip to Europe would have to be delayed a few days. That night, my story was on the news. The next morning, it was in newspapers all over the place.

If Southland had never threatened me, I never would have announced the burglary. I would have kept it to myself. But now there was at least one benefit from the break-in: Southland would probably not make any announcement about me. The company would look pretty stupid slamming an athlete who couldn't make a trip because his house had been burglarized.

Still, I would not forget the experience with Southland, and it was a sign of things to come. The negative media before, during, and after the Olympics would affect the way I was treated by corporate sponsors. At least, some sponsors. A vicious cycle had started. Negative media keeps potential sponsors away, and the lack of sponsors leads to more negative stories. In the end, no matter what is true and what is false, negative stories create a negative image. The public generally believes what it reads.

Here's how bad things got. On his Halloween show, David Letterman invited members of the studio audience to come on stage in costumes. A little boy was wearing a track outfit and four gold medals.

"And who are you supposed to be?" Letterman wanted to know.

"Give me twenty bucks and I'll tell you," the kid said.

In other words, Carl Lewis doesn't say or do anything before being paid. This was the image that had been stamped on me, and getting rid of it would not be easy. Ironically, the money image would keep me from making money. Potential sponsors were lost, and some were as big as they come. The biggest was Coca-Cola.

Before the Games, Coke had wanted to sponsor me. I had been offered a pretty good deal, but didn't want to sign until after the Games. Then came the negative publicity, and Coke backed off. I was disappointed because a company as big as Coke, with its powerful ads and positive image, could have helped turn things around for me. I had always done a lot of charity work for children, and I thought that Coke would want to work with something like that. We talked about showing me working with kids, playing with kids, running with kids, showing me the way I really was, not the way reporters made me out to be. A series of commercials and ads like that would have been great for Coke and me. But the offer never came through.

The *LA Times*, which had been after me all year, was among the leaders in the "Poor Carl" stories that made the rounds for a few months. Poor Carl, he's not getting the sponsors he expected. Poor Carl, he's not making the money he wanted. Poor Carl, poor Carl . . .

One *Times* writer, Rick Reilly, wanted to know, "Does Carl Lewis have a bad rap with America?" After describing what had happened on the Letterman show, Reilly quoted me saying, "People don't hate

Carl Lewis," and quoted Joe Douglas saying, "People love Carl
Lewis."

"Perhaps," Reilly wrote, "but if America loves Carl Lewis, Madison Avenue must be playing hard to get." In other words, no sponsors. One contract to promote a Japanese athletic drink, Suntory, and
he has retained his lucrative endorsement contract with Nike, but
that's it.

"Some marketing experts say Lewis would be too high at almost
any price. They say he has a soured image in the country. . . . Although Douglas has booked Lewis on every national talk show in
recent weeks in order to revive his image, most agents believe it is
too late."

Despite all this, my life was just fine. In fact, I was having a great
time, thrilled to be done with the pressures of the Olympics. And the
financial situation was much better than most people realized.

Finally, the frustration of all the false rumors, the lies, and the
negative reporting caught up with me in early 1985. Before a meet in
Dallas, I called my parents from my hotel room. The night before, I
had been thinking about the way I had been raised, the things I had
learned from my parents, the way I believed in doing the right things,
whether it came to religion, family, sports, friendships, whatever.
And yet I was alone in a hotel room, wondering where everything had
gone wrong. I was at the top of my sport, known around the world,
but something was missing. I wasn't being treated fairly.

Reporters had done everything they could to tear me down, it
seemed, and the way I was being treated was starting to take a toll.
Not that all reporters were bad. I had gotten plenty of positive press,
too, especially in other parts of the world, and I didn't want to be
overly sensitive about the negative press. I had made plenty of my
own mistakes, and reporters were by no means the sole source of my
problems. But they were a big part of them. I had gone through
different stages of ignoring reporters, trying to understand them,
trying to joke with them, being quiet, being loud, but now I had
settled on the only approach that made sense: being angry.

On the phone, I told my mother what I had been thinking, and she
got all worked up about the reporters. She hated them, couldn't stand
them, didn't appreciate anything they were writing, and didn't like
the way most of them acted around us. For months, my mother had
wanted me to lash out at the press, and I thought that was the thing

to do. But my father had cut that off. He didn't think that would be a good idea. Express your feelings in a low-key way, yes, but don't lash out. That will only make things worse. That will only lower you to their level.

This time, my father's protest was not enough. I was ready to say something to the reporters, and my mother was saying, go for it. My father said, if you have to make a statement, go ahead, but be careful. Don't alienate the reporters more than necessary. I started planning a statement.

After running my race—easily winning my first sprint of the year in a 60-yard dash—I walked straight toward a crowd of reporters and broadcasters who had been waiting for me.

Without any prompting, I said, "I felt good about the race, pleased with my start, and I felt good about the reception I received." Then I changed gears. "I want to say one other thing. I have been a bit appalled and a bit flabbergasted by the media's mistreatment of me. But I'm going to keep on trucking. I am who I am, and that's who I'll stay, and that's who I'll be. That's all I have to say."

The reporters were a bit stunned, but I was not going to say anything else. Some of them went after Carol, who had just jumped 22 feet, 3 inches, to break her own American record in the long jump. Simple, Carol told them. Carl is misunderstood.

"It makes me laugh," Carol said. "People write things about Carl who have never met him. Then the American people form opinions about him because of those things that are written."

A few days later, I was at a banquet in New York to accept the Jesse Owens Award. We were in the grand ballroom of the Waldorf-Astoria Hotel. The banquet made me think back to the days when I met Jesse, the way he had inspired me, and I was able to forget, at least for a night, how tired I was of all the Jesse comparisons. Ruth Owens, Jesse's widow, made the presentation and said how touching it had been for her to see me on the track in Los Angeles. "Jesse would have been proud," she said.

When it was my turn to speak, I thought about all that had happened the last year, and how it had all happened so fast. The hype. The Olympics. The medals. The rumors. The negative press.

I thanked Mrs. Owens, then said something about athletes, something I had not planned. "We are people, too. We make mistakes. But we do our best."

The applause was generous.

"Looking back," I told a reporter that night, "I think one trouble was just the fact that I had been No. 1 in my events for three years, and there was nothing new to say about me. When you can't find something new, it's time to find something wrong."

So many reporters had been competing with each other for something new, something nobody else had written, that they started going overboard, believing rumors they heard and printing them as fact.

Also, it seemed like reporters not only wanted to compare me to Jesse Owens, they wanted me to *be* Jesse. He was poor and quiet and usually did what was asked of him. That was probably because he competed during a time when blacks were expected to be poor and quiet, and were expected to do what was asked of them. But I was not Jesse, and I was not living in the 1930s. I was not poor, not quiet, not doing everything that was asked of me. I was raised by middle-class parents, taught to speak up, and educated about the civil rights movement my parents had experienced firsthand. Of course, this was not the night to mention any criticism that had anything to do with Jesse. First of all, the Jesse comparison had not turned negative because of anything Jesse ever did. It was the fault of reporters who insisted on wearing out the comparison, expecting us to be alike off the track just because we accomplished some of the same things on it. But this was a night for saying nice things about Jesse, a night to be excited about winning the award, and to show that excitement.

Being in the public eye was tough, and I had learned some lessons the hard way. But I would survive. Overall, I was happy, and I would continue to be happy.

It wasn't long after the Jesse Owens banquet that I was able to joke with reporters about the image problems. When I was asked about all the Michael Jackson quotes—for the zillionth time—I said: "Do I want to be as big as Michael Jackson? Well, actually, it's Prince now."

Talking about Michael Jackson and Prince was kind of funny, because I was trying to start an entertainment career of my own. Not that I wanted to be Michael Jackson or Prince. I was not looking for any new comparisons. But I had done some singing and acting before the Olympics, and I enjoyed both.

Acting classes had been great. I spent a month in New York with an acting coach named Warren Robertson. Every day, I'd wake up, eat, and go to class. It was just like being back in college, only better—no tests, no NCAA rules, nobody telling me where to go and when to be there. The classes were tough because Warren expected a lot out of his students, but I enjoyed stretching my imagination and moods. Being on a stage and being somebody else made me learn more about myself. One day I could be Gale Sayers in a scene from *Brian's Song*. Another day I could be Hamlet, holding Yorick's skull in my hand. I could be anybody. Of course, I had always been fueled by crowds (well, at least, since I got over the fright that froze me during that high school awards banquet in New Jersey). Warren's reviews were very positive.

"I couldn't believe anyone who had never acted could be that focused," Warren would say. "He's got a honing instinct that eliminates all excess and waste and goes straight to the essence. He touches an audience for the same reason Travolta does: that balance between the aggressive side and the receptive, sensitive side. It fulfills the need for both that we have as an audience. Carl may not think he's vulnerable, but you can feel a sensitive side in his presence. . . . He could become the first great actor who was an athlete, because he's secure enough to risk."

But now I wanted to concentrate on singing. It was something I enjoyed, and the combination of singing and acting would be good, something I could use for a long time. I had never wanted to limit myself to track. There had always been more than that in my family, and there would always be more than that in my life. Plus, singing would be a nice change of pace from all the negative stuff that came after the Olympics. If I had allowed myself to get too caught up in all that, I would have gone nuts. Singing would be a great challenge, a great outlet, and fun.

Before the Olympics, Narada Michael Walden asked me if I would be interested in singing on an Olympic album that was being planned. He knew that I did not have much musical experience, a few years in the school choir back in Willingboro, and six years of cello lessons. That was it. But Narada said we should give it a try. He would help me through it, pay the recording costs and everything. So we came up with a song called "Goin' for the Gold." First, we did a rap version. Then we did a singing version, and that's the one we released. We sold some copies on the West Coast, and more in Europe, but we weren't much of a threat to hit the charts. "Goin' for the Gold" never made it onto the Olympic album, but we had fun with it, and it got the word out to anyone who might be interested: Carl Lewis can sing.

At a few meets, I sang the national anthem. I probably did not practice as much as I should have before the first time I did that, and it didn't help that ten seconds before I sang, I found out that there was no music to accompany me, but I survived. The *New York Times* said, "There are many stories of singers who have forgotten the words to the national anthem. Lewis remembered them all. . . . His voice was pleasant and every note seemed on key." Not a bad review for a newcomer.

In Houston, I met some people in a band, Electric Storm, and we did a live show together. Pop, rhythm and blues, a little of everything. All the guys in the band were young, some very talented, and we had a blast. Track was still my priority, though, so I could sing with the band only when it didn't interfere with my schedule.

In mid-1985, that changed. I pulled a hamstring, had to stop training before the national championships, and was left with more time than usual for things other than track. In addition to singing with the band, I had been taking voice lessons in Houston, and I wanted to record another song. Next thing I knew, I had a deal to do a whole album.

A Japanese company agreed to give me a fifty-thousand-dollar production budget for an album, as long as I could get a band and a studio. That was fine. Electric Storm would love it, and we had a friend at a studio in Houston. He could keep our costs down. A budget of fifty thousand dollars is not much for an album, but we could get it done. We called it a deal.

Japan was becoming my home away from home. I always enjoyed going there, probably because it seemed like I was always wanted, and in some ways, I was accepted more readily in Japan than in my own country. The only problem in Japan was my name. I was usually called "Car Rewis." People had trouble pronouncing my name, but I certainly understood. I have a lot of trouble pronouncing names of people from other countries, too, and even with the little communication problems we sometimes faced, the Japanese made me feel very comfortable.

The album, called *The Feeling That I Feel*, wasn't bad. It just wasn't good. There were two problems: lack of time and lack of experience. We had to do everything in less than a month, which was way too fast, and we ended up working twenty-hour days to finish on time. That might have been okay if at least some of us knew what we were doing. But we were all inexperienced, especially me. The first time around, we should have gotten more help from people who had recorded an album before.

Still, I was able to take the band to Japan for a little tour, which was great exposure for my new career. When we returned to the States, one of the guys in the band started expecting too much of me, wanting me to finance every musical dream he had ever dreamed, and I wasn't going to do that. I left Electric Storm and decided that my next move would be solo.

Another offer came pretty quickly, again from Japan. An overnight mail company called Sagawa Express, the Japanese version of Federal Express, had signed me to a two-year endorsement deal, and now Sagawa wanted me to sing a song to be used in my next commercial. Mr. Sagawa, the head of the company, was one of the most straightforward, dynamic corporate executives I had met, and he owned part of a record company. Mr. Sagawa did everything first-class, and he wanted Quincy Jones or Stevie Wonder to produce my song. He got Quincy Jones, and we did two songs, "Love Triangle" and "Love Will Do." Finally, I was working with some of the top studio musicians in the business, and I learned a lot about what it takes to produce good music: the time commitment, immeasurable amounts of energy, a lot of money for production, and surrounding yourself with the best people you can find. Producing these two songs really made an impact on me.

Next, I did a single in Belgium, called "Break It Up," which was released all over Europe and went gold in Sweden. Back home, I put together my own band, the Carl Lewis Band, and worked with a great bass player, James Garner. We did some original stuff for another album. We did some live gigs in Houston, and two on the road, in Baltimore and San Francisco. Then we went our own ways.

By then, the successes and failures of the 1984 Games seemed like ancient history. The four gold medals were tucked away in a safe-deposit box in a bank vault, and the image problems that came with them were locked away, too. I was not going to dwell on the negative stuff. Other people could say whatever they wanted to say about me, but I had moved on to other things, and I was comfortable with myself and all that had happened. Acting and singing had taken me into new worlds, allowing me to explore beyond the limits often placed on an athlete. I had found new ways to express myself. I had found more and more time to learn and think about my religious beliefs. And I had been spending more and more time with my family, especially my parents, sharing with them anything good that was happening with me. Nothing meant more to me than being able to give something back to Mom and Dad. I had always wanted to make them happy, had always wanted to make them proud, and after all we had been through together, they knew me and understood me better than anyone else possibly could. They were the most important people in my life, and it was important to me that they always knew that.

NINE

≡

Home Again

On Christmas Day, 1985, my parents came from Willingboro to Houston for the holidays, and we were all ready for some nice family time. I had bought my father a big-screen television, and he was excited about that. But he wasn't feeling right. He was weak, and all he wanted to do was go home, rest, and be entertained by his gift.

None of us thought much about it when Dad went back to New Jersey the day after Christmas. Whatever he wanted to do was fine with us. But after resting at home for a few days, he didn't feel any better. My mother urged him to see a doctor, and he did. Then he went for a second opinion. Then my mother called me.

"I hope you're sitting down," she said.

"What is it, Mom?"

"Your father has a tumor. We don't know the details yet." She was struggling. "We need to find out more. He's going in for tests. But they found a tumor in his colon."

I was shocked, of course, and there wasn't much I could say. But we had to be optimistic. That was the way my father had raised us: Think positively, stick together, things will work out. This was different than anything we had ever faced before. But the Lewis approach was the only approach we knew. We would do whatever we could for each other, and we would get through this. Dad would get through this.

A few days later, however, we were told that the tumor was malignant. Cancer was attacking Dad. Just like that, everything that ever seemed important to me was not important anymore. The only thing I cared about was being a son, my father's son.

I was appearing at a charity telethon in California, and I caught a late-night flight to New Jersey. All I wanted to do was spend the day with my father. This was the first time I had confronted a hospital in a situation like this. I had been sick a few times, and had visited friends when they were sick. I had made a number of appearances at hospitals, visiting children. That was always emotional, but not nearly as tough as this. I had never seen my father like this, and I was scared. My father was only fifty-nine. I was not ready to lose him.

Cancer had spread to the liver and the lymph nodes. But we were still optimistic. We had to be. The doctors said that Dad's heart was in great shape, and that would help. They would start chemotherapy.

Dad lost a lot of weight. But the treatments did not affect him as badly as they do some people. By the spring, he was ready to do what he liked best. He wanted to see a track meet, so he and my mother came down to Texas for the Houston Invitational. Anyone who knew Dad knew he was sick, but everyone kept telling him, "Oh, you look so good. It's great to see you. We were worried about you"

This was just the lift Dad needed. Soon he visited me again in Houston, alone this time. Then he wanted to see me compete in the national championships, so he went out to Eugene, Oregon. Dad was just bouncing around the stadium, talking to all his friends, carrying on as if he were running the place. He enjoyed watching me win the 100 and the long jump. I was third in the 200, but Dad was not quite as concerned with the order of finish as he had been in the past. Now, it was just seeing me compete, just being there, being involved, that mattered.

The Goodwill Games were next on my schedule, in the Soviet Union, and Dad wanted to go there, too. "We should do everything we can, go everywhere we can," he said. For the first time, we realized why he was so eager to travel again. He knew he might die, and he wanted to fit in whatever he could. My mother was a wreck.

We all were. But we would keep busy, keep moving, keep competing, and we would try to enjoy the time we had together.

After the Soviet Union, I had some meets in Europe, and my parents went along. But Dad had to go home earlier than planned. He was exhausted. When I got back to the States, I was told that the chemotherapy had not been enough. The cancer was spreading again, and at the end of September, the doctors told us they had done all they could. They said they had no clue how long Dad would live. It could be six weeks or ten years. But there was nothing more they could do.

We had to start preparing for the worst. I visited as much as possible, sometimes at the hospital, sometimes at home in Willingboro. On Christmas, 1986, exactly a year after my father had felt sick for the first time, his temperature shot up, and he was miserable. But he begged us not to take him to the hospital. I had just given him an easy chair, and all he wanted to do was sit in it, by the Christmas tree, with his family. We practically had to drag Dad to the hospital, and he was almost crying. But he had to go. He wasn't able to eat, and he needed a doctor.

The next few months, I went to see Dad every other week. He was definitely losing his battle, but there was nothing he could do. It was so hard to see him like this, such a strong person looking so weak. His love for his family was the only feeling he was able to keep strong.

One day when Carol and I were leaving New Jersey for Houston, we were on the way to the airport, and out of nowhere my father blurted out, "I love you two. I'll always love you." Dad wasn't the kind of person who expressed himself like that too often, and I wanted to remember this. In the backseat of my mother's car, I pulled out a pen and a piece of scrap paper, and I scribbled my father's words. "I love you two. I'll always love you."

May 5, 1987. I was home in Houston, and my Uncle Abraham called. He wanted to know which funeral home we were using. *Which funeral home? Why is he asking that now?* Just then, Mack and Carol came in the back door, and Carol was sobbing. I put down the phone and yelled, "What is going on?"

"Dad died," Carol said.

I had pretty much figured that out, but I had to hear it. I returned to the phone, but nobody was on the line anymore. I walked to the back of the house, to my exercise room, and I stood there, crying, alone. I thought I had prepared myself for this. But there is no way to prepare for what I was feeling. I didn't know what to do. Carol immediately left Houston to be with our mother. But I wasn't ready. I needed a day by myself.

No matter what I tried to do, I could think only about my father—the old days in Willingboro, the lessons he taught me, the way he pushed me to always do my best, no matter what I was doing, all the trips we had made, all over the world. My father was very sensible and very sensitive, and he could sit and talk to anyone, about anything, all day long. But if you ever talked bad about him or did something against his beliefs, that was it. He was done with you.

He taught us to do what we think is right. "Not what you want to do," he would say, "but what you think is right." Period. "And if you're doing what you think is right, what you honestly, deep down believe is right, then don't take any shit about it from anybody."

That had been his philosophy in 1984, when so many people were saying bad things about me, and so many reporters were writing and broadcasting so much crap about me. Dad said, "You're not doing anything wrong, Carl. You haven't done anything to hurt anybody. You're not bad-mouthing anybody. You're not mistreating anyone. Not doing any of that stuff. You're doing just fine. Be yourself, and don't worry about what's going on around you. Everything is going to turn around."

My mother was not as calm about the way I was treated during and after the '84 Games. She wanted to go off on everybody who said or wrote bad things about me, just wanted to call everybody she could track down and let them know what she thought of their criticisms. But my father said, "No, you don't need to do that. None of that stuff matters. As long as Carl is doing what he believes is right, we don't have to answer to anybody, and we won't."

Now, as I was getting ready to leave for the airport, I pictured the way my father had enjoyed the '84 Games, especially the 100-meter finals. I dug through the piles of videotapes in my room, found the tape of that race, and popped it in the VCR. I watched it over and over. My father was such a big part of that race, everything leading up to it, the energy I felt that day and the excitement that came with winning.

My father had given me so much, in so many ways, and now I wanted to give something to him. How about the 100-meter medal from '84? It is the one thing I could give him to represent all the good things we did together, all the positive things that happened to me because of him.

I had never before taken any of my medals out of the bank vault where I kept them. But that day, on the way to the airport, I stopped at the bank to get the medal, and I put it in the pocket of my suit jacket. I would take it to New Jersey—for Dad.

The night before the funeral, we were all at home in Willingboro, and my mother was giving directions. She thought it would be nice if I sang at the funeral, and she asked me to pick a song. I decided to write one of my own, and she said, "Fine." Sitting in the chair I had given Dad for Christmas, I started reflecting, and one of the first things I thought of was that day in the car when my father told me and Carol that he would always love us. That was the inspiration for my song. And once I had that, the words came pretty easily.

> *From the first time I remember*
> *all I saw was you.*
> *And as my days grew longer*
> *you pushed my dreams on through.*
> *And all that you told me*
> *helped pave the way*
> *for me to be me*
> *and show the world our ways.*
>
> *I'll always love you*
> *is what you said to me.*
> *And though your life was short*
> *your list of love will always be.*
>
> *As time goes on*
> *we'll miss you.*
> *Gone away*
> *your spirit's still true.*
> *Now we must go on*
> *forever and a day.*
> *Cause our Lord*
> *has called.*
> *And you're home again.*
> *Home again.*
> *You're home again. Today.*

Then I would speak to my father for the last time: "I'll always love you, too, Dad."

The day of the funeral, when our family was viewing the body, I pulled out the medal to place in my father's hand. Willie Gault was the only non-family member in the room at the time, and that's the way I wanted it. I did not want people outside the family to know what I was doing.

My mother asked me if I was sure I wanted to bury the medal, and I was. It would be my father's forever. "But I'm going to get another one," I told my mother. Turning to my father, I said, "Don't worry. I'm going to get another one." That was a promise—to myself and to Dad. He was lying there so peacefully, his hands resting on his chest. When I placed the medal in his hand, it fit perfectly.

TEN

≡

Nike

WITH ALL my emotions caught up in our family situation, I went a few weeks without paying much attention to business. Joe Douglas mentioned something about a letter from Nike. The company was threatening to cut off my contract, but I figured that Nike was just playing games with us, and I didn't give it much thought.

Don Coleman, the Nike representative who had handled my contract for years and had been real nice to my family, was at my father's funeral, and he certainly didn't act like anything was wrong between us. But it turned out that Nike was serious. Their letter, written two weeks before my father died, said that Nike was immediately terminating my contract. Nike said they had "substantial evidence" that I had breached the contract. "If you believe we are in error," wrote Mark Thomashow of Nike, "we invite you and your attorney to contact us and arrange for a meeting." Nike claimed I had competed in a few meets without wearing Nike clothes, as my contract required.

But there was so much more to it than that. Nike was my biggest sponsor, and if the people there had taken any time to think about my side of the situation, they would have known I would not intentionally jeopardize my contract by wearing something I wasn't supposed to wear. Some of the Nike people had lost interest in me over the years, and I had been through some ups and downs with the company. But I wasn't stupid. I knew I had to wear Nike stuff.

By this time, my Nike contract was a lot better than the $200,000 deal I had signed back in 1981. Joe Douglas had stepped in, claiming that Nike had taken advantage of me. I had agreed to the original deal without any help from an agent or attorney, and Joe didn't think that Nike had been fair. The company saw his point and did not want to lose me, so Joe was able to renegotiate and get me a much better deal. The result was a six-year contract from the beginning of 1983 through the end of 1988. The annual base pay was now up to six figures, and it went up even more after the 1984 Olympics. Winning four gold medals also meant a lot of bonus money, and my annual pay from Nike almost doubled. For a track athlete, it was a huge contract.

There were all sorts of other benefits for me, my family, the Willingboro Track Club, the University of Houston, and the Santa Monica Track Club. Each had its own deal with Nike. Everybody got in on the action in one way or another because Nike wanted to keep us all happy. This was not the kind of contract I would take lightly. It was the kind I wanted to keep.

But there had been problems, and that was a shame because everything with Nike had started out so well. Don Coleman had been like a big brother to me at the Pan American Games, when I was so young, and our friendship had grown after that. My sophomore year in college, when Don was just starting out with Nike, he had come through for me with $5,000 and bonuses from Nike after other companies had let me down.

For a few years, my relationships with Nike and Don were as good as they could have been. They expected a lot out of me, but they gave a lot, too. Everything with Nike was great. Phil Knight, the founder and president of Nike, invited me to appear with him at an annual stockholders' meeting in Oregon, and I did. I planned on staying with Nike my entire career.

Don liked and trusted me so much that he often let me in on company secrets. One time, on a plane coming back from Europe, Don showed me a list of Nike track athletes and their salaries.

"I like him," Don said, pointing to an athlete on the list. "I think I'll give him a raise." Then he would point to another name, and say,

"Nice guy, he calls me a lot. I'm going to get him a raise, too." Or, "This guy is a jerk, doesn't check in enough—no raise." Don might have been joking about the way he chose people for raises. At least, I hoped he was. But this would later serve as a symbol of the way Nike did business. Everything was so arbitrary, and personal relationships sometimes interfered with good business. If you were hot and Don liked you, you would be in great shape. If not, you might as well find another company.

I was hot through the '84 Games. Then came the negative publicity, and Nike didn't know what to do with me. I was still used in ads, and Nike told me the ads did very well. But Nike wanted more say in everything I did. The company wanted to hire a public relations firm for me, and I didn't want that. I didn't want Nike to run my show. I just wanted to continue the relationship the way it had been. I'll do my part, you do yours.

Nike also sponsored the Santa Monica club, and that started out as a good relationship, too. But later, there were contract problems between Nike and several individuals who competed for Santa Monica, and that complicated the relationship. David Mack and Johnny Gray had the most trouble with Nike, but there were others, including my sister, who were not satisfied with the way Nike treated them.

In early 1985, Don Coleman started questioning the loyalty to Nike of some Santa Monica athletes, including me, and threatened to cut off Nike from the club. Don was complaining that he could not get along with Joe. Later in the year, we got a letter from Howard Slusher, a Nike attorney, who wanted to discuss his "concerns" with the relationship between Santa Monica and Nike. A lot of them focused on Joe. Slusher claimed that Joe interfered in relationships between Nike and athletes, failed to cooperate in arranging appearances and press conferences, and generally attempted to make life difficult for Nike. Of course, Joe had a very different story, and I believed him before I believed Nike. If there were times when Joe was difficult to deal with—and I'm sure there were—it was only because Joe's top priority was always making sure that we would be ready to perform the best we could. That meant training when necessary, resting when necessary, and sometimes turning down offers for appearances or business, even when they were good offers. Those are things that must be done to stay the best in the world at something, and those are the things that were most important to me and Joe. Nike didn't always understand that, or didn't care.

By the time Joe and I got the letter telling us our contract was being terminated, my relationship with Don was completely different than it had been in the beginning. We still spoke and did business when we had to, but he was not my friend anymore, not the person I had thought of as a brother when I first got to know him. Don had taken advantage of me too many times. Nike had leaned on him too many times to get me to do things I didn't have to do, an extra appearance here, a few minutes there. Whenever Nike wanted something extra, Don was supposed to come through. He didn't know how to say no to his bosses, and he didn't know how to accept a no from me. He just kept pushing and pushing, and I got tired of that.

Nike was no longer using me in advertising because company officials were still concerned about my public image. The public was "fickle" about me, Nike people were telling each other. But Nike was still paying me a lot of money. Once the company decided not to use me for advertising, I was thought of as a big waste of money. Nike had been looking for ways to dump me, and now the lawyers thought they had enough to do it.

Joe Douglas and I didn't contact Nike for a meeting. We didn't see any point in that. The company had made a decision, and now we had to make one. We decided to sue, and I was not going to be the only one going after Nike. Johnny Gray and David Mack also wanted to sue for the way they had been treated, and the Santa Monica club joined our case, along with a company I had formed.

My attorney, David Greifinger, filed the lawsuit in federal court in California. David has been with the Santa Monica club almost as long as Joe Douglas, first as a runner, then as the club's attorney. In 1973, as a high school student just outside of Los Angeles, David heard about the club and went to Santa Monica to meet Joe. He started training with Joe, and has been with him ever since. After running cross-country and track for UCLA, David went to law school at nearby Loyola University, and it wasn't long before he started helping Joe with legal matters. David had a summer internship with a big law firm in Los Angeles, and that's all it took to know he didn't want to work for a firm. He would rather work with athletes, throwing a few

T-shirts, his jogging gear, and a pair of corduroys in a bag, and spending months on the track circuit in Europe. He still runs some long-distance races, primarily in California, so he trains with us all the time. David also does our legal work at home, and he is a vice president of the club. He does some general practice work on the side, but not much. Representing me and the club is more than enough work, and I couldn't imagine the club without David being around. He is just about everywhere we go, and he is a lot of fun, his wit and sarcasm always helping to keep things light. Until there is legal work to be done. Then he is all business.

There was a lot of legal jargon in the court papers David filed against Nike, terms like "anticipatory breach of contract . . . promissory estoppel . . . quantum meruit . . . declaratory relief." But as far as I was concerned, the case was a lot simpler than all that. The bottom line was that Nike did not want to pay me anymore, so the company was claiming I did things that I didn't do—or, in some cases, had good reasons for doing. The company thought it had a right to stop paying me. I didn't see it that way. I wasn't going to give in without somebody outside Nike hearing my side of the story. We asked for a trial with a jury.

I was not the lawsuit type. I had sued only once before when a joint venture I had formed to buy and distribute Nike products went bad. This was not Nike's fault. It was the fault of a businessman named Randall Slavin and his company, Justin Morgan, Inc. After a lot of legal hassles and a trial in Los Angeles, the judge agreed with me. Slavin and his company were eventually ordered to pay me more than $729,000.

Still, I wasn't eager to sue again. I didn't want my business in a court file and in the newspapers. But I felt that I had no choice.

Nike made the next move, with a countersuit against us. Then we started the legal wrestling. We went through months of depositions, with Nike's attorney, Kirk Hallam, asking all sorts of questions, making all sorts of suggestions, basically doing whatever he could to make us look bad in transcripts of sworn interviews that would be used in our case.

Nike's big blow was that I had worn a black suit without the company logo on it during a few track meets. The company claimed that this was a violation of my contract. Actually, it was just an indication of how petty the company had become and how eager it had been to unload me.

I had gotten the suit from a woman named Nancy Frickel, who handled marketing for Nike in Belgium, when I was there to film a music video for my song, "Break It Up." Nancy showed up at the health club where we were making the video, and she had some Nike wear, including the black suit. I didn't think much about it then, but it turned out that only the bottom half of the outfit had a Nike logo. The top didn't. That was sin number one: wearing something in a video that didn't have "Nike" on it.

Then I wore the suit in a few meets back in the States. If I had thought that there would have been any problem with that, I would not have worn it. It would have been just as easy to wear something else. But the outfit had come from someone with Nike, so the thought of it being an issue never even crossed my mind. Simple as that. I was getting a lot of money to wear Nike, and there was no reason why I would intentionally jeopardize the arrangement. Anyone in his right mind would wear Nike or Adidas or Puma or whatever anyone wanted him to wear for the type of money I was getting. It was easy money. Too easy, Nike had decided. The company collected photographs and statements from people in its camp to prove that I had worn something without the company logo on it. That would be the most damaging evidence against me.

Another big complaint was that I was not wearing Nike clothes in a picture used to promote a charity event. The event was a worldwide Peace Run, organized by Sri Chinmoy and some of his followers. During several months in 1987, thousands of runners were going to cover twenty-seven thousand miles in more than fifty countries, passing a torch from runner to runner, carrying a message of peace all over the globe. The Sri Chinmoy Oneness-Home Peace Run would be the longest relay of all time, and for a great cause. It was Sri Chinmoy's version of "We Are the World" or "Hands Across America." The Peace Run was supported by quite a few celebrities, including Nobel Peace Prize–winner Desmond Tutu, television host Dick Clark, actress Joanne Woodward, Canadian Prime Minister Brian Mulroney, United Nations Secretary General Javier Perez de Cuellar, America's Cup winner Dennis Conner, musician Clarence

Clemons, singer Whitney Houston and her Grammy Award–winning producer, my friend Narada Michael Walden.

It was an impressive group, and I was proud to be part of it. I was supposed to light and carry the first torch to begin the run at the Statue of Liberty in New York. Organizers of the event put out a press release, quoting me as saying, "The Peace Run is intended to celebrate the invincibility of the human spirit and inspire us to overcome the barriers to a lasting peace among the peoples of the earth." This was about as wholesome an event as you could find, and I never would have guessed that being involved could cause me any trouble. But Nike tried to make it into trouble.

In addition to the press release, organizers sent out a photograph of me with Narada and Clarence Clemons. Each of us was wearing a sweatshirt with a globe on it and the words, "Sri Chinmoy Oneness-Home Peace Run." That was my crime, in Nike's eyes. The company considered this an athletic event and claimed that I should have been wearing Nike. I didn't consider it an athletic event, and knowing that I was obligated to wear Nike only during athletic events, I didn't even think about whether I should have been wearing Nike. If the company was so concerned about my image, which its people claimed from time to time, then it should have been pleased to see me as part of such a positive event.

In addition to the Big Two (the black outfit and the peace run sweatshirt) Nike spent a lot of time in depositions trying to make me look bad for little things. Everything they brought up was either not true or easily explainable, but the Nike attorney kept trying to put his slant on things. I guess that's what civil lawsuits are all about.

Why hadn't I met Phil Knight in New York for a Broadway show? He had been expecting me. Well, actually, I had never said I was going to be there.

Why did I skip a meet in Seoul after Nike told me it was important to be there? And was this the same time I was in a hospital for a nose job? Had I put self-improvement ahead of my sponsor? No. Again, Nike was complaining about me missing a commitment that I never made. I never said I was going to be at the meet in Seoul. I was exhausted from a long trip just before that, had told Nike I wasn't going, and had been told that there was no problem with that. As far as the nose job, yes, I had one, but not to get out of a meet.

There were plenty of other attempts.

Kirk Hallam kept wanting to talk about a clothing line Joe Douglas and I had discussed with Nike. Some company officials had agreed that a Carl Lewis line might be a good idea, but it never got off the ground. Nike ended up not wanting to do it. Now Hallam tried to make us look bad by drawing us into comparisons with basketball great Michael Jordan and tennis star John McEnroe, both Nike athletes with clothing lines. Hallam wanted us to say things to create something like the Michael Jackson comparisons of 1984. He even asked about the Michael Jackson comparison. Anything to bring up the image problems of 1984. Anything to make me look like the bad guy.

Hallam took the depositions of about ten people, including me and my mother, Joe Douglas, Johnny Gray, and David Mack. He also took a sworn statement from Kirk Baptiste, who had left the Santa Monica club but was still with Nike. It bothered me that Nike used my old teammate and friend against me, and that he agreed to help in their case, but that's what happened. Nike contributed to the downfall of a close friendship, coming between me and Kirk. Joe Douglas and I had to answer the most questions from Hallam, three days worth for each of us, all under oath with a court reporter taking down everything we said.

These sessions were mostly serious, sometimes sarcastic, and every once in a while, funny. But for the most part, they were a pain. Now I knew why people don't like being involved in lawsuits.

With the case dragging on longer than we hoped it would, we started thinking about a settlement. I had a new shoe contract with Mizuno, a Japanese company, and I didn't want the Nike case to distract me while I trained and competed. The Olympic Games were on the horizon again, and I had to focus on what was most important: preparation and competition.

I can't discuss the terms of our out-of-court settlement. That was part of the agreement. But I was satisfied. This would finally put an end to all the turmoil that followed the 1984 Games. It had all been tied into so many things that made so little sense—lies, distortions, and other crap that flies around the corporate world and the press boxes of America. But I was ready to put that all behind me, ready to stop thinking about Nike, ready to look forward, not back.

CHAPTER
ELEVEN
≡
Drugs and Dodging

A FIRST step forward would be to do something about my public image. If I wasn't going to accept the press's view of who I was, I would have to do the best I could to let people know the real Carl Lewis. Everything was fine in the rest of the world, but in my own country I was still having problems with the coverage I was getting. I would have to be more accessible, more open, and I was willing to give that a try. I would also accept some of the blame for the image that had developed. I had made some mistakes, just as anyone would, and if I could talk about them, that would help. There had been times when I wanted to blame everything on reporters, but that wouldn't be entirely fair, and it would only cause more problems. I wanted to be humble, not bitter. Placing some of the blame on myself would be one way to show my humility.

Joe Douglas spent a lot of time arranging meetings with reporters. If one had been particularly tough on me, Joe would call and say, "What's the problem? Let's talk about it. What are your complaints? Maybe you could meet Carl and talk about them, get to see what he is really like." Better communication would help the reporters as much as it would help me.

So many of the people who had written bad things about me had never even met me. At least half of the negative stories, probably more, fell into that category, so I increased the number of one-on-one interviews I did. There was now more time available for that. When a reporter got time, he felt wanted, and when he felt wanted, he wrote nicer things. I guess that's just human nature.

I also started doing more television than I had done in the past. On television—especially live television, with no editing—people would see the real me, not the way somebody chose to write about me. Doing too many interviews with print reporters and not enough with television was one of the mistakes I had made in 1983 and 1984.

One of the regular features in my interviews now was a discussion of the way I had matured since the '84 Games. I had been through a lot, learned a lot, grown up, and everybody wanted to talk about that. *The New Carl Lewis.* That was the big story angle. In a way, that provided an easy out for reporters who had covered me all along. Even if they wrote nice things about me now, they would not have to admit to themselves or their readers that they might have been somewhat wrong about me in the past. They wouldn't have to say, "Maybe Carl was a decent guy and we just didn't know him." They could stick to their old stories, and at the same time, justify their new approaches by saying that *I* had changed.

That was fine with me. The bottom line was that reporters started treating me a lot better. My father had been right when he encouraged me to be patient. I had waited out the problems, and now I would have a chance to turn my image around.

The new headlines said things like, "Carl Lewis Loosens Up," "Carl Lewis Takes a Great Leap Forward in an Effort to Repair His Public Image," "Carl Lewis Is Singing Different Tune." Amazingly, a writer here and there would focus on what the media, not I, had done to my image. One story that went over the wires and appeared in a number of newspapers said, "What has happened to Lewis since the Games says a little about how the media, for better or worse, makes and breaks heroes."

People finally were realizing that I was human, not a robot. I had ups and downs like everyone else, did good things and bad things like everyone else, did smart things and stupid things like everyone else. I had humility and I had confidence. I had strengths and weaknesses, talent in some areas, trouble in others. I was a mixture of things, not a one-dimensional freak. In that respect, I was just like most other people, and that was a key. Reporters willing to spend time getting to know me, willing to try to understand my thoughts and actions—they were the ones who started treating me as a person, not a freak, and they were the ones whose stories started putting my image back together.

Of course, there were still going to be negative writers and negative stories. But things were getting better.

At the 1987 Pan American Games in Indianapolis, I met the biggest crowd of reporters I had seen since the Olympics in Los Angeles. I sat with Coach Tellez in a press conference bigger than any I had seen since the pre-Olympics press conference, the one where I was criticized for being late, too flashy, out for money. Back then, I could have said nothing and I still would have been creamed for my words. Now the situation was entirely different.

I said: "We're all older now. It's a whole new ballgame. Since '84, I've changed. I'm more mature, I'm a little more confident in myself, I'm happier. I also understand better that everyone has their lives to live and their jobs to do." I was talking about reporters, trying to make them realize that I did not hold any grudges. "I don't believe that anybody is out to get anybody else. I understand that better now. In '84 in LA, I tried to achieve in track and others tried to achieve in writing stories. Those things are our jobs."

After attending the press conference, Bill Dwyre, the sports editor of the *Los Angeles Times,* wrote: "What a difference 1,095 days make. Three years ago, in the aftermath of Lewis' grand appearance at the Olympics . . . the thrill of victory disintegrated into the agony of bad press."

What Dwyre wrote was especially nice considering that his paper had been one of the most critical in '84.

"The new Carl Lewis met the press here," the story began, "and the press was his. On the surface, Lewis' news conference at the Pan Am Games was intended to give reporters a chance to question the 1984 Olympic star about his attempt at breaking the world record in the long jump here. But this meeting of longtime adversaries turned out to be much more than track and field chit chat. This was a Carl Lewis intent on mending fences, on winning friends and influencing people. His emphasis was on burying hatchets, letting bygones be bygones, kissing and making up."

After a quote from me talking about staying in track and field at least through the 1988 Olympics, probably longer, the story ended with this: "So it appears that the press will, for at least a few more years, have Carl Lewis to kick around. The question after Thursday's event here, however: Will it want to?"

The summer of '87 would be a big season for me because I was coming off a knee injury that had pretty much ruined my previous year. Tendinitis had made my left knee very stiff and sore, and I had ended the season early with minor surgery. After disappearing from the track scene for a little while, I wanted to make sure everyone knew I wasn't done, wasn't over the hill. I kept saying, "I'm not dead and I'm not old," but I would have to prove it to the skeptics. I wanted to have a great year, partly because the year before had been so rough, partly because it was now the year before the Olympics. Once again, the ability to focus would be more important than anything else.

Some interesting things were happening in my biggest events, the 100 and long jump. In the 100, Ben Johnson, who had placed third in the '84 Games, was making a strong move to challenge me as the best sprinter in the world. He was stronger than ever, and faster than ever. From 1980 to mid-1985, I had run against Ben seven times in the 100, including the '84 Olympics, and had beaten him all seven times. But then Ben started coming on. He was unbelievably strong and quick out of the starting blocks, and he beat me five out of the next six times we raced. For the time being, he could claim the title, "World's Fastest Human," and he boasted about that whenever he had a chance. By 1987 I was tired of hearing about Ben and wanted to reclaim the number one ranking in the world.

I wasn't worried about my ranking in the long jump. That was pretty secure. In my first outdoor meet of the season, I went beyond 28 feet on all six jumps, and I knew I was ready. That was fortunate because Larry Myricks and Mike Conley, my chief competitors, were jumping well. At the national championships in June, all three of us went past 28 feet, the first time ever that three people went that distance in the same competition. My knee wasn't feeling as good as I would have liked, but I was able to win. That put my long-jump winning streak at fifty, and once again set off all the questions about breaking Bob Beamon's record.

"Is this going to be the year?"

"Maybe," I said. "It's definitely possible."

Reporters asked the same question in dozens of different ways, and

I kept trying to explain that records were not the most important things in the world.

"Are you finally going to do it?"

"It's in me," I said. "I know that. But that's not my focus. I know I can jump over 29 feet. The talent is there and I've worked hard at it. But I'm not possessed by the thought of a world record."

"If you don't ever get it, won't you feel like something is missing?"

"Not really. I'm just going to perform the best I can. That's the way it's always been. Records are for other people to talk about, not me. If I never set a record, I still think people will remember me. They'll remember the Olympics and they'll remember that I lasted a long time. I was consistent."

But no matter what I said, the anticipation was there for the record to go in August at the Pan Am Games. Part of the reason was location. We were going to compete in the Indiana University stadium. Five years earlier, I had jumped 30 feet there—at least, a lot of people thought I had, including me—but an official called me for a foul, saying a toe had gone past the takeoff board. But there was no mark on the Plasticene at the end of the board. That's why Plasticene is used in long-jumping. It's a rubbery, claylike substance that shows a mark when the jumper has gone too far before jumping. When that happens, the runner has fouled. There was no mark that day, but the official didn't care. He had seen a foul, and he wasn't going to change his mind. At the Pan Am Games, people remembered that jump and wanted to see something incredible happen. Some people even *expected* it to happen. This was like the '84 Olympics all over again.

The day of the long jump, the wind went wild. It blew like crazy and kept changing directions, making it impossible to plan a jump. Just when I thought I was ready to go, the wind would do something else, and I would have to start focusing all over again. The conditions were the same for everyone, of course. We would all struggle, and I had to be realistic. I couldn't imagine going 29 feet in these conditions, and even if I did, it would be wind-aided, so it wouldn't count.

The best I could do was 28 feet, 8½ inches, which was a record for the Pan Am Games, the sixth-longest jump in history. But it was not the world record. It was not what everybody had been waiting to see. They would have to keep waiting.

Next up, a week later, were the World Championships in Rome. I would face Ben Johnson, and that was going to be the big story of the meet. Our rivalry was big news now. We had raced three months earlier in Spain, and Ben had just barely beaten me. Actually, there had been a dispute over a photo finish, but Ben was awarded the victory with a time of 10.06 seconds. I was clocked at 10.07. I was still ahead of Ben lifetime in the 100, but the margin was now eight to five, and Ben had won four in a row. I had not beaten him since 1985.

The long jump in Indianapolis had proven that I was back from my knee injury. But now I wanted to prove that I could do my best on the track. I wanted to be back on top, and I wanted Ben to know he was in for a battle. The rest of my career would be dedicated to my father. I wanted to compete more recklessly than ever before, and I wanted to do the absolute best I could every single time I stepped on the track. That's what my father had always wanted.

Ben thought he was going to keep cruising, and I had to show him that he was wrong. He was not going to fly right past me and right through the Olympics. No, I was not going to allow that. To set the tone, I needed a victory in Rome.

The meet was one of the biggest of the decade, with almost 2,000 athletes from more than 150 countries. In a way, it was bigger than even the Olympics because politics had been keeping some of the best athletes in the world out of the Games. The Americans had boycotted in 1980 and the Soviets had stayed away in 1984. The last time all the best athletes had been together was in 1983 at the first World Championships, in Helsinki, so promoters in Rome were looking for something big to happen. More than anything else, Primo Nebiolo, the head of the IAAF, the international track federation, wanted a world record. We were in his home country, at his meet, and he wanted something that would be remembered for a long time. At a dinner before the meet, Nebiolo pulled me aside and told me how much he wanted to see a record. It didn't matter to him if I did it in the long jump or the 100. He just wanted a record. "This is going to be the greatest meet of all time," Nebiolo told me. A few minutes later, I saw him talking to Ben Johnson, probably saying the same things.

The Stadio Olimpico was packed for the 100-meter finals. Almost sixty-five thousand people were there to see the big race, and they got exactly what Nebiolo wanted, a world record. Ben absolutely exploded out of the blocks—maybe even false-starting without being caught—and he never slowed down. Well, maybe a little, but not much, not enough. I was able to pick up a little ground down the track, but not nearly enough to catch Ben. He ran a 9.83, a full tenth of a second better than Calvin Smith's world record, and the stadium scoreboards flashed "Nuovo Record Mondial," new world record. The place went nuts. I had run the best legal time of my life, a 9.93, tying Smith's four-year-old record, and it still wasn't good enough to beat Ben. It wasn't even good enough to come close.

A lot of people started questioning Ben's start, wondering if he had come up with an illegal technique that would not be detected. If anyone moves before the gun sounds, a false start is supposed to be called. In some big meets (including this one) an electronic device in the starting blocks is used to assist the person who calls false starts. The device measures the pressure of a runner's feet against the blocks, and if the pressure is released before the gun sounds, it is considered a false start. A second gun sounds and the race is halted. It then must be started again. But that is not the only way for a false start to be called. It can also be called if the starter sees something illegal that is not detected by electronics.

Ben did something unusual. He lifted up with his arms and body quicker than anybody else, but apparently was able to maintain pressure against the blocks as he did so. That's what people told me right after the race, and that's what it looks like on films I have seen since then. No false start was detected by the electronic device, but it still should have been called. Sometimes the human eye is more reliable than electronics. There was actually a meeting of officials to review whether Ben had false-started, but I have been told that Nebiolo quickly put an end to that. He wanted the world record and it would stand. End of discussion. A Swedish newspaper reported that Ben had, in fact, false-started without being caught.

But there was nothing I could do. The Italians were too busy celebrating the record, Nebiolo was too excited about having it at his meet, and he was too powerful for anyone to challenge him. Plus, the possibility of a false start was not nearly as important to me as another problem with Ben. I had been hearing that he was on drugs. People on the track circuit had whispered here and there that Ben was using steroids, doing whatever he could to bulk up, speed up, and beat me.

He was on a single-minded mission. Beat Carl. Be number one. Do whatever it takes.

A lot of what I heard about Ben centered on his coach, Charlie Francis. The word was that when Charlie is involved, doing "whatever it takes" includes doing drugs. Charlie's reputation was one of the worst on the circuit. He was known as "a drug coach." Ben was not the only Canadian athlete suspected of using steroids, and the others I had heard about also trained with Charlie and Ben.

Sometimes I heard very specific information about what Ben was doing, sometimes I heard only vague comments. But I had heard enough to convince me that something was going on. The track circuit is a tough place to keep a secret, and too many people were talking about Ben.

One of the most interesting stories had started in Rome just hours before Ben got his world record. Pat Connolly, a former Olympian who had coached the great American sprinter Evelyn Ashford, and was now coaching a number of other athletes, overheard a quick but meaningful comment on her way into the stadium. She was stuck for a minute in a crowd of people trying to get from a warm-up track into the stadium, and Pat found herself standing behind Charlie Francis and another coach, Chuck DeBus. Chuck is also a coach who has been mentioned in stories about steroids. Some of his former athletes have talked extensively about his involvement with drugs, and he has been investigated by The Athletics Congress (TAC). Pat didn't hear a complete conversation, but she did hear Charlie say to Chuck: "They can say anything to me they want. I'm just going to say that Ben had gonorrhea."

To the casual listener, that would not have meant much. But Pat was not a casual listener. She knew about Charlie and she had heard a lot about drugs. Years before, Charlie had approached Pat, introduced himself, and asked her how in the world Evelyn Ashford had been beating East German sprinters. Charlie had told Pat that he had been in East Germany and knew how drugs were being administered to athletes there. He was amazed that Evelyn had beaten an East German, and he wanted to know what drugs Evelyn was using. Charlie wanted to work with Pat to beat the East Germans at their own game, the use of banned drugs. Pat told Charlie to get lost. She was furious that he would assume Evelyn was on drugs—she was not, Pat told him—and Pat was furious that Charlie would invite her into the world of drugs, assuming that she would want to be involved. Now, in Rome, Pat knew what Charlie was all about, and she knew that his comment to DeBus was serious stuff.

Charlie was worried about Ben being caught with a masking agent in his system, and just in case, he was ready with an excuse. Charlie had to be talking about a drug called probenecid, which is sometimes used to treat gonorrhea. Probenecid increases the effectiveness of penicillin.

Some athletes have used the drug as a masking agent to hide other drugs. The presence of probenecid in a urine sample apparently makes it difficult, if not impossible, to detect traces of certain steroids. There had been articles in the sports pages about this, and Pat had read some of them. What Francis was saying must have been that, if probenecid were found in Ben's urine sample, Francis would deny that it was there to cover for other drugs. He would say it was there because Ben had been suffering from gonorrhea.

Minutes before the biggest race of the World Championships, one of the biggest of my career, Joe Douglas had approached me on the track. He was a wreck. He had heard something very disturbing, but he wouldn't tell me what until after the race because he didn't want to distract me. But it was too late. I was already distracted. What the heck was he talking about? I hoped it wasn't anything really bad. I wished Joe had waited to say anything at all.

After the race, Joe told me that Pat Connolly had passed along the conversation she overheard. It was just talk, of course, not absolute proof. But I had already heard way too much about Charlie and Ben. That's what made the story from Pat so upsetting.

All the talk about Ben seemed to be reinforced by a change in the way he was acting. In the past, he had been pretty quiet, but perfectly nice. Now nobody knew what he was going to say, or how he was going to react to something as simple as a hello in the lobby of a hotel or at the track. Ben would often ignore other athletes or coaches or anybody else in his path, and sometimes he would snap without anybody knowing why.

In public, Ben was a lot bolder than ever before. He was still stuttering, as he had been for years, and he still struggled in front of a lot of people or in front of television cameras. But now he was telling reporters he was on top of the world and he wasn't going to take any shit from anybody. That is exactly how Ben put it in a live television interview. Ben said after the race that it might be another fifty years before anybody broke his record, and "if anybody's going to break it, they're going to have to beat me." Then he talked about how "awesome" he was. This was not Ben talking. This was steroids. Ben was more aggressive than he had been, partly because of the steroids, partly because he had probably been told he had to be more aggressive if he wanted to be the best in the world. Charlie Francis would undoubtedly tell him something like that.

All the behind-the-scenes talk about Ben and drugs left me in a tough spot. Should I say something about Ben, or should I keep my mouth shut and let the authorities catch up with him? The situation was complicated by the fact that I didn't trust the authorities. There had been strong indications that some of the people in charge of track and field, both worldwide and in the United States, had been covering for athletes using steroids. I had pretty good information on this from athletes, coaches, and people who conducted and evaluated drug tests. I might not be able to prove that what I heard was true, but I had heard enough to be suspicious. I truly believed that certain athletes were protected, and I wondered what, if anything, could be done about that. Should I raise the issue publicly, prompting reporters to ask questions and forcing the top officials in our sport to give answers? Or should I leave it alone?

There was no easy answer. Speaking out could, in the long run, help our sport. But speaking out would leave me open to a lot of criticism. People would say, sour grapes—Carl lost to Ben, and now he's complaining. Why doesn't he stop shooting off his mouth? Can't he accept that he lost?

I decided to take my chances. I felt that I had to talk. It was time to take a stand on something that mattered, just as my parents had done back in Alabama when they felt that they had to, just like any of the Lewis children did when the situation called for it, no matter what the immediate consequences might be. The idea was not to cause trouble, but to call attention to a serious problem. Maybe I could help solve it.

Ben definitely was not the only one doing drugs. There were other drug-users who won gold medals at the world championships. One of the winners even admitted it to some of my Santa Monica teammates. Another winner had needle marks high on the back of his leg. Mentioning the names of these drug-users would not have helped anything then, and I'm not sure that it would serve any purpose now, so I don't want to do it. The important thing was to raise the issue. It had been ignored by too many people for too long.

In an interview with a British television station, ITV, I talked about the drug problem, saying that some world champions were taking drugs to improve their performance and that the problem was worse than ever. There were even "designer drugs" or "masking agents" being used to keep athletes from testing positive.

"I feel a strange air at these championships," I said. "A lot of people have come from nowhere and are running unbelievably. It's worse than ever. There are gold medalists at this meet already that are on drugs. . . . We have always run away from the problem. We haven't been facing the issue. . . . I'm not bitter or angry at anyone in this sport. But there is a problem, and it is a problem that we must resolve to clean up the sport. . . . The leaders of the sport have to try to clean things up."

No, no, no, I kept repeating to reporters, I was not going to name names. I was not going to single out which athletes were using drugs. That was not the point. The issue was bigger than that. We needed a new approach to stop the use of drugs.

A few days later, I was back in the stadium for the long-jump competition, and reporters chased me down for more talk about drugs. They didn't have much to ask me about winning the long jump. Four times I had jumped past 28 feet, and a jump of 28 feet, 5½ inches, gave me the gold medal. The world championship I had won four years earlier in Helsinki was still mine, but that was not a big story because I had been expected to do that. I was always expected to win the long jump. As far as reporters were concerned, the only good long-jump stories left were "Lewis finally breaks Beamon's record" and "Lewis loses for first time since 1981."

In Rome, they had neither of those stories, so what they really wanted was more on the drug story, something they could use to get on the front page. I said that I favored more testing to identify drug users, and that people who are caught should be banned for life from our sport. But I wasn't going to add to the controversy. The issue had been raised, and that had been my goal. Any new controversy would have to come from someone else, and there were plenty of people—

athletes, coaches, and officials—already criticizing me for what I had told the British TV station.

Some of the people trying to brush off my comments were calling them vague and unsubstantiated, and they were asking each other, "Why should we listen to Carl unless he gives some specifics?" That was an easy way to reassure each other that our sport was fine, and always would be, and it was an easy response to reporters looking for reaction to my comments. But a response like that certainly wouldn't help our sport move forward. There were also plenty of comments about "sour grapes," just as I had expected. But I could live with that.

Next, I was going to call for an independent drug-testing agency. We needed an outside organization, not the track federations, to test for drugs because the federations simply were not getting the job done. They felt that they had too much at risk and couldn't afford to have top athletes getting caught on drugs. That would make the whole sport look bad. But the drug issue had always been very important to me, and if necessary, I was willing to pay a price in order to get out an anti-drug message. We could not afford to ignore the message because it had been buried too long. We needed to take a stand.

"Dodging" was the next big challenge for Ben. He wanted to dodge me, running in races all over the world, collecting as much money as possible along the way, without having to face me. After his big win in Rome, he did not want to risk losing. Losing would hurt his value. It would cost him money. So with the help of Charlie Francis and manager Larry Heidebrecht, Ben did everything he could to avoid me. In the three weeks following the World Championships, Ben and I were entered in the same meets a few times, but never faced each other. Meet promoters could not get Ben to race me.

In Rieti, Italy, a regular stop on the summer circuit, I was told I could not run the 100 because Ben was running it and didn't want me in the race. Joe Douglas told the meet organizer that we don't play that game. If Ben wanted to dodge me, that was his business, but unless promoters wanted me to leave, I was running the 100. Eventually, separate heats were arranged, one for Ben, one for me. What a ripoff for people who wanted to see a legitimate race.

A few days after that, I entered the 200-meter race at the Grand

Prix Final in Brussels. Knowing that Ben was in the 200 there, I figured he could not get out of racing me. It was too late for Ben to switch events. But when I arrived in Brussels, I learned that once again Ben's people had found a way. I was in the main draw with the serious runners. Ben was in a specially arranged 200 against a bunch of guys who didn't have a chance.

In Lausanne, Switzerland, Ben was very unhappy when he heard that I was in the 100, and he threatened to pull out of the meet unless I was yanked from the race. Jacky Delapierre, the meet promoter, wanted me in, though, and he refused to let Ben tell him what to do—well, to a certain degree. Delapierre offered to put us in separate heats. He wanted to handle the problem the same way it had been handled in Rieti and Brussels. But Ben wouldn't do that anymore. Both times that we had run separate heats, my times were better than his, and fans considered both events as wins for me. Ben didn't like that. This time, if I was going to run the 100, he wanted to run a 60-meter race. That is an indoor event, but Ben got what he wanted, a 60-meter outdoor race created just for him.

At least Delapierre went after Ben. Delapierre told a bunch of reporters what Ben was doing, and the word got out in local newspapers. The fans did not appreciate the way Ben was handling things. When he was introduced at the stadium, the Swiss crowd whistled, which is like the American boo. After Ben won his ridiculous little 60, the crowd whistled again, and Ben took off, leaving the stadium without the traditional victory ceremony.

Ben kept telling people he was not afraid of me, saying I was "nothing." Then why was he avoiding me? Why did he keep telling meet promoters what he wasn't willing to do? The reason was a typical reason in sports, whether we're talking about "professional" sports or "amateur" sports. The reason was money. Everything Ben was doing related to money. He wanted a series of match races against me, but not yet. Heidebrecht was talking to Joe Douglas about waiting until before the 1988 Olympics, when interest in track and field would be at its greatest. Meet organizers would pay huge appearance fees to get us, television networks would love it, and sponsors would want in on the act.

Of course, this wasn't fair to fans who wanted to see us race now, but Ben and his manager didn't care. This was a big change from 1984, when the media made me out to be the lone money man in a sport meant for pure competitors, the greedy American carrying capitalism into the wrong arena. Now all I wanted was a race. Ben, the world champion with who-knows-what in his body, was the one with his eye on the bottom line.

The talk about a series of match races escalated in early 1988. At one point we were told we would get close to one million dollars for three races, two 100s and a 200. A package was almost ready to be signed, we kept hearing from promoters, but in the end it fell apart. For one thing, Ben would not agree to a drug-testing procedure I demanded—for both of us. Finally, we settled on one race, me and Ben in the 100 in Zurich, Switzerland. For the first time since the World Championships in Rome in August 1987, the fans would have a chance to see the race they had been waiting to see. And I would have a chance to get even. We would go to Zurich in August, about five weeks before the Seoul Olympics.

The buildup was incredible. Newspapers said we would each get $250,000 for the race, which wasn't right, but it was fine with us that everyone was saying that. The more speculation, the more hype, and the more hype, the more money we would actually make. That's because our payments were tied into television money. Each of us—Andreas Brugger (the meet promoter), Ben, and I—would get a cut of the money paid by television stations to broadcast the race. At first, Brugger wanted to split the money evenly—a third to the meet, a third to Ben, a third to me. But Joe Douglas objected. He was not going to let Ben get an equal share. Ben's appearance fees generally were lower than mine, and that was just how we wanted it. Meet promoters all over Europe were used to that, and we did not want to set a precedent in Zurich. We did not want word to get out that Carl and Ben were getting equal slices of the pie. That would hurt my market value. Brugger and Ben's people eventually gave in, and Joe and I got what we wanted, the biggest slice of the pie. All the speculation and hype was great, more and more television money came in as the race approached, and we ended up doing very well.

The Zurich stop is always one of the biggest on the European circuit, but this year it was bigger than ever. From the moment I arrived in Switzerland, every move I made was captured by cameras and scribbled in notebooks, and Ben was getting the same treatment.

It was like preparing for a heavyweight championship bout. That was the atmosphere.

"I don't think he can beat me again," Ben told reporters. "I've proved it so many times already."

"I'm ready," I said. "I'll do my talking on the track."

As usual, Ben was first out of the blocks, and, surprise, surprise, he was called for a false start. It was obvious this time, and we were called back to start the race again. If Ben jumped the gun a second time, he would be disqualified. But that was not likely, not in such a big race. Again, Ben was first out of the blocks, legally this time.

He got ahead of me by about a meter and led most of the way, but I caught him with 10 meters to go. That's when I nailed him. Ben faded, and with two meters left, knowing I had it, I shot my arms into the air. The celebration was on. I hugged Carol, who had been waiting for me past the finish line, and she picked me up, spinning me in front of a pack of photographers.

My time was 9.93, the same as my time in Rome. Calvin Smith finished second with a 9.97, and Ben was third in 10 flat. This was one of the most enjoyable races I had ever run. Nobody in the world had run better than 9.93 that year, so heading into the Olympics I was back on top. My confidence level was exactly where it needed to be. Meanwhile, Ben was struggling. He was talking about being out of shape and needing more training. With five weeks left before the Olympics, he thought he had enough time to peak, but I didn't think he could do it. Nobody who claimed to be out of shape could get ready in such a short period of time.

A few days later, though, I picked up some information from inside Ben's camp, and I started to wonder. The information came from Jack Scott, a physical therapist. Jack was in the strange position of having worked with both me and Ben. I had met Jack in 1987 at the U.S. national championships in San Jose, California. When I hurt my leg, he offered help, showing me a new machine called the My-O-Matic. It sends an electrical current through the leg, like a muscle stimulator would, only the current is so low that it doesn't actually stimulate the muscle. I don't know all the medical jargon involved, but Jack did, and his machine helped quite a bit. He later gave me a My-O-Matic to use at home, and we became friends.

Then Jack started working with Ben. Dr. Jamie Astaphan, Ben's doctor, had invited Jack to the Caribbean island of St. Kitts. That's where Ben trained before the race in Zurich, trying to strengthen his left hamstring, which was giving him trouble. Jack went to St. Kitts and, just as he had done for me, introduced Ben to the My-O-Matic. That helped. But there was more.

Here is what Jack told me after the race in Zurich.

Astaphan had approached Jack, told him he was fed up with Ben and would rather work with me. There had been a confrontation between Ben and Astaphan. The day of the race, when Ben was supposed to be getting a massage, he was instead looking for a meet organizer. Ben thought he had been shorted some of the money promised him, and he was on a mission to get his money. Astaphan kept telling Ben to get his rubdown, but Ben wanted his money. He ignored Astaphan, leaving the doctor to say, "What an idiot. If only I had Carl."

Astaphan wondered aloud if there were any way that Jack could convince me to work with Astaphan. If Astaphan could get me on the same "stuff" he was giving Ben, there was no way I could lose. Astaphan told Jack that drugs were the reason Ben was so good. He was talented, yes, but he's great because of drugs. If I could get Carl on drugs, Astaphan claimed, he would run 9.5. He and Ben wouldn't even be close.

Jack was shocked that Astaphan could be so disloyal. After working with Ben for five years, the doctor was ready to jump ship if he could get a better athlete. Jack didn't like that. He thought that Ben was with the wrong person, partly because Astaphan was feeding him so many steroids, partly because he was feeding him so much bullshit.

When Joe Douglas and I discussed this, I kept asking the same questions: Why would Astaphan tell Jack Scott all this? Why would Jack tell us? Why would Astaphan be so eager to work with me instead of Ben? We got together with Jack again, and started putting the puzzle together.

Astaphan had spent years searching for a stud. Working with a great athlete would help build his own image, and if he could create a positive image, he could get bigger in sports, maybe even in the United States. That was his ultimate objective. Ben was a stud. But he wasn't really getting Astaphan anywhere. A few dollars here and there, maybe, but nothing huge. Astaphan wanted something bigger.

Maybe he felt that I could get him into America. I had a bigger name than Ben, so I could make Astaphan a bigger name. I think he finally figured out that Ben was a joke, and he decided, "Let me get somebody who is really going to do it for me." I don't think Astaphan was concerned about what I could run, or what he could do for me. I think he was concerned about what he could get out of it.

The talk with Jack Scott was the last piece of evidence I needed. Before this, I had pretty good information that Ben had been doing drugs. Now I knew for sure, and going into the Olympics, I would not be able to forget it. To win the 100 in Seoul, I would have to beat a druggie.

I still didn't know what I could do about it. Probably nothing. My relationships with reporters were better than ever, and I was able to drop a few more hints about what was going on. But I had made my comments in Rome, and if people were really interested in cleaning up the sport, that should have been enough to create some sort of action, if not a serious investigation. A year had passed without much of anything happening.

It was time to avoid controversy, time to focus on the Games. It was time to get myself ready, not time to worry about what other people were doing. I would have to let things run their course. If Ben had gotten away with drugs for so long, there was little chance he would stop now. There was even less chance that someone would do anything about it, and almost no chance that he would ever be caught.

TWELVE

≡

Joe DeLoach

IN ADDITION to my own preparation for the Olympics, I had a special project. His name was Joe DeLoach. Joe was a high school senior when I first met him in 1985. Coach Tellez was recruiting Joe, and wanted me to go with him to Bay City, Texas, to meet the DeLoach family. Great athlete, great guy, great talent, Coach Tellez said of Joe. But I had just read a newspaper article that said Joe probably wanted to go to Southern Methodist University, SMU. So I said, "Forget it. I'm not wasting my time. Bay City? To push Houston on a high school kid who has all but committed to SMU? Give me a break." I had better things to do. But Coach Tellez insisted, and I went with him. He had also convinced Kirk Baptiste to go. Might as well hit the wide-eyed high school kid with the one-two punch, a gold medalist and a silver medalist who had done so well for themselves by going to the University of Houston.

Joe has eleven sisters, a brother, and a whole bunch of nieces and nephews, so his house was packed when we got there. This was not a typical recruiting visit. It was more like a family reunion. And an autograph session. I signed autographs for parents and kids, aunts and uncles, sisters and brothers. It was incredible. All this excitement because young Joe was getting so much attention. He had played wide receiver on his high school football team and had been recruited by a bunch of college football coaches, but Joe had ruled out football. He wanted track to be his future.

Mrs. DeLoach was concerned, as any mother would be, about Joe being away from home. This was a religious family in a small town. To them, Houston was big and far away, though actually it is only about eighty miles from Bay City. Joe was a nice guy, and I told Mrs. DeLoach, "If Joe comes to Houston, I promise you I'll take care of him." I would look out for Joe, help him adjust to college life and the track team.

The next week Joe signed with Houston. He was impressed with Coach Tellez's knowledge and wanted to learn from him. We were all excited because we had recruited a great athlete. But the excitement did not last long. A coach from Rice University turned us in for an illegal visit. I did not realize it when I made the visit, but I had violated NCAA rules by going to Joe's home. As a former Houston athlete, I was not allowed to recruit Joe like that. Only coaches could.

We fought the NCAA because it was such an innocent violation. It was no big deal, we thought. If we had known we were breaking a rule, why would we have done it? I was too well known for Coach Tellez to take a chance like that, and I certainly would not have signed all those autographs, solid proof that I had been there. But the NCAA officials would not budge. They told Joe that, if he went to Houston, he could not compete there as a freshman. The school could appeal to the NCAA, seeking to make Joe eligible as a sophomore. But Joe also had a simpler option. He could go to any other school and compete right away.

Once the NCAA gave its ruling, a lot of schools were on Joe again, trying to change his mind about going to Houston. But Joe showed a lot of character by sticking with his decision. He would come to Houston without a scholarship and would sit out his freshman year while the NCAA considered an appeal. Joe was not allowed to train with the varsity so he competed for the Houston club team. He was in shape sometimes, out of shape others, but his performances were consistently mediocre, and he didn't feel like part of the team. He was running against guys with much more experience. He had some injury problems, so it was a tough, lonely year for him. Joe was a pretty quiet guy and he was down a lot. I was still training with the varsity and club teams, and now I was an assistant coach for the varsity. Coach Tellez put me on his staff so we would not have any more trouble with the NCAA. I encouraged Joe when I could. But there was not a whole lot to say. He was in a tough spot for a year, and we all knew it.

There were times when Joe considered leaving Houston. I wanted to talk him through those times, wanted to make good on my promise to Joe's mother that I would take care of him, but Coach Tellez told me to leave Joe alone. I was the one associated with Joe's eligibility problems and Coach Tellez did not want it to look like I was still "recruiting" Joe, even though he was already at school. I felt terrible about not being able to do anything for Joe.

Kirk had been in Bay City, too. But I was the one who took all the heat. Reporters would ask me: Did Joe get a raw deal from the NCAA? It was really your fault, not his, that a recruiting rule was broken, right? I talked to Joe's parents to let them know how sorry I was about what had happened, but I didn't know how they felt about me. Talking to them became very awkward for me, and more than ever, I felt responsible for helping Joe achieve his goals. If nothing else, I wanted him to be happy at Houston, glad that he made the decision to go there.

A rumor that Joe was going to transfer to UCLA floated around from time to time. So in January 1986, midway through Joe's freshman year, I was very relieved when the NCAA announced its decision on his appeal. Joe could compete at Houston starting his sophomore year.

He got off to a slow start when he finally joined the varsity, and Joe was still kind of a loner because of all the problems his freshman year. Joe had a flash here and there, but no consistency. He qualified for the NCAAs but did not make the finals. He never reached his potential that year because he didn't have the drive he needed. Joe had all the talent in the world. But something had to be done with his training, his attitude, his focus.

Joe had been training with other guys on the team. But now, during his junior year, he would be my special project. I said, "Joe, from now on you train with me. All the time. Every day. You need to stay focused. You need to do it. And you can make it. You can win nationals, go to the Olympics, whatever you want to do."

Coach Tellez was thinking the same thing, so I started training with Joe. We stretched together, practiced starts together, ran sprints together, spent almost every day together on the track. We talked a lot about focusing, staying relaxed, being confident.

Joe was still pretty quiet around me, kind of shy. But that changed the night 1987 turned into 1988. I had a New Year's Eve party, and a lot of guys from the team came over. None of them knew Cleve was loading up the margaritas with Everclear, the 190-proof grain alcohol. We got toasted, just blasted. Joe still doesn't remember how he got home, but he certainly didn't drive. He was hilarious at the party, finally opening up and showing he could be as wild as the rest of us. Not that we drink a lot. But this was a special occasion. We had a great time and Joe was finally comfortable around me and the other guys on the team.

By early 1988, the year of the Seoul Games, everything seemed to be going well. But then Joe added another distraction, starting to work at a blood bank. Ten to fifteen hours a week, at about six dollars an hour. Joe was really proud of the white jacket, like a doctor's jacket, he wore at the blood bank. One day, Joe was late for practice, finally showing up in his white jacket, and I just went off on him about the job. He needed to be thinking about track and classes, not blood. But Joe needed the money and felt he should have a job in case the track season did not go well. I offered to loan him money and, after a few weeks, I finally got Joe to quit the job and focus on training again. Joe never took me up on my offer for a loan, but he always knew I was there if he needed me. I was able to help him more and more, finally fulfilling my promise to Mrs. DeLoach and erasing any guilt left from my contribution to screwing up Joe's freshman year.

The indoor season started well for Joe. He won the 60-meter and 200-meter sprints at the Southwest Conference championships. At the indoor nationals, he was fourth in the 60, but then hurt his leg in the 200. His right hamstring, the one that had bothered him the year before, got really bad. For such a young guy, Joe had already been through a lot of adversity. He was used to it by now. But how much could he take? Joe really started to lean on me, and all I could tell him was: Keep it simple. Do what the trainer says. Go to treatment. But don't worry. Just get better and come back strong.

I made sure to spend extra time with Joe whenever I could, and I said, "Joe, all the hard work is going to be worth it. You have to

14

15

I was overwhelmed with excitement, joy, relief—all the possible good feelings wrapped up in one—when I won the 100-meter finals in the 1984 Olympics. During my victory lap, I borrowed a flag from a spectator. I had no idea that some reporters would blast me for doing that. On the victory stand, I congratulated a little-known Canadian named Ben Johnson, who had placed third.
(14- DUOMO/Steven E. Sutton;
15- DUOMO/David Madison;
16- DUOMO/Steven E. Sutton)

16

17

In the 1984 Olympic long jump, I did what I had to do to win. That was not good enough to satisfy everyone. But in the end, I was able to smile. I had won four gold medals. (17-DUOMO/David Madison)

18

19

Winning big in the Olympics meant that I would be very busy. There were banquets (here I am with Mrs. Jesse Owens, accepting an award named after her late husband), trips (I always got a great reception in Japan), and lots of television appearances, sometimes being interviewed, sometimes interviewing others (here I am with Santa Monica teammate Johnny Gray). (19- DUOMO/Paul J. Sutton; 21- Burt L. Davis)

20

21

There was a time—before our lawsuit—when I could smile for Nike.
(DUOMO/Paul J. Sutton)

It was against NCAA rules to pay me while I was competing for the University of Houston, but Nike did, and they even put my deals in writing. First, a company memo listed terms of a one-year agreement. A later contract included big money for winning Olympic medals. In both cases, Nike paid bonuses for placing in collegiate meets. (Ron Garrison)

Confidential

44 Club Road, Suite 320
Eugene, Oregon 97401
Telephone 503/484-6358

MEMORANDUM

TO: John Gregorio and Ron Addison
FROM: Don Coleman *D.C.*
DATE: January 20, 1981
RE: Tentative Consultant Agreement with Carl Lewis

CONSULTANT AGREEMENT
Contingent Upon Approval of Both Parties Involved
(Carl Lewis and BRS, Inc.)

Terms of Agreement:

    1. One year payment of $5,000.

    2. Bonus of $500 if first in the NCAA

    3. Bonus of $500 if first in AAU

    4. Bonus of $1,000 if first in World Cup

    5. Bonus of $3,000 for World Record

    6. Four AAP Trips

    7. Bonus of $1,500 for American Record

23

DC/jkf

    D. Bonuses shall be paid for achievements in specified events
follows:

    1. 1984 Summer Olympic Games:

        Gold - $40,000.00; Silver - $15,000.00;
        Bronze - $10,000.00

    2. Pan American Games:

        Gold - $2,500.00; Silver - $1,500.00;
        Bronze - $1,000.00

    3. World Cup/World Championships (World Games):

        Gold - $5,000.00; Silver - $2,500.00;
        Bronze - $1,000.00

    4. The Athletes Congress National Championships:
        (Outdoor/Indoor)

        Gold - $1,000.00/$750.00; Silver - $750.00/500.00;
        Bronze - $500.00/300.00

    5. National Collegiate Athletic Association Championship:
        (Outdoor/Indoor)

        Gold - $1,000.00/750.00; Silver - $750.00/500.00;
        Bronze - $500.00/250.00

24

At the 1987 World Championships in Rome, Ben Johnson was huge. He beat me, setting a new world record in the 100. His size, along with what I had heard from people close to him, made me conclude that he was using steroids. (25- DUOMO/Steven E. Sutton; 26- DUOMO/Paul J. Sutton)

25

26

27

Joe DeLoach (*left*) and I stayed close, like brothers, before the 1988 Olympics. In addition to being friends, we trained together, often under the direction of Coach Tellez (*center*). (University of Houston photo)

At the end of the 100-meter final in Seoul, Ben Johnson shot his arm into the air, pointed his index finger triumphantly, and turned his head to look over at me. I couldn't believe what was happening. (28- DUOMO photos; 29- DUOMO/Steven E. Sutton)

30

My friend André Jackson with Ben Johnson in the drug-testing area at the 1988 Seoul Games. At the time, André had no idea he would be labeled "The Mystery Man." I do not know the identity of the woman with André and Ben, but she was in the area and wanted to be in a picture with Ben.

31

32

Joe DeLoach went out and ran the race of his life in the 200-meter final in Seoul. I was second. When it was over, we were both a bit stunned. "You better believe it," I told Joe. "You won." (DUOMO/Steven E. Sutton)

Winning medals often translates into selling shoes. After the Seoul Games, Joe DeLoach (*left*), Danny Everett (*right*), and I did some publicity work for Mizuno shoes.

34

There are no hugs for me and Ollan Cassell these days. But years ago, when he presented me with a medal at the 1983 World Championships, we looked like buddies. (DUOMO/Paul J. Sutton)

35

For my lawyer, David Greifinger, a three-piece suit is running
shoes, corduroys, and a Santa Monica T-shirt. But don't be fooled
by his attire; he still takes care of business. (Ron Garrison)

36

E.

D.

Long-jump sequence. (DUOMO/Steven E. Sutton)

C.

B.

A.

Landing in the pit. (DUOMO/Steven E. Sutton)

believe me." I went to all his meets because I had to let him know I was in his corner. I had to instill in Joe the belief that no one can succeed without help, and he had to know I was sincere about wanting to help him.

We stayed close, like brothers, and that helped both of us. Joe had never spent a lot of time with his own brother. Now I was like an older brother with enough experience to help him realize what could be done with his piles of potential. Joe would call and we would talk about anything. He told me things he wouldn't even talk to his parents about, and I would do the same, talking to him for two or three hours at a time about life, school, girlfriends and, of course, track. I wanted him to think that track was important—very important. He had to treat it that way to do well. But track certainly was not the world, and Joe had to keep that perspective. That would help to keep him from getting too uptight before a big race.

At the outdoor Southwest Conference meet, Joe surprised even himself by running a 19.98, the fastest time of the year, to win the 200. Finally, Joe realized he could beat anyone in the world. It was the first time he was convinced he could make the Olympic team. All he had to do was reproduce that time or better it.

But the next week, a Mississippi State sprinter named Lorenzo Daniel busted Joe's bubble, running a 200 in 19.93, which meant Joe no longer had the fastest time of the year. With the NCAA outdoors approaching, everyone was looking for Joe and Lorenzo to square off in the 200. I couldn't make the meet in Oregon because I had to compete in California, and I was really upset when I heard that Joe completely blew it, not even qualifying for the finals. He was last in his preliminary heat, which was ridiculous for someone with his talent.

I called Joe, and his explanation was so lame. "It was cold," he said. "I didn't take enough time to warm up. Mentally and physically, I just didn't feel good. The gun shot and I just couldn't get in sync. Everybody beat me."

Everybody? The U.S. Olympic trials were only a month away and the 200 was supposed to be Joe's best event, so I went nuts on him. "JOE!" I shouted. "What are you doing? This is big time. This isn't some little meet. What are you thinking about?"

I didn't get much of an answer, but Joe came back with a great race in the 100, winning in 10.03. What was this guy's deal? He was out to

lunch for his best event, the 200, then he won the 100, which surprised everyone. The Joe DeLoach roller coaster was down and up
again. The 100 boosted his confidence, but Joe was still perplexed,
not as mature as he should have been. He was latching onto whatever
event was working for him at the moment. "If I'm going to make the
team for the Olympics," he wondered, "should I do the 100 or 200?"

That was easy. He could make it in both. But he was so scared as
we prepared for the trials. No matter what Joe did on the track, he
was always asking questions. "What was it like in '84, Carl? Don't just
tell me it was a breeze. Tell me what's going to happen. What should
I expect? What do I need to think about?"

"In order to make the team," I told Joe, "you have to go to the trials
and treat it like it's nothing, no big deal, not a big meet. You can't be
scared, and you can't be distracted."

That sounds a lot simpler than it is. At the trials, one of the biggest
problems for some athletes is that they put too much emphasis on
trying to make everything perfect. Before a race they wonder if they
warmed up too much, or not enough. At meals they are afraid that
they are eating too much, but the last thing they want to do is be short
on energy. At night they are talking about getting too much sleep, or
not enough. It is easy to worry too much about things that are not
going to make a bit of difference, and I wanted Joe to avoid doing
that.

All around him, athletes would be engulfed in one of the most
pressure-packed situations of their lives, and some of them would be
acting pretty strange. Joe might see an athlete so nervous that he is
throwing up on the track. He would see someone lose a race and start
sobbing. Then he would see someone else lose a race and laugh,
trying to drown out disappointment with silliness. The trials is blood-
and-guts time, and everyone deals with it his own way. The best way
for Joe would be to ignore the swirl of emotions around him.

Joe definitely had enough talent to make the team. I wanted to
make sure he knew that. "You'll be fine if you don't get distracted,"
I told Joe. "Just don't get involved in the emotions."

At the trials, I was with Joe every step of the way. We warmed up
together, and I kept telling him, "It's no big deal. It's no big deal."
But I would have to do more than that to calm him down.

The first day, to make Joe relax, I went out to the meet wearing a pair of tights and an old T-shirt from high school, just to show Joe it was no big deal. Who cares if all the photographers follow me around and I'm wearing stuff from high school? It was just another meet.

Joe seemed to be ready for the 100 finals. But he didn't do as well as he should have, finishing fifth. I was first, and was really happy when I looked up at the clock to see my time. 9.78 seconds (wind-aided). One of the first things that flashed through my mind was the way the people at Nike had given up on me, writing me off as a has-been.

Well, now I had a little something for Nike. I saw Don Coleman, the Nike representative, in the first row, close to where my mother was sitting in the stands, and I grabbed Joe to walk over there with me. Don was sitting with some other people from Nike. Holding a little American flag someone had given me, I reached past a few people to say hello to my mother, and Don was just staring. I took the flag, handed it to him, and said, "Here, courtesy of me and Joe DeLoach." Then I pointed at our shoes. I was wearing Mizuno spikes, as I had done since the problems with Nike, and that didn't mean anything to Don because he was used to that. But Joe was wearing Mizunos, too. As a member of the Houston team, he had been wearing Nike. Don knew what I had done—I had switched Joe to Mizunos—and he didn't like it a bit. "Motherfucker," he growled at me. But I just smiled back at him.

To people in the stands or watching on TV, it looked like I was just visiting with a friend. Actually, I was shoving it in Don's face, saying, Screw you, look at the time and look at our feet.

Don went to Coach Tellez the next day, and asked him why Joe had changed to Mizuno. Don wanted Joe to switch back to Nike before the 200 final, and he appealed to Coach T for help.

Coach Tellez called Joe Douglas to talk about this, and Joe told me what Coach T was saying. Coach T and Joe Douglas were going to talk to Joe DeLoach to get him to switch back to Nike. I begged Coach Tellez not to do that. I didn't want anything to distract Joe before the 200. On the practice track, Coach Tellez and I had a heated conversation about this. I said, "Leave Joe alone. Don Coleman and Nike won't do anything. They *can't* do anything."

The whole time Coach Tellez and I were debating this, Joe was warming up on the track, just jogging alone with no idea what we were talking about. Finally, Coach Tellez agreed with me, and Joe stayed in Mizunos.

Joe won the 200, I came in second, and we hugged. "God, I can't believe it," Joe said. "I made it. I can't believe I'm on the team."

I said, "Okay, keep your cool." People thought I was always standing next to Joe at the trials only because we were great friends. But I was also telling him everything to do. It got to the point I was saying, "Joe, bow; Joe, wave; Joe, smile; Joe, turn. . . . You got to give it up to get it back."

Joe is a bright, perceptive guy, and that is why I wanted to work with him. He had so much potential but so little experience. All he needed was a little help from someone who had been there, a little help dealing with TV and the crowd. Joe knew he should take a bow. He just didn't know when.

Joe went down on the track and said a little prayer. I saw Joe's high school coach, Marshall Brown, so I said, "Let's go over and speak to him." Joe thought that would be nice, but he didn't know I had another reason for the suggestion. By chance, Don Coleman and Marshall Brown were standing near each other, and I really wanted to see Don again. As we jogged over, Joe realized what was going on, and he was just as pleased as I was to make sure Don had another chance to see his shoes.

I looked at Don and said, "A clean sweep." First and second for Mizuno. Forget Nike. Don just looked at me with hatred. He could have cut me with his eyes.

The crowd was still cheering as we headed back to the field. "Make sure you wave to everybody," I told Joe. "And get out in the middle of the track. Wave your hands and take a nice bow. Just give it up." Once we were out there, I backed off so Joe could do his bow, and he was great.

Someone told him to take a victory lap, and he asked me if that was okay. "Sure," I said. "But make sure you keep waving. Always give smiles. If you see somebody you know, give an extra little stare because people notice that. They think that's nice. And then the person you stared at goes home feeling good."

Joe executed like a real veteran. He was ready for the Olympics.

THIRTEEN

≡

The 1988 Olympics

THE SEOUL Games were going to be the low-key Olympics for me. No controversy, no statements that would get me in trouble with the press, no skipping jumps, no matter what the circumstances. Nothing but concentration and performance. I decided that I would even check into the Olympic Village. I wasn't going to stay there, but by checking in, I would not have to deal with a repeat of the nonsense I heard in 1984. There would be no controversy about why I wasn't staying in the village because as far as anybody else had to know, I was in the village. Taking care of that wasn't as simple as it sounds, though. When I arrived, I couldn't get in. Didn't have the proper credentials. The security people recognized me, they knew exactly who I was, but that didn't matter, not in Seoul. Every detail had to go by the rules, and the people who kept track of the rules were as rude as they come. Anyway, when I finally got in, after two days of waiting, I went right back out of the village. I had planned to stay with my family, Joe Douglas, and a few other people in a rented house. That had been arranged by Bob Carey, one of my closest friends with Lay Witnesses for Christ. The house was part of a Baptist missionary, so I didn't think anyone would look for us there, and the people staying there were extremely nice. It was a perfect place to relax between events.

The overall feeling at the beginning of these Games was a lot different than it had been in 1984. Back then, I kept saying that I did not necessarily have to win four golds for the Games to be a success, but nobody bought that. Most people were locked into the thought that anything but four golds should be viewed as some kind of failure. Now, I felt that just being back at the Games was a major accomplishment, and people seemed ready to accept that. When I said, "No one can expect me to come back and win four golds," that was taken as a reasonable statement. I was entered in the same four events—the 100, 200, 4 × 100 relay, and long jump—but they were no longer lumped together the way they had been in '84.

The 100 was me against Ben. That was the event getting all the ink. The 200 was a little bit of a mystery. Nobody was too sure what would happen, and people weren't talking about that race the way they were talking about the 100. The relay was turning into a bit of a drama, with all sorts of problems behind the scenes. Publicly, it looked like a little personality clash was causing problems, but there was a lot more to it than that. There was no reason why the United States should lose a sprint relay, but the way things were going, anything could happen. The long jump was the only event in which I was really considered a heavy favorite. I still had not lost since 1981, and it would take a major upset to beat me. This was an exciting event for me because nobody had ever won back-to-back Olympic long jumps. Nobody had ever won back-to-back 100s either.

The 100 was my first event.

It was hard to focus when I saw Ben Johnson on the track. I noticed that his eyes were very yellow. A sign of steroid use. "That bastard did it again," I said to myself. The one man I wanted most to be in the crowd could not make it. My father. I did not want to let him down.

The gun was fired. I didn't see Ben coming out of the blocks. But knowing the way he gets out, I knew he would be in front. That was fine. I got out well, too, and knew I would catch Ben in the second half of the race. Fifty or sixty meters down the track I glanced to my right and saw Ben in front, maybe by five feet. He was mine. He needed a bigger lead than that. But about eighty meters down the track—with the finish line flying toward us—I looked at Ben again, and he was not coming back any. Ben had pretty much the same lead

all the way through, and I knew I couldn't get him. Damn, I thought,
Ben did it again. The bastard got away with it again. It's over, Dad.
God, I wanted to win it for Dad. But that was impossible now. It
wouldn't happen.
Ben crossed the line with a time of 9.79 seconds. He had again
lowered the world record. I was second with a 9.92 . . . my best time
ever . . . but not good enough to win.

After the race ended and I left the Olympic Stadium, I returned to
our rented house. I walked into the kitchen and found Narada's wife,
Anukampa, fixing dinner. She was staying with us in Seoul, in what
was a very full house. It was me; my mother; my sister Carol; my
brother Mack; Fran, who is married to my brother Cleve; Fran's
sister, Deborah, who doubles as my secretary; Joe Douglas; Joe De-
Loach; André Jackson, a family friend; and Anukampa.

That is not her given name. It is the name she got from Sri Chinmoy. When I am with Anukampa or Narada or anyone else who
follows Sri Chinmoy, I am Sudhahota, and some other close friends
who have nothing to do with Sri Chinmoy also call me by that name.
Sometimes that seems kind of strange, going from one identity to
another, as it did now, walking into the kitchen. Just a few hours
before this, I was Carl Lewis, going at it with Ben Johnson in front of
a huge crowd, with so much at stake. Now, I was Sudhahota, alone in
the kitchen with a close friend. But I couldn't shake the thoughts that
I had taken with me from the track. I couldn't forget what had happened to Carl Lewis, and how it had happened.

"It is so unfair," I told Anukampa. "You try to do the right thing,
you try to be honest and hardworking . . . but there seems to be no
justice."

I didn't have to explain what I meant. She knew. Everyone around
me knew about Ben and his drugs. We had all talked about that, and
it was obvious now that I was talking about Ben. In her diary, Anukampa would later write that she could see the hurt in my face and
feel it from my heart. Trying to make me feel better, she told me what
she had been thinking since the race: "Where is the honor for Ben?
This man has to live with a lie. There is no integrity, so I can't imagine
him feeling any joy. Is this an achievement a man can truly be proud
of in his heart?"

No, definitely not, not in his heart. I agreed with Anukampa that below the surface, Ben must face the fact that he was living a lie, and accepting something like that must be tough. It must cause at least some regret. I wondered which would be tougher to deal with, the feelings I had this night or the feelings Ben would have as he passed the years with his constant companion, his lie.

The next day was qualifying for the long-jump finals. After that, I went with Anukampa to see Sri Chinmoy, who was waiting for us at a hotel. I had invited him to Seoul to see me compete, and I was very pleased that he had come. After the race with Ben, he wanted to see me as soon as possible. Sri Chinmoy told me that the result of the race had not, and would not, register with him. Something had been wrong. He felt that Ben Johnson had looked and acted "abnormal," and he said that Ben had not been full of joy on the victory stand. I told Sri Chinmoy that Ben had probably been using drugs, and Sri Chinmoy was bothered by that.

"I had an interesting experience during the victory ceremony," Sri Chinmoy said. "I want you to know what happened. I stood for the Canadian anthem, but I was holding an American flag. A Canadian patriot standing beside me whispered that I should put the flag down, and I didn't like that. 'Not for long,' I told him."

Sri Chinmoy said that my father's soul was watching from the inner worlds and was very proud of me. My father, he told me, knew that all would be well. Then I told Sri Chinmoy and Anukampa about a dream my mother had had the night before the race with Ben. It seemed real to her when my father spoke to her, telling her not to worry, everything would work out just fine. Everything would be all right.

The way Anukampa recalls it, "Sri Chinmoy acknowledged this tale and gave more words of encouragement. He ended the conversation with his main theme throughout the meeting—gratitude to God. Whatever turned out for Sudhahota there must be a sense of gratitude to the highest source, the Supreme."

I thanked Sri Chinmoy for the time he spent with me. He had been such a calming influence, just as he had been back in '84 when he helped me through some difficult times at the Games, just as he always had been. *Whatever turned out for Sudhahota there must be a sense of gratitude to the highest source, the Supreme.* He was always able, in a few words, to snap the world around us into perspective. We went back to the house, as Anukampa says, "a little late but a great deal lighter in heart."

The next day would be the most demanding day of track and field in my career. I had to run two qualifying rounds of the 200, with just over an hour of rest between them, then after less than an hour, I had to start the long-jump finals. Luckily, I was able to get through it okay. The 200s took a lot out of me, but I didn't have much trouble with them. Then I got a little break from the long-jump officials. I had been scheduled to jump first, but just before the start of competition, they switched me to last, which meant extra rest. I was able to sit and stretch, then jog a little, while eleven other athletes jumped in the first round. Then it was my turn.

Everything was fine until another official arrived midway through the competition, telling me I had to switch back to first in the jumping order. By then, it didn't really matter, though. I felt good, and had a jump that nobody was going to beat. On my fifth jump, I had a bit of a scare, twisting my right ankle. Coach Tellez told me to skip my last jump, but I wouldn't do that, not after all the problems caused by skipping jumps in '84. I sprinted down the runway for my last jump, but couldn't explode off the ground properly, and fouled. Still, I had taken all six attempts. There would be no questions about skipping jumps, no challenging my motives. I had the four longest jumps of the competition, and won with a jump of 28 feet, 7½ inches. Mike Powell (27 feet, 10¼ inches) took the silver medal and Larry Myricks (27 feet, 1¾ inches) took the bronze. It was an American sweep, the first in any event in Seoul.

I still had two events left, and I needed rest, but in the middle of the night, about 3:30 in the morning, Seoul time, I was awakened by the phone. It had to be important because there weren't many people who had our number, and why would any of them call now? It had to be something that couldn't wait until morning. It was Cleve, calling from home. Tracy Carruthers, working for NBC in Seoul, had just called our travel agency in Houston, trying to track me down. She had been all excited. Someone in the 100-meter finals had tested positive for steroids, and NBC was pretty sure it was Ben Johnson. They weren't certain yet, but they were pretty sure. They wanted to arrange an interview with me, as soon as possible.

I certainly wasn't going to do any interviews until a normal hour of the day, and I wasn't going to say anything about Ben until we knew for sure what the deal was. Joe Douglas and I called NBC, Joe's office in Santa Monica, my office in Houston, anywhere we could call to find out some more information. By now, everyone in the house was up, and there was a lot of excitement. What justice, if Ben had indeed been caught. What a shock, too. All these years he had been getting away with using drugs. Finally, this might be the end of the line for him. But we needed more information.

It took a few hours, but the news came out on television, little by little. First it was that someone in the 100 might have tested positive. Then it was that someone in the 100 *had* tested positive. Then it was reported that Ben was the one who got caught. Tests showed that he had used a steroid called stanozolol. Ben denied it, of course, but he would be disqualified, stripped of the gold medal and banned for two years from international competition. His own government in Canada would also penalize him, cutting off a monthly payment Ben had been getting while he trained and competed. And I would be awarded the gold medal.

Call it fate or luck or justice or whatever you want to call it, but the gold medal I had wanted so badly would be mine. The gold medal I had promised my father would be mine. It was unbelievable.

I wasn't surprised that Ben had been using steroids. The tests just confirmed everything I had heard. The big surprise was that he was finally busted. This would have to be the biggest story of the Games . . . but this was supposed to be my low-key Olympics. Now, what do I do?

Joe and I decided that I would say nothing. I didn't want to get involved, didn't want to rub Ben's nose in the mess he had created. There would be plenty of other people to do that.

But the phone calls would not stop, not at Joe's office in Santa Monica, not at the agency in Houston, not at our house in Seoul. And it wasn't like I could hide forever. I would be competing again, so reporters would be waiting for me. That night, I was scheduled to speak for the Lay Witnesses for Christ. We were going to have an "Evening with the Olympians," just like the session we had during the '84 Games to share our religious beliefs. I would have to say something about Ben at some point. After waiting much of the day, watching the news unfold on television, Joe and I decided to issue a statement. No rushing into interviews, no emotion-filled responses.

Let things settle down a little, take some time to figure out what you really want to say, then put out a statement. That way, there would be less chance of saying the wrong thing. We had learned a lot of lessons in '84.

My emotional response would have been something like: "Ben deserves everything he gets. If you live by the sword, you die by it. He ran with the steroid sword, and he fell on it . . . finally. Nothing but a drug addict, and he finally got caught."

But that wasn't the thing to say. Instead, my statement said: "I feel sorry for Ben and for the Canadian people. Ben is a great competitor and I hope he is able to straighten out his life and return to competition. I do not think it would be appropriate for me to fuel this controversy by commenting further."

One of the first reporters who got the statement from Joe, a reporter who knew us pretty well, said something like, "Okay, Joe, that's fine. Now, what does Carl really think about all this? When is he really going to talk?" It was that obvious that we had turned bland, that obvious that we were doing whatever possible to low-key it. But I wasn't going to say anything else. Not at this point.

I would allow other people to refer to Ben's positive test as vindication for me. They could recall the comments I had made in Rome, and say, "Aha, maybe Carl did know what he was talking about. Maybe he wasn't just shooting off his mouth. Maybe, just maybe, we should have given him a little more credibility than we did." That would be for others to say. I would just sit back and watch. And yes, enjoy. But not too much. With two more events to go, this was not a time to celebrate. I had to stay focused.

Looking out from the pulpit of a big brick church, with a choir next to me and about a thousand people watching, I spoke, softly and calmly, on behalf of my family and the Lay Witnesses for Christ. It was my only public appearance of the day, and I tried to put the Ben Johnson situation in perspective. I talked about the influence of my father, and the way I had buried the '84 medal with him as a tribute to his love and guidance. Then I said, "The Lord speaks to us in many ways," and I talked about my mother's dream the night before the 100-meter finals.

"My father came to her in her dreams. He told her to make sure that I knew he was proud of me, and that whatever performance I made, don't worry about it. He said everything would be all right. He said it again: Everything would be all right. . . . Today, we found out that it was." I thought of my father, thanked the Lord for all his blessings, and smiled a huge smile. That was enough about the race with Ben. I wanted to talk about things that really matter. I wanted to talk about faith.

The night before the 200-meter final, a friend came up to me and said, "Two down." The long jump and the 100 were mine. "Can you win the 200?" I would have to beat Joe DeLoach.

"I honestly believe I can," I said. "I'm going to give it my all, and I know I can run 19.80 tomorrow. I don't care how many jumps I've taken, how much running I've done." I had a swollen ankle after spraining it in the long jump. "I don't care about all of that. I can run 19.80, and I don't think Joe can run that fast."

The next day, Joe ran flawlessly in the semifinals, winning his heat, and he was bubbling like a ten-year-old who was just handed a stack of candy bars. My semifinal heat was not nearly as inspiring. I did not feel good on the track, and two hours before the final, looking at Joe, I realized for the first time that I could lose the 200.

And that's how it turned out. Joe—the high school kid from Bay City, the ineligible freshman, the blood bank employee, the some-times-confused competitor—went out and ran the race of his life. I was still ahead coming out of the turn. But I knew I wasn't going to win. My legs were not coming up like they should. I felt fatigue with about fifty meters to go, and Joe caught me with thirty meters left. He stayed aggressive, ran all the way to the tape, and that was that. He had a 19.75, a new Olympic record, and the gold was his. I ran 19.79, better than I thought I would need to win, but only good enough for second.

Four years earlier, at the Games in Los Angeles, I think the other sprinters were intimidated by me. They were too afraid to challenge me, too afraid to beat me. But Joe knew me too well, so there was no intimidation factor. Somebody else might be close with fifty meters to go, realize what is happening, press too hard and . . . boom, I'm gone, still relaxed and smooth while he cusses himself out for getting too tight and blowing it. Not Joe. He was very aggressive at the end, doing exactly what he was supposed to do.

After crossing the finish line, I looked at the clock, saw Joe's time and thought, God, he ran fast. Before I thought about me losing, I thought about Joe winning. I hugged him, and Joe said, "I can't believe it." He had finally won the big one. He was an Olympic champion. But he didn't know what to feel. Joy, of course, because he had won, but he kept saying, "I can't believe it."

"You better believe it," I said. "You won."

Meanwhile, I struggled with my own thoughts. The first thing that went through my mind was: It's over. Finally. There had been so much pressure for so long. I was exhausted and relieved to be done. But I was not used to losing. I ran a good race and lost, and that had never happened. Taking a victory lap with Joe, it still did not sink in that I had finished second, and I had trouble grasping that thought until we were called to the victory stand. Joe climbed to the top of the stand, leaving me to look up at him, proud of my friend's great accomplishment but not as happy as I had hoped to be.

The next few days, Joe and I did not know how to act around each other. He did not know how I felt about losing and I did not know how he felt about beating me. This was the Games now, not the trials, so this was for keeps. We got along, but we didn't talk as much as usual, and staying in the same house with me and my family made it even tougher on Joe. Everyone else in the house had been pulling for me in the 200. They all liked Joe and were happy for him, but the house was a lot quieter than it would have been if I had won. It was an awkward situation for all of us.

Finally, I found a way to start joking with Joe again, breaking the ice during a TV interview. Joe and I were being interviewed together, and the guy asked me how I felt about Joe getting the gold. "Well, he won it," I said. "I got the silver, but, hey, I can't complain. Joe lives in Houston, and he already told me he'll let me see his medal sometime." Joe busted out laughing, and that was the end of any tension between us.

Finally, we did not have to look at the 200 as two individuals placing first and second. There was another way to look at it, and that's what I focused on. *One team* placing first and second. The Santa Monica Track Club, which Joe and I both ran for, gold and silver in the same race. Not bad for a little club started by a high school teacher in California. The men's track-and-field competition was turning into a Santa Monica showcase.

By the end of the Games we would have six gold medals, out of ten for the entire U.S. men's track-and-field team. Two golds for me and one for Joe DeLoach. Two golds for Steve Lewis (no relation, other than teammates) in the 400 and the 4 × 400 relay. And a gold for Danny Everett, who was also on the 400-meter relay team. In addition, there was my silver in the 200, and a bronze for Danny in the individual 400. There were other great American champions, of course—Roger Kingdom winning his second gold medal in the high hurdles, Andre Phillips beating Edwin Moses to win the intermediate hurdles—and Santa Monica missed a few opportunities for more medals. One of the youngest members of the club, Kevin Young, was fourth in the race that Phillips won, and one of the oldest members, Johnny Gray, was fifth in the 800. But what a performance for Santa Monica. We were thrilled.

There was one other event that could have made a big difference for me, the Santa Monica club, and, most importantly, the United States. The relay. We should have won another gold medal in the 4 × 100 relay, an event traditionally dominated by the U.S. But we had a lot of problems with the relay team, and the result was a disaster.

For the most part, the problems were not reported in any detail. When they were talked about and written about, they were dismissed as the result of a "personality clash" between me and the coach. Actually, there was a much darker side to what was going on. The U.S. coach for sprints and relays was Russ Rogers, the former Fairleigh Dickinson coach who had offered me the moon to go to his school back in 1979. Russ and I were not the best of friends. I guess it had been hard for him to like me after I chose the University of Houston over Fairleigh Dickinson. And after Russ had left me, as a teenager, waiting in New Jersey after telling me he was taking me to Europe, it was difficult for me to respect him or trust him.

In Seoul, it was easy to dismiss the relay problems as a case of Russ against Carl. Russ wanted to do things his way, Carl wanted another way. Russ wanted practice at certain times, Carl didn't. Russ didn't want Joe DeLoach on the relay team, Carl did. And everybody else was picking sides.

That was a convenient way for Russ and the other U.S. team officials to define the problems. It was easy to dismiss them that way, because who cares about a little feud between an athlete and a coach? Happens all the time. But there was so much more than a "personality clash" involved in this mess. I was willing to leave it at that, but only because I did not want to create a big stir during the Games. As it turned out, there were a few touchy moments, anyway, such as me yelling at Stan Huntsman, head coach of the U.S. team, on the practice track, and Stan and Russ banning Joe Douglas from the facility. Joe showed up anyway because nobody had bothered to tell him he had been banned.

But I was determined not to let the situation really blow up. These were the low-key Olympics, I had to remind myself, and I would have to keep my mouth shut. Had I been completely open about the real story, there would have been nothing low-key about the way people would have reacted.

The whole thing goes back to the U.S. Olympic trials. After the 100-meter finals, Stan Huntsman and Russ Rogers had a meeting with the top sprinters and told us their plan for picking members of the relay team. The top six finishers in the 100 would go to Europe to train with the national team, and based on who was running the best, the relay team would be picked. That's what Stan said, and Russ agreed to that. The top six finishers were me, Dennis Mitchell, Calvin Smith, Albert Robinson, Joe DeLoach, and Mike Marsh, in that order. According to the plan, Emmit King, who finished seventh, and Lee McNeill, who was eighth, would not have a chance. But that's not the way it worked out, partly because Russ Rogers tried to play businessman instead of coach.

Russ pulled aside Mike Marsh and told him that he would probably end up being an alternate. He would be on the Olympic team, but he probably wouldn't compete. Mike was between his junior and senior years at UCLA, and was obviously excited about being in the Olympics. He is a former high school state champion in California in the 200, and in college, he is a two-time Pac-10 Conference champion in the 100. But the Olympics—that was going to be the highlight of his young career. So this news about being an alternate was disappointing. Still, Mike was determined to do the best he could in Europe. If he had some good races there, and trained well, then maybe Russ would change his mind and give Mike a shot, maybe let him run in a preliminary round, if nothing else. (In the Olympics, the members of a relay team can be switched between heats and before the finals.) For Mike, just being in an early round would be a great experience. If you run in a heat but not the final, you can still get a medal. A winning team gets up to six medals.

So Mike thought he still had a chance . . . until Russ started playing businessman. He told Mike he wanted to represent him in some European meets before the Olympics. Russ wanted to pick the meets Mike would run in, negotiate his appearance fees, and pick up his money for him. He wanted to do everything any good agent on the track circuit would normally do. I wasn't surprised when I heard this. Russ had been an agent for years, even though a college coach is not supposed to do that. It was common knowledge on the circuit that Russ collected money for his athletes, and I knew from my own experiences with him that Russ talked more about money than he did about coaching. Russ is not a coach. He is a businessman. That put Mike in a tough position. The message was clear: "If I didn't use Russ as my agent," Mike says, "I wasn't going to run in the Olympics. I couldn't believe it."

Mike had already been running for Santa Monica, and he didn't want to leave the club—not for Russ, not for anybody. So Mike called Joe Douglas to tell him what Russ had said. Joe said to forget about Russ, and Mike did. That was the end of his Olympic dream. Later, Mike approached Russ at the meet in Zurich, and he told Russ he was ready to practice at any time, ready to run a relay whenever Russ wanted him to, but Russ just blew up at him. Mike didn't have to practice or run a relay now. He was out of it. He would have to live with a simple reason for missing a chance to run in the Olympics: "Russ was all into the money thing."

That was not the only case of Russ using his position as Olympic coach to convince an athlete that he, Russ, should be his agent. With one of the other athletes, Dennis Mitchell, the plan worked. Dennis grew up in New Jersey, and I've known him since he was ten years old. When I was in high school, I helped coach the youngest members of the Willingboro Track Club, and Dennis was one of them. Later, my parents coached him. Now, Dennis was a great college sprinter at the University of Florida, and he had a year of eligibility left, but so what? Russ wanted to be his agent. He didn't care about the fact that college athletes are not allowed to have agents. The more athletes an agent has, the more money he makes. Russ wanted more athletes. Dennis had been using another agent, Tony Campbell, but he had been having some problems with Tony, and Russ used that as part of his pitch.

"Every manager does it in their own way," Dennis says. "That's just the way of the world. If you have problems with your manager, there's always another manager to pick you up." Russ told Dennis he could make more money for him than Tony Campbell did. "He talked about money a lot. That's every manager. Their basis for being (in Europe) is to make money. I don't think the things Russ was saying, another manager wouldn't say." But Russ was the Olympic coach. "Russ was trying to pick up as many of those athletes as he could for the next year," Dennis says. "He wanted to pick up everybody . . . all the high-powered Olympic athletes. Russ went for his own individual gains that he could get from the Olympics."

Once we were in Europe, competing before the Games, there were other problems with Russ. First of all, he completely abandoned the plan he had agreed to in the meeting at the trials. It had been decided that the top six sprinters could train and run on their own in Europe until a meet in Brussels. Then Russ would pick the four athletes who had been running the best, and those four would run together in Brussels. Based on that, Joe DeLoach and I trained and competed with Santa Monica, not Russ. We didn't see any reason to go with him, especially after the things he had said to Mike Marsh and Dennis Mitchell. If Russ wanted to handle his relay team as a business, we didn't want to do business with him. Plus, Joe and I had been passing batons for years, knew how to do it, and didn't think we needed instruction. We could practice with other members of the relay team in Brussels, and again once we got to Seoul. Of course, Russ said he didn't appreciate us not being with him in Davos, Switzerland, where other members of the U.S. team were training, and he started looking for excuses to keep us off the team.

One way would be to keep us in the dark. He told us nothing about when and where the U.S. team would be running or what was expected of us. I had told Russ that as long as we knew ahead of time, Joe DeLoach and I would be happy to run with the U.S. team before the Games. We wouldn't be in Davos, but we would join up with the team for a meet. Russ wasn't interested in that. If he kept things to himself, he could later say that we had not cooperated, that we weren't willing to run when and where he wanted us, so why should he do anything for us?

His strategy became clear during a meet in Sestriere, Italy, so we did some quick thinking—and running—to let him know it wasn't going to affect us. I was scheduled to run a 200, and that was it, but then I saw something strange. Some members of the U.S. relay team were warming up together, practicing with a baton. That was strange because Russ had not said anything about the team running in Sestriere. If I had known, I could have run with them. But now Russ was pulling a little stunt. He was going to run the team without me, as if he were punishing me for not training with him. The final straw was when I saw that Emmit King and Lee McNeill were warming up with the U.S. team. They had been seventh and eighth in the trials, and seventh and eighth were not even supposed to be considered for spots. How could Russ totally contradict the plan he had endorsed? The only thing I could come up with was that Russ (Russ the agent, not Russ the coach) had been representing McNeill. One of the other athletes training at Davos had explained to me that Russ had promised Lee he would run at least a preliminary heat in the Olympics. In other words, "I represent you, you'll run. I represent you, you'll have a good chance to get a gold medal." Another one of those deals.

Santa Monica had not been entered in the relay in Italy, but once I saw what Russ was doing, I wanted in. We threw together a team—Mike Marsh, Mark Witherspoon, Joe DeLoach, and me—and we lined up against the U.S. team. That shocked a lot of people, including Russ, and he was pretty upset about it, especially when Santa Monica won the race.

The leadoff leg was an interesting matchup: Mike Marsh for us, Dennis Mitchell for the U.S. team—two guys Russ had put the squeeze on. Mike had turned Russ down, choosing to stay with the club. Dennis had given into the pressure and gone with Russ. Now they were in the starting blocks against each other. The last baton exchange was also quite interesting. Calvin Smith was passing to Albert Robinson, and they dropped the baton. All that practice with Russ, and the U.S. team was disqualified. So much for "practice makes perfect." Russ was fuming.

Back on the practice track at Davos, Russ told his athletes what assholes the Santa Monica runners were for going against the U.S. team, *his* U.S. team. "Russ expressed his opinion that they shouldn't be doing that," Dennis Mitchell says. "And the athletes agreed. . . . If they didn't want to run *with* us, they should have stayed out of the race."

I could see that point. But when Joe DeLoach and I tried to run for the U.S. team in Brussels, Russ told me I couldn't run because I had not been practicing with the team. He said that someone who had not been with the team would be likely to get injured or cause an injury, and he could not risk an injury to one of his athletes. That was one of the worst excuses I had ever heard. I had been running relays my whole life. In fact, Calvin Smith and I had exchanged the baton dozens of times over the years. He was always third leg, and I was anchor. We had never had a problem, so why in the world would we have one now? Simple. We wouldn't. Talking about an injury was just a way for Russ to rationalize. Joe Douglas tried to reason with Russ, but that didn't work. Then I called Russ in his hotel room, and when he stuck to his bullshit, I cussed him out.

Next, I called Stan Huntsman, and I said, "That's it, I'm not running the relay. The hell with it. I have too much to think about, and Russ is ruining everything." Stan didn't know what to do. He tried to change my mind, saying the team needed me. I had been running anchor for the U.S. for years (winning at the '84 Games and at the '83 and '87 World Championships) and there was nobody else Stan wanted in that spot. "Sorry, Stan, I'm out. You can thank Russ Rogers."

Then Russ told reporters he had been willing to let me run in Brussels, but he had not been willing to let me *and* Joe DeLoach run. Russ had not told me anything like that. He had talked about the risk of injury. But now he was starting to play the media game. He wanted to make it look like my only complaint with him was that he would not let my teammate run. If he could make me look selfish, he could win some points in the media, and that's the way the story started to be written: Carl wants Joe on the team, Russ won't take him, so Carl is mad. True, I wanted Joe on the team. I thought he deserved to be on it because, back at that first meeting during the trials, Stan and Russ had said that the people running best in Europe would run the relay. Joe was running great, but he wasn't even getting a chance.

The press accepted the Joe DeLoach issue as the reason for the "personality clash" between me and Russ, and it was easy for Russ to convince other members of the team that my desire to have Joe on the team was the major problem. Dennis Mitchell says I was being selfish, going for "personal gains," just as Russ had been doing when he was rounding up athletes as an agent. Well, if "personal gains" means wanting to win the relay for my country, then it is true that I was after those gains. Nobody wanted to win another relay for the

U.S. more than I did. But the way the team was being handled, I wondered if that would happen.

I went back and forth on whether I would change my mind and decide to run the Olympic relay, and in the end, there were two deciding factors. First was my desire to help the national team. There were so many problems, it seemed that the team would need me in '88 more than it had in the past. I had to look beyond any problems with the coach and remember that this was going to be the Olympics, the biggest meet of them all, and I wanted to make sure the U.S. had its best team on the track. The second reason was Joe Douglas. He kept telling me I had to run the relay. When I was leaning against it, saying I would give up the relay and focus on my three individual events, Joe looked ahead and said, "No. You shouldn't give up your chance to compete in an Olympic event just because of a problem with the coach. This is too important. Forget about the coach." So, yes, I would run the relay, I finally decided. I would try to keep my distance from Russ, but I would run the relay.

Russ made it difficult. He knew that Joe DeLoach and I were not staying in the Olympic Village in Seoul, so he would change practice times, thinking we wouldn't find out. Then if we missed practice, he could say that we weren't doing what we were supposed to do. Nice little trick. Luckily, Joe and I had friends in the village, and they called our house to tell us what was going on. Russ looked so surprised when we showed up for practice. He hadn't told us when it was going to be, so how did we know?

Finally, I blew up at Stan Huntsman. He had promised to keep an eye on the relay situation, promised to step in with common sense and fairness, but he was letting Russ totally run the show. I saw Stan at the practice track when I had reached my boiling point. I went right at him. "Stan, I've always supported you, but you're not doing anything. How can I respect you as a man when you're not doing what you said you would do? I *can't* respect you, not anymore. I put my trust in you, and you violated my trust. You're full of shit, and as far as I'm concerned, I have nothing more to say to you."

I turned and walked away, leaving Stan next to my sister.

"Well, Carol," he said, "you want to be head coach of the men's team?"

She walked away, too, and I went on with my workout.

The next day, Russ gave me an ultimatum. Not directly; he didn't have the guts to do that. He delivered his message through the press, telling reporters: "If Carl continues to disturb the team, I will have to take him off. The next incident he does to disrupt the team, he's got to go. I have no choice. He's at the end of his rope. The only thing he can do is hang himself."

At our next practice, Russ rushed over to me, all panicky. He didn't want any more problems, so he made an offer. He would let my guy, DeLoach, run in the finals as long as his guy, McNeill, could run in the heats—and no more problems in the press. That was his way of striking a deal. He could appease McNeill by letting him run in the heats, which meant he could get a medal, and we would still be able to run the best people in the finals. That was not the ideal situation, but it seemed to be acceptable.

Now Russ wanted to do a little public relations work, and he wanted me to do it with him. With reporters and photographers gathered around us, we shook hands and he said that everything had settled down. I hated being in the spotlight with Russ, but I let it go. My biggest concern was getting the best team in the finals, and I finally had a commitment on that.

"It doesn't matter whether Russ and I are best of friends or worst of enemies," I said. "What does matter is that we have the best possible relay team."

It would have been a lot more interesting to tell the real story—the *whole* story. But that would have completely ruined any chance of the team sticking together, so I said what I felt I had to say.

"Everything is okay," Russ said. "And we're going to set a world record."

That was the one thought we had in common. If everything went the way it should, with the best people running, we would be in great shape to break the world record. No team had beaten the 37.83-second relay we ran in the '84 Games, but with the right team in '88, I thought we would have a chance to cut half a second off that time. Then again, in '84 we knew we were running the best team we could put on the track—the top four finishers in the U.S. trials, no questions asked, no conflicts of interest involving the coach. This was completely different. If we could get to the finals and break the world record, our success certainly would not have anything to do with Russ.

Russ waited until the last minute to announce the team for the first preliminary round: Dennis Mitchell, Albert Robinson, Calvin Smith, and Lee McNeill, in that order. Calvin was the only one with any relay experience in big international competition. In the final, Joe DeLoach was going to replace Robinson and I was going to replace McNeill. As long as everything went right, all six of us would get gold medals, and we would have a shot at a world record in the final. But nothing went right.

In the very first race, Calvin and Lee messed up their baton exchange, with Lee running out of the passing zone, and the U.S. team was disqualified. The baton has to be passed from one runner to the next in a 20-meter zone, and Lee was beyond the 20-meter mark before he had the baton from Calvin. At first, the U.S. team claimed victory. An official had indicated no violation, and when the results were posted, the U.S. was in first place with a time of 38.98 seconds. But teams from three countries—the Soviet Union, France, and Nigeria—protested, and they were right. Tapes of the race showed that the pass was illegal, and we were disqualified, just like that. Without even stepping on the track, I was out of my final event.

Should all the blame be put on Russ Rogers? No, not all of it. I'm sure he wanted to win, but then again, it was one of his guys, a guy who didn't even belong on the team, who had screwed up the race. After finishing eighth in the U.S. trials, Lee McNeill should not have even been in South Korea. That was what the coaches had said back at the trials. But Russ had changed the selection process to accommodate one of his runners—one of his *clients*. That's not the way to run an Olympic team, and now we had to pay the price. We were out. After winning this relay in thirteen of the previous sixteen Olympics, the U.S. would not even run in the finals.

What a bizarre ending to a drama that had been building for months. What an outrage.

Even with all the craziness of the Games—Ben being caught, losing the 200, the relay fiasco—I was able to get through it all without any trouble. Everything was much more positive than '84, and that would help tremendously in the long run. *Sports Illustrated* is a perfect example of what I mean. The same *Sports Illustrated* that was so unfair to me in '84.

Kenny Moore, who covers track and field for the magazine, wanted to interview me at the end of the Games, but I declined. Nothing against Kenny. He's a former Olympic runner himself, and a good guy, but after what *Sports Illustrated* did to me in 1984, I was not interested in doing anything for the magazine. So I was amazed when I saw Kenny's story. It was the most positive piece *Sports Illustrated* had done on me in years.

The headline was "MAN, NOT SUPERMAN . . . Ben Johnson's demise revealed a more endearing Carl Lewis." All of a sudden, I was a nice guy again. Early in my career, *Sports Illustrated* had written about me as the kid next door, the type of kid you want your son to be. Then Gary Smith painted me as a complete asshole. And now I was a nice guy again. In fact, according to Kenny Moore, I was finally "revealed" as the person I had always been.

It was the end of the story that amazed me, and made me feel really good. "Lewis is much the same man he was in 1984, though certainly the death of his father hurt him and moved him to a greater sense of purpose in his sport. It's time to reexamine our perceptions of Lewis. When these bewildering Olympics recede enough to allow us a sense of proportion, we may not remember Johnson being found out as much as Lewis being revealed as the gentleman he has always been."

FOURTEEN

≡

Year of the Steroid

IF 1988 was the year of the Olympics, then 1989 was the year of the steroid. One positive drug test changed everything. Not that Ben Johnson being caught encouraged the use of drugs. If anything, all the negative publicity about Ben did just the opposite, so that's not what I mean. I call it the year of the steroid because public awareness of the problem increased so greatly. A reporter with a hot steroid story was a hero in the newsroom. A politician with some rhetoric on the issue was a lock for some good press. Educators had to deal with the problem, finally admitting that it exists in our schools, even on the high school level. The most disturbing stories I heard were those about kids taking steroids, sometimes just to bulk up and impress girls, sometimes to get ahead in sports. And all this talk about steroids was in no way limited to track and field. All sports were open territory now. Football, for example, took more than its share of the headlines.

So much had changed since the Los Angeles Games. Remember when Dr. Robert Kerr admitted that he had given steroids to a number of medal-winners? Well, back then, that was worth only a few lines in the sports section, and nobody followed up with any real digging into what he had said. Steroids were not an issue, and nobody gave them much attention. Now, in the year of the steroid, a story like Kerr's would be huge. All of a sudden, the problem of steroids, which had existed for years and years, was on the public agenda, and it didn't just creep onto the agenda, it *exploded.*

There were allegations and investigations, confessions and denials, debates and testing plans, hearings and interviews. Turn to the sports page, and you were almost guaranteed to find something about steroids. For years before this, we had been bombarded with cocaine stories. Those were still around, but now they shared space with steroid stories. Everywhere we looked—steroids, steroids, steroids.

There were all sorts of stories. The Soviets punished 290 athletes after positive drug tests. A U.S. Senate hearing was told that at least two American women gold medalists took steroids before going to Seoul. The laboratory that tested Ben Johnson at the 1987 World Championships in Rome was dropped by the International Olympic Committee for failing to meet standards. An American hurdler was suspended for failing to take a drug test when he was supposed to. Congressmen were told about steroid problems in professional football. U.S. and Soviet officials agreed to a new drug-testing plan. Then the Soviet Union lost its place in the World Cup when a shot-putter failed a random drug test. After retesting urine samples from the 1988 Games, a German professor claimed that more than fifty male athletes had used steroids during training.

The list goes on and on and on. After spending so much time fighting against drugs, I thought the explosion of the steroid issue was good for sports. The more exposure it got, the better the chances that something might be done. Behind the scenes, I talked to as many people as I could to keep up with what was going on concerning steroids, and I followed the newspapers to see what was being said publicly. It was wild to see how many stories unfolded, and to follow them.

Personally, the initial blasts in the year of the steroid meant a squabble with the most successful female athlete of the Seoul Games; a lot of back and forth with investigators in Canada; the introduction of a "mystery man" and talk of sabotage in the Seoul drug-testing room; and some party politics on Capitol Hill. Some of this was big news, some of it was trivial. Most of the stuff about steroids was serious, but sometimes the behind-the-scenes stuff got pretty funny.

For me, the year of the steroid started with an appearance at the University of Pennsylvania, where I was invited to talk to a group of students. I was telling them all the usual things—stories about the Olympics, living with the legends of Jesse Owens and Bob Beamon all the time, what it's like to earn a living in our so-called "amateur" sport. But it didn't take long for the students to start asking about steroids.

Somebody asked me if Florence Griffith Joyner used drugs. She had made the transformation from being just another Olympian to being one of the most incredible athletes in the world, and it was a change that came too quickly for the imagination. Her physical appearance alone—muscles popping everywhere—made a lot of people wonder. Then there was her voice, much deeper than it had been in the past. Steroids often affect a woman's voice that way. I asked the college students, "What do you all think?" I wanted a show of hands. First, how many people think she did use drugs? A lot of hands went up. How many think Florence didn't use drugs? Most people kept their hands in their laps. The response of the students was an overwhelming: "Yes, we think she used drugs." To acknowledge that I had basically dodged answering the question myself, I said, "I guess I should have raised my hand, too."

Then I tried to answer as honestly as I could without totally blasting Florence. I didn't have any reason to do that, not in front of this crowd. I didn't come right out and say, "Yes, Florence used drugs," but my answer made it sound like that's what I was doing. I didn't think much of it. This was just a talk to students, no big deal. Then I found out that a student had taped my comments and used them for a story in the school newspaper.

In response to the question about Flo-Jo, I was quoted as saying: "I actually do know, and I know from some very reliable sources, but see, it's a very sensitive situation. Because I think in the United States, we have probably more women on drugs than men, and they really play a mean game. I don't think we should really blame Florence. I think that's the situation of her former coach. Not her coach now, Al [Joyner]. I think that [former] coach should be put out of the sport because I believe he tries to put everyone he knows on drugs."

When the student paper came out, the story was picked up by the wires, and a lot of newspapers used it. But it certainly wasn't the first time Flo-Jo had been accused of using drugs. In Seoul, that had been a big story, especially when Joaquim Cruz, a Brazilian runner who had attended school and trained in the States, implied on television that Florence and her sister-in-law, Jackie Joyner-Kersee, used drugs. Cruz said that Florence looked like a man and that Jackie looked like a gorilla. Pretty harsh words. Florence and Jackie denied using drugs and said they were terribly hurt by the accusation. That was the end of that.

In response to the new round of Flo-Jo stories, Joe Douglas released a statement quoting me as saying that I didn't think it was proper to accuse people of drug use in the press and that I didn't have personal knowledge of drug use by Florence or her former coach, Bob Kersee. If my comments were construed that way, the statement had me saying, I was sorry.

Actually, this was a very kind statement, considering that I had heard enough about Florence and Bob Kersee to believe that they had been involved with drugs. When the statement said I didn't have "personal knowledge" of drug use, that meant, no firsthand knowledge. In other words, I had never seen either of them use drugs. But I had the same type of information I had had about Ben Johnson in 1987, comments I picked up from other athletes and coaches I trusted who had more direct knowledge through conversations with Florence and others around her. It was a common belief on the track circuit that Florence had used drugs.

The talk about Florence was strong enough that I had decided to avoid being associated with her, whenever possible. I did not want to be photographed with her for any advertisements and did not want to make any personal appearances with her. Sometimes this was a problem because we both endorsed Mizuno shoes. The Mizuno people sometimes asked me to do things with Florence, but when I objected, they seemed to understand my feelings. They had heard some of the same things about Florence that I had, and they told me that they knew about Florence's reputation on the circuit. It was nothing new. The reputation existed even when Mizuno signed Florence to a contract, but Mizuno wasn't worried.

In May 1989 I was asked to appear in Japan at a big charity event for children. I wanted to go, but when I heard that Florence was also going, I had to make special arrangements. The organizers wanted me to be one of a few celebrities leading teams of children in a relay race. I would lead a team, former baseball great Hank Aaron would lead a team, a Japanese golfer would lead a team . . . and Florence would lead a team. Sorry, I said, but if Florence is in, I'm out. The organizers told me I could participate in other parts of the program and skip the relay.

The solution wasn't as simple when Joe Douglas told me he wanted to put out a statement in response to the Pennsylvania situation. At first, we disagreed about whether anything more should be said, but Joe wanted me to apologize. In terms of public relations, he thought I should. Joe didn't want me in the middle of a controversy. But I didn't want to take back what I had said. I wanted to stand by it, and still do. Joe had heard a lot of the same things about Florence that I had, and he also believed that Florence and Kersee were involved in drugs, but that wasn't the point now, Joe said. He wanted me to quiet down the uproar over my comments, clearing Florence in the press, if not my mind. Finally, I gave in, letting Joe put out the statement. The words weren't mine, but if Joe wanted to release them, fine, it wasn't that big a deal, and I wasn't trying to pick a fight.

Flo-Jo and her attorney, Rafael Chodos, started talking about a lawsuit. The attorney wrote me care of Joe and David Greifinger. Chodos objected to my statements, said that he and Florence were considering a lawsuit for slander, and finished by writing, "Our decision will be based in part on your response to this letter." Chodos wanted to know my "reliable sources" and what "evidence" I had. After all the hassles with the Nike lawsuit, I didn't particularly want to be involved in another lawsuit, but if that's the way it was going to end up, Florence would have a lot more to lose than I would.

First of all, I would explain what I knew, and that would hurt Florence even more. There would be evidence from people who had trained with Florence, coached her and lived with her. There would also be damaging evidence from one of the top TAC officials, who, despite his anti–Santa Monica feelings, has told us more than he probably should have about Florence.

Secondly, my lawyers would be able to take sworn statements from Florence and the people around her. That would mean a lot more negative publicity for Florence, and the truth would come out. I doubted she would want that. Denying a comment made on television, the way she did after Joaquim Cruz spoke out, or denying a comment made before a group of college students is one thing. Being placed under oath and forced to testify is something entirely different. I chose not to respond to the letter from Chodos, and that was the last I heard from the Flo-Jo camp.

The Flo-Jo controversy was nothing compared to what was going on in Canada. The official name of a Canadian government investigation into the Ben Johnson affair was "The Commission of Inquiry Into the Use of Drugs and Banned Practices Intended to Increase Athletic Performance." Most people just called it the Dubin Inquiry, after Ontario Chief Associate Justice Charles L. Dubin, who was in charge. Dubin, in his late sixties, had conducted other big investigations, one into air safety, one into a children's hospital, so he knew what he was doing. This was not going to be a little investigation used for public relations; it was going to be serious business. As Canadian Sports Minister Jean Charest said when he announced the investigation, the main concern was the integrity of sport in Canada. Dubin would have subpoena power to call witnesses and demand documents, and he would do things his way. He would listen to athletes, coaches, and everybody else, but he would have no reason to yield to pressure from any of them. He would be independent. In Canada, Dubin would be a one-man, independent agency, not exactly the independent agency I had been suggesting, but at least a start. Dubin would not conduct drug tests—the most important task for an independent agency—but he would uncover evidence about drug use.

Before the inquiry started, Ben was sticking to all the denials he had made since being caught in Seoul, saying he had never "knowingly" used steroids. I kept seeing the same quote from Ben: "I have never, ever knowingly taken illegal drugs, and I would never embarrass my family, my friends, my country and the kids who love me." What a lie. The more I saw it, the more I thought about going to Canada and telling the inquiry what I had heard about Ben and Charlie Francis and the whole mess. But I didn't really want to be involved and didn't think I was needed. There should be plenty of evidence without anything I could say.

As athletes, coaches, and doctors testified, it became clear that Ben would have a tough time sticking to his denial. Too many people were talking, telling the truth, or at least parts of it, under oath. They were all saying, yes, Ben took steroids, and, yes, he knew what he was doing. The first major blows came from Charlie Francis, who detailed Ben's drug use.

Ben had used steroids and other performance-enhancing drugs since 1981. So had other athletes Charlie coached. That was the good part of Charlie's testimony, his willingness to admit what he and his athletes had done wrong. Then came the part I didn't like. Charlie painted our entire sport as drug-infested, and said that Ben had to use drugs to keep up. "Either he wanted to participate at the highest level or he didn't," Charlie said. "He could decide he wanted to set his starting blocks in the same place as the others or one meter behind. It was pretty clear that steroids were worth about one meter at the highest level. It was pretty clear he wanted to participate."

This was nothing more than a poor rationalization, a lousy excuse. The whole sport is not on drugs. There are plenty of clean athletes who train and compete by the rules. It was the steroid user who started a meter *ahead* of everyone else, not the nonuser starting *behind* the rest of the field. But it appeared that Charlie wanted to give the whole sport a black eye.

Charlie went on to admit that steroids had been a major part of the training program leading to Ben's world record in Rome, and he described other periods of steroid use between the 1987 World Championships and the 1988 Olympics. Charlie had injected Ben with drugs, and he had watched as Ben and his teammates took turns injecting each other. There were also pills. Charlie talked about a variety of drugs: Dianabol, testosterone, furazabol. And he said that his athletes had also taken a human growth hormone.

Then Charlie came up with another diversion, and this one was even wilder than the talk about starting behind if you don't take steroids. Charlie said that it had been years since Ben had taken the steroid stanozolol. That was the drug found in Ben's sample at the Olympics, and Charlie said he had no idea how it got there. Well, maybe one idea, he said. It must have been sabotage.

This discussion came toward the end of Charlie's testimony. One last, desperate attempt to find an excuse for Ben's positive drug test. When Charlie said that he believed Ben's test had been sabotaged, he included me in his conspiracy theory. The theory went like this: An "unidentified stranger" had sat with Ben in a waiting room before he was tested. The stranger and Ben talked, watched television, and drank beers together. One of the drinks could have been spiked by the stranger. He could have placed a steroid in it. He had no other reason to be in the waiting area. And—here is where the plot thickens—two witnesses told Francis that the stranger had spoken with me in another area of the waiting room. Conclusion: Carl is the bad guy, and we have to find the unidentified man.

Reporters had a fresh dose of mud, and Canadians had a story they wanted to believe. The newspapers went wild with this stuff. They wrote about the "mystery man," and some dubbed him "Mr. X." A Canadian businessman offered ten thousand dollars for the mystery man to testify.

When the story broke, I was in Los Angeles, filming a commercial. Reporters from all over the world tried to reach me, but I wanted to stay out of this, so David Greifinger talked to the reporters, telling them it was ludicrous to implicate me. "Charlie and Ben should own up to the fact that what they did was wrong, should promise never to do it again, and move on with their lives," David said. "By continuing their present course of action they are just embarrassing themselves further."

The funniest part of the conspiracy theory was that Francis could not even get his "facts" straight. First, he testified that Ben had described the mystery man as a 6-foot, 160-pound black American. Then Francis said that, according to two people who accompanied Ben to the testing area, the man was white. Finally, Francis said that they later agreed he may have been a light-skinned black man. I was surprised that nobody described the mystery man as being purple with yellow stripes. That would have made the story even more spectacular.

The mystery man is André Jackson, the friend who stayed with my family in Seoul. He is in his mid-twenties and black, as dark-skinned as I am, which makes it tough to mistake him for being white. I've known André for about five years. He loves to travel, so he often shows up for track meets. He has become friends with a lot of people on the track circuit. Seoul was one of the few trips André actually planned ahead. Usually, he just shows up.

I'm not sure how André got into the drug-testing area. Either he had one of my passes for admission to the area or he got one from an Olympic official. The passes were amazingly easy to get, considering how strict the overall security was. Anyway, I was surprised when I looked in the waiting area and saw André sitting with Ben. Once I had

provided my urine sample, I left the drug-testing room and found
André to ask him what was going on.

André did not really have any reason to be in the drug-testing area.
He was just going to wait for me, to see what goes on in drug testing,
then leave. Certainly, he never expected to be caught in the middle
of an international scandal. But a few minutes after André got into the
waiting area, and before I got there, Ben entered the room, along
with his physical therapist, Waldemar Matuszewski. Ben and André
greeted each other. They had met not long before in a nightclub in
Zurich. André and Ben had joked with each other because they had
both been interested in the same Swiss girl. (André got her phone
number; Ben did not.) Ben had no idea that André and I were friends.

The waiting room was separate from several other rooms in the
drug-testing area. It had a couch, a television, a trainer's table, and a
refrigerator full of beer, juice, and water. The drinks were there to
help an athlete replenish his fluids and produce urine. The quicker
we can fill a bottle, the sooner we can leave the area. From the
moment Ben entered the room, he was complaining about leg cramps.
He pulled off his sweats, climbed up on the table, and kept complaining. His therapist hooked up some sort of machine and started
rubbing Ben's legs with it. That is when André decided to stick
around. He had heard me and others on the track circuit talk about
Ben doing drugs, and he was suspicious about this machine. André
had seen the therapist carry a black medical bag into the room, and
he wanted to make sure that the therapist did not give Ben anything
more than a rubdown before Ben urinated into his drug-test bottle.

Ben asked André to get him a beer, and he did. By this time, Ben
was lying facedown on the couch, pointed toward André, who was
sitting on the floor next to the couch. André had a beer for himself,
and they talked about the club in Zurich. Yes, André said, he had
kept in touch with the girl they had met. Ben said he was glad the big
race was finally over. He just wanted to get out of Seoul, and get
home. He did not seem to be excited about winning the biggest race
of his life. He just wanted to get out of there. He couldn't wait to buy
another car, a Ferrari, he said. Then he asked for another beer.

But his legs were still cramping. Ben kept asking, "Where's Jamie?"
meaning his doctor, Jamie Astaphan. He got angry when he was told
that Astaphan was having trouble getting into the testing area. Several officials came into the room to take pictures with Ben while the

therapist kept working on Ben's legs. André thought Ben was stalling, waiting for something from Astaphan before giving his urine sample.

Without knowing André and Ben were in the room, I glanced through an open door as I walked by, and couldn't believe what I saw. I had no idea what André was doing with Ben, but I'm never surprised when André shows up, no matter where it is, floating around, doing whatever he wants, being in places he doesn't belong. Some people just have that knack. André and I looked at each other, not saying anything, but Ben must have realized that we knew each other. He became real quiet, still answering when André talked to him, but much less responsive than he had been. A few minutes later, after sitting with Ben for almost an hour, André left. Ben still had not given his sample, despite having downed six or eight beers, according to André.

The next day, I was with André out by the warm-up track when Ben's physical therapist, Matuszewski, approached us. Matuszewski gave André his business card and asked if André would send copies of some pictures he had taken in the waiting room. André had taken the pictures because, in case anything strange happened, he wanted to be able to show me the people who had been in the room and the machine Ben had been using on his legs. We didn't know it then, but those pictures would prove to be an exclusive glimpse of sports history: snapshots from the final minutes before Ben Johnson turned in his drug-tainted sample in a bottle.

It did not take long for the Canadian investigators to rule out Charlie's sabotage theory. But it will take years for friends to stop teasing André Jackson about his few days of fame as the Mystery Man.

In March, a few weeks after Francis appeared in Canada, I was invited to testify before the U.S. Congress. The House of Representatives was considering a bill to forbid the mail-order sale of steroids from Canada and Mexico in the United States. It sounded like a good start, and any public hearing on steroids was a positive thing. The more that people hear and learn about steroids, the better the chances that steroid use will decline.

It is unfortunate that so few people seemed to care about steroids until Ben got caught. For years, politicians certainly did not care about steroids. Most of them did not even know what steroids were. But now that steroids were in the news, the politicians could look good by doing something about them. The Dubin Inquiry was getting lots of headlines. The Athletics Congress had recently adopted new random drug-testing programs. And the National Football League had just announced that it would suspend players who test positive for steroids. Now Congress could get in the act.

Before the hearing, I went to breakfast at a Capitol Hill hotel with Joe Douglas, who had flown in from California, and Paul McNulty, a lawyer who helped arrange the hearing for a House subcommittee on crime. Paul explained the bill and we discussed what I would say. I would make an opening statement and congressmen would ask questions. They would not put me on the spot by asking me to name other athletes using steroids or anything like that. The subcommittee members wanted me there mainly to gain publicity for them and their bill.

I wrote a few notes on a legal pad. "We perpetuate use for kids when they see Ben win." Everyone should be able to understand that. Kids are the key to the whole steroid issue. They have to learn the dangers of steroids. They have to realize that steroids can harm them and maybe even kill them. Then kids will not use steroids. Paul said the congressmen would want to hear about the 100-meter final with Ben because that was something everyone could relate to. "Ben's changes," I jotted down. "What the effects are." I also wrote, "Doctors are a part of a major problem. We must not let them hide."

Then I wrote a reminder to say something that had been bothering me since TAC announced its drug-testing plan. "An independent agency to test all sports." As I had said so many times, without such an agency doing the tests, an organization like TAC has no credibility. I don't trust TAC to treat all athletes fairly. How do we know TAC would not cover for an athlete? I wrote "independent agency" twice on my sheet of notes, once in the middle, once at the end, and that made Joe Douglas happy. He is not a big TAC fan, either.

The hearing room was packed. One by one, congressmen greeted me and said a few words before the hearing was called to order. Pete Stark, a California Democrat who introduced the bill, said he was offended by a mail-order form one of his constituents had received. The congressman gave me a copy of the form, which listed all sorts of steroids and syringes—thirty-two products in all. It was shocking because I did not know steroids were sold like this. In bold letters, the form said, "Anabolic steroids legally sold in Mexico . . . Come direct to us . . . Say no to drugs . . . Say yes to steroids." Congressman Stark told me, "We're going to put the guy out of business." Fine with me. I would be more than happy to play a small role in that.

After opening remarks from a few of the congressmen, it was my turn. Actually, Tommy Chaikin, a former South Carolina football player who had detailed his steroid problems in a *Sports Illustrated* story, was scheduled to testify before me. But he did not show.

First, I tried to put the steroid problem in perspective. Children are facing a tough choice in athletics. Do they want to take steroids or not? Certain coaches will try to push young athletes into taking them, so we need to go after coaches who are involved, not just athletes and doctors.

Most of our world-class athletes, especially in America, are not using steroids. But enough people are using them to have an impact on international competition. Sometimes an athlete takes steroids to beat another individual. Sometimes it is to win for the country. Sometimes it is for financial gains. There are many reasons.

So it is very important that we continue to fight the steroid problem. Kids get constant reinforcement not only that steroids are going to help them, but that taking steroids isn't bad.

I talked about the need for an independent testing agency and touched on the other points in my notes.

If I said one thing in my opening remarks that probably surprised people, it was that Ben Johnson would not have been in the Olympic finals, probably would not have been on the Olympic team, had he not taken steroids. The steroids made that much of an impact over a seven-year period in his career. We are talking about someone who went from possibly fiftieth or sixtieth in the world to number one in the world. He set a world record, but his coach and others have admitted he was taking steroids. So Ben has changed the course of history by pumping his body with drugs. What a terrible example for kids. They are going to think taking steroids is the right thing to do unless you get caught.

A few more comments from the question-and-answer session would make the news: I said that at least five to ten track-and-field medals in Seoul went to steroid-users. Some of them were gold medals, definitely. I talked about a West German athlete who took so many steroids that needles could no longer break through the scar tissue on her buttocks and in her hip area. That area was as hard as a rock. She ultimately died from the effects of steroid use.

There were two things that impressed me most about my hour with the congressmen. One, they were starting to treat steroids the same way they treat drugs like cocaine. It is good to clump together steroids and cocaine because they are both so dangerous. The congressmen began to see the poison that is being spread in our society. Two, I was pleased that I was the Olympic athlete chosen to talk about steroids. I had received a lot of criticism over the years for talking against drugs, especially after the comments at the 1987 World Championships in Rome, and all I had been trying to do was help my sport. Finally, a very important group supported my commitment to the fight against drugs. That meant a lot to me.

The comments of a Kentucky congressman meant even more: "I realize that you haven't been totally without controversy, and some of it deals with your outspokenness," Romano Mazzoli, a Democrat, said to me. "Let me tell you, in a world in which that is a rare commodity, I would hope that you are never bludgeoned into a kind of verbal submission. I hope that you always are willing to stand up for what you believe is correct."

At this point, Ben had not appeared yet at the Canadian inquiry, and he had not said anything to reporters about the testimony that had been heard. He would have his chance later, but not before Dubin filled the record with enough evidence to make a convincing case.

Angella Issajenko, Canada's best female sprinter and a teammate of Ben's, talked about doing drugs with Ben. Reading from a diary, she was able to offer quite a few details. Tim Bethune, a former 400-meter Canadian national champion, said he had seen Ben get an injection in Astaphan's office, then asked to be put on Ben's program. Bethune said that he quit taking steroids after he found out the pills he was getting came from a bottle labeled "For Veterinary Use Only." One of Ben's Olympic teammates, Andrew Mowatt, recalled Ben begging him for an injection. Mowatt quoted Ben as saying: "C'mon, I need a shot. Be a friend. . . . I'll give you a shot if you give me a shot." Desai Williams, the other Canadian who made the 100-meter finals in Seoul, said that Astaphan had given him and Ben a honey-and-vinegar mixture that was supposed to keep them from testing positive for drugs. But they did not use the drink. Desai placed seventh and was not tested.

Then came a witness who damaged the Canadian federation as

much as he damaged Ben. Peter Dajia, a shot-putter suspended for using drugs, said he had been reinstated by the Canadian Track and Field Association after he threatened to expose the use of steroids by Ben and others. That was powerful testimony, but I wasn't too surprised. For years, I had heard various stories about different track-and-field federations covering for drug users.

There was plenty of other testimony against Ben, including a chemist who ruled out Charlie's sabotage theory, so Ben was nailed. Period. Only two key figures were left to testify: Astaphan and Ben.

Astaphan had been threatening not to show for the inquiry. He had been trying to sell his story to a magazine and had been demanding a large fee to appear in Canada, but eventually he testified, apparently free of charge. Astaphan said he had given steroids and other drugs to Ben and thirteen other Canadians. He said he had injected Ben between fifty and sixty times, and Ben knew exactly what he was taking. The doctor even had a tape recording of a telephone call that seemed to prove that Ben knew. Astaphan's rationale for steroid use was the same as Charlie's, that everybody uses it. He told the inquiry his little axiom: "If you don't take it, you won't make it."

Next, Astaphan came after me and the Santa Monica club. He turned around the story about what he and Jack Scott had talked about, claiming that Jack had approached *him* the previous summer, on our behalf, to tell Astaphan we had expressed an interest in working with the drug doctor. Astaphan said he had ignored Scott.

Scott, of course, denied that, and so did everyone connected to our club. That was a low blow on Astaphan's part. But that's the way he operated. Ben and Charlie and Astaphan had been caught up for so long in such an incredible web of lies. Once the sabotage theory failed to blemish me, why not try something else?

Ben would be next on the stand, a week after telling a reporter in Italy that he had high hopes of clearing up his position, whatever that meant. "I'm looking forward to a comeback," Ben said. "My dream is to compete in the next Olympics. I want to face Carl Lewis again." But he had a long way to go before that, and it wouldn't be easy, especially for someone who had relied on drugs for so long.

With tears in his eyes, Ben finally admitted that he had taken steroids for eight years, and he accepted the blame. Ben's attorney, Ed Futerman, asked him if he had a message for young athletes who admired him. Yes, Ben did. "I want to tell them to be honest and don't take drugs. It happened to me. I've been there. I know what it's like to cheat."

Futerman steered Ben through only ten questions. They worked together, trying to save what was left of Ben's image. When Ben was asked why he had lied for so long, sticking by the statement that he "never, ever knowingly" took steroids, he said: "I was ashamed . . . I was just in a mess."

There would be other witnesses, more testimony. But when Ben stepped down from the stand, I considered one of the worst episodes in the history of track and field to be over. I thought the year of the steroid was over. But I was wrong.

CHAPTER
FIFTEEN
≡
The Athletics Congress

THE TOP organizers and promoters of American track and field were excited about the 1989 national championships. In mid-June, less than a year after the Seoul Games and only days after Ben Johnson testified about steroids, public interest in track would figure to be high. This would be the biggest meet in the United States since the 1988 Olympic trials. Surely, thousands of devoted track fans would flock to Houston to watch their favorite athletes compete. And thousands of people with only limited interest in the sport would turn out to see Olympic stars who had all but disappeared since NBC stopped delivering them by satellite from South Korea into millions of American living rooms.

Even the location of the national meet was a plus. With Joe De-Loach and me having attended the University of Houston and still living in town, meet promoters were counting on people wanting to support the local gold-medal winners. Radio spots advertising the meet mentioned me and Joe. A color picture of Joe was printed on brochures used to sell tickets. And the official meet program, to be sold at Robertson Stadium, included a nice feature story on Houston track, focusing on me and Joe.

In welcoming remarks prepared weeks before the meet, Allen E.

Murray, chairman and president of Mobil Corporation, sponsor of the championships, wrote:

"There's a special pleasure in holding this meet at the University of Houston—a school that has produced at least one individual NCAA champion for track and field in every year since 1979. The record for these Houston Cougars has been studded with championships for a long time, and they've surely had to build a slew of new trophy cases since head track coach Tom Tellez arrived in 1978.

"Everyone in Houston shares the University's pride in former Cougars Carl Lewis and Joe DeLoach—who've combined for eight Olympic medals, including four in last year's Games at Seoul. Carl Lewis has been called the most celebrated track and field athlete in U.S. history—and he's the best example I've ever seen of a competitor who invariably gives everything he's got."

There was only one problem. I was not going to give everything I've got. In fact, I was not going to give *anything* I've got. Neither was Joe DeLoach. We would boycott the championships to protest the way The Athletics Congress (TAC) governed track and field in the United States. For years, I had disagreed privately with TAC officials, especially executive director Ollan Cassell. Now it was time to let the public know that something was wrong. If Ollan and his buddies continued their course, then American track and field would continue to struggle.

Since the beginning of the year, I had been telling reporters some of the things that bothered me about TAC. The problems fell into three categories: poor promotion, foolish financial decisions, and a drug-testing policy that, at best, lacks credibility. All are symptoms of a larger problem: poor leadership, starting right at the top. Broad reform is needed to make track successful in the States. But I doubt we will see such reform unless we have new leaders.

At an indoor meet in January, I had talked about the lack of leadership and the fact that TAC was killing track in the States. But the issues were hardly ever addressed publicly. In the past, I had taken little jabs at TAC here and there. Now it was time to take a stand.

My plan to boycott hit the newspapers in May, and reporters finally had a reason to start asking their own questions about TAC.

The organization was formed in 1979 after a federal law required separate governing bodies for each Olympic sport. For almost a century before that, the Amateur Athletic Union (AAU) had been responsible for eight different sports. But Congress wanted each sport to operate on its own, so TAC was established to regulate track and field. TAC promotes training programs and competitions for about 150,000 individual members and about 2,500 clubs, schools, and other organizations. "Democracy is the keynote," TAC says of its leadership style. But if that is the goal, it certainly is not the reality.

The first few stories about the boycott blew it out of proportion, making it look like I was plotting with all sorts of major athletes to ruin the meet. Actually, only a few Santa Monica athletes would be involved. But TAC officials were scared. They told Joe Douglas they would do what they could to get along with us if we would turn down the heat. Joe leaned on me to make a public statement to ease the impact of the boycott, and I did.

In the next round of stories, I denied that I was feuding with TAC and said I was skipping the meet because of scheduling problems. The Associated Press ran a national story that quoted me saying, "I have no personal problem with TAC. I hope the meet sells out, and if they ask me to help promote it, I will."

The meet did not come close to selling out and nobody asked me to help promote it. But Joe Douglas was satisfied with the comments. We had gotten the attention of TAC. And anybody who follows our sport knew I was boycotting. That was the story people would remember, not the kiss-and-make-up story the week of the championships.

In retrospect, I may have made a mistake pushing the we-can-get-along theme. At the time, I thought that trying to get along might be productive. But I was wrong. No matter what I said publicly or privately, TAC did not want to consider real changes. It just wanted to avoid bad publicity.

In addition to giving up a shot at being national champion in the 100 and long jump, I was also skipping my chance to qualify for a U.S. team that would compete in several international meets, including the World Cup, scheduled for September in Spain. Long before that, the Santa Monica club figured to clash head-on with the U.S. national team. The national team was scheduled to compete in Birmingham, England, the week after the TAC championships. Originally, only national teams from the United States, the Soviet Union, West Germany, and Great Britain were expected. But when meet promoters heard that Joe DeLoach and I would not be running for the U.S. team, they invited us to compete on a Santa Monica relay team. We happily accepted, excited about the chance to beat a TAC-picked team and maybe break a relay record.

The one thing I have in common with Ollan Cassell is that we both competed for the University of Houston. He was an All-American in the 100 and 200 in 1963 and 1964, and he made the 1964 Olympics as a quarter-miler, winning a gold medal in the 4 × 400-meter relay. By the time TAC was formed, Ollan was one of the most powerful people in amateur sports, having served as chief executive of the AAU. He became TAC's first executive director, and he has held the position ever since.

My criticism of Ollan might get a lot of attention. But I am far from the first to disagree with him. In 1986, a letter signed "Committee for TAC Reform" made the rounds on the track circuit, accusing Ollan of a number of offenses, including the mishandling of funds. Ollan has always denied doing anything wrong, and the specific charges were not proven. But questions about his style of absolute rule, if nothing else, have lingered.

Ollan wants to live in the past, ruling like a king scared of losing his empire. He acts like any change will bring him less power, which it should. He is not willing to accept any suggestions from outside his little circle of friends, no matter how reasonable the advice may be. As a result, our sport is failing miserably in the States. Track and field is not becoming more popular, as it should.

Part of the problem is promotion. TAC has not done anything to create public interest in track. Maybe that is because Ollan and other leaders are so set in their ways, maybe it is just that they are not capable of coming up with new ideas. Either way, it is time to give someone else a chance to control TAC. We need fresh faces and new ideas.

Maybe a new leader would be willing to consider my proposals for change, which would include profit-sharing and retirement plans for athletes, and a new national agency to test athletes for drugs.

Even without profit-sharing or retirement plans, the money issues are numerous. What is TAC doing with all the money it takes in from sponsors and promoters? Why does TAC insist on operating behind a facade of amateurism when our sport is so obviously professional?

After decades of struggling in the States, our sport is finally starting to get the financial backing it needs. The Turner Broadcasting System is paying to televise meets and Mobil has committed to being the primary sponsor of the Grand Prix circuit. I don't know how much TAC takes in from those deals, but it is not pocket change. Where does the money go? TAC does not spend enough of it to promote meets and does not give enough to individual meet directors. As a result, American meets lose athletes to the European circuit, where much bigger appearance fees are offered. European promoters, with huge budgets, know they have to pay well to get the athletes they want.

One of the most frustrating things about TAC is that no matter how many times we ask, its leaders never explain how they spend their money. They should open their books and let the athletes take a look. Show us where the money comes from, how much there is and where it is going. TAC chooses which meets will be part of the television package. But less than half the revenue from televising each meet goes to the individual meets. TAC never talks about where the rest goes.

The people at TAC like to dismiss my complaints by saying, "Carl is just being selfish." But that makes no sense. I get paid very well. My money is there, and it will be there long after I stop competing. That's not what bothers me about TAC. If Ollan listened to what I'm saying, he would realize that my proposals have little to do with personal gains. Rather, they focus on increasing public interest in our sport and making it a better sport for all competitors, not just the top athletes.

Take my plan for the way TAC should split its money with athletes. The top ten competitors in every event—sprinters, marathoners, discus throwers, whatever—should be paid equally. That would encourage athletes to focus on a variety of events, and they could afford to do so, training instead of working at jobs. Right now, most of the money goes to sprinters and some long-distance runners. As a result, the United States is not developing, for example, discus throwers, javelin throwers, or women shot-putters.

I have also lobbied to get a pension plan for athletes. I'll be just fine when I retire. But what about the eighth-ranking intermediate hurdler who holds down two part-time jobs; the shot-putter who trains and competes for years before just missing the cutoff for the Olympic team; the veteran marathoner who represents his country in grand fashion but never saves enough money to be comfortable? These people need financial help. By providing it, TAC could establish a lot of positive feelings within our sport, and the new, *professional* atmosphere would help move our sport forward. We need to escape from the Dark Ages of so-called amateurism, the same way golf and tennis have progressed.

And, as I have said so many times on the drug issue, what we need is a national, independent testing agency. For years, athletes have openly talked about how easy it is to beat TAC's tests, and some have even alleged that positive drug tests are being ignored to protect certain athletes. Those are serious charges, and tough to prove. But having an independent agency to conduct and report the results of drug tests would go a long way toward eliminating any questions of improper tests or handling of results.

Of course, that would mean the loss of some control for Ollan Cassell. And that brings us right back to the source of so many of the problems with track and field in the States.

My ideas for reform are just a starting point, of course. Maybe there are better ways to implement change. But without talking about that, without even entering a discussion on the possibility that changes are needed, Ollan and TAC responded by attacking me, not the issues. I tried to avoid talking too much publicly about personal problems with TAC. I wanted to address issues, not personal problems. But the whole TAC situation has been a combination of both. I have had plenty of problems with people at TAC, especially Ollan, who spends too much time sticking his nose into the personal business of individual athletes.

Over the years, Ollan has cost me some large endorsement deals by interfering with people who had been negotiating with Joe

Douglas. This goes all the way back to 1982 when Ollan steered away a potential sponsor, saying that I could not appear in an advertisement because that would be a violation of collegiate rules. He failed to mention that I had already declared my decision not to compete anymore as a college athlete, so NCAA rules no longer applied to me.

More recently, Ollan contributed to the loss of other major sponsors, including an Italian clothing company. Several times, potential sponsors have told me that TAC officials pressured them to stay away from me. That is not exactly my idea of free trade, which is the American way.

But it has been the TAC way. Another example: Just before the 1989 TAC meet, Ollan wrote a letter to Pierre Weiss, executive director of the French athletics association, trying to influence where *certain* U.S. athletes would compete on the European circuit. Several people who read the letter immediately concluded that Ollan was after me and Santa Monica, and they sent the letter to me.

"You may have seen some press coverage concerning one of our clubs for attempting to challenge the membership and acting as if they are the governing body for the sport in this country rather than The Athletics Congress," Ollan wrote to Weiss. "You understand this cannot happen and member federations around the world must . . . not give comfort to those athletes and those clubs once a decision has been made by the federation."

Time after time, Ollan has found ways to come after me. One of the most amusing was after the 1987 World Championships in Rome. Ollan wrote me to lodge an official complaint because I had not worn my complete uniform during the victory ceremonies after the 400-meter relay and the long jump.

"You realize that once an athlete has been selected for the National Team, they are obligated to wear the official uniform in competition as well as on the victory stand," Ollan wrote. "Could you let me know why you did not appear in the official presentation suit as provided by the team management?"

If this was the burning question on Ollan's mind, it must have been a pretty slow day at the TAC offices in Indianapolis. My response, Ollan concluded in the letter, would be provided to the International Competition Committee at TAC's next annual convention. It was just another way for Ollan to flex his muscles. I saw no point in responding to such an unimportant issue when the major issues in U.S. track were being ignored.

I soon heard that more big-name athletes had decided to pull out of the national TAC meet. Renaldo Nehemiah and Greg Foster, two of the best high-hurdlers in the world, scratched. Olympic gold medalist Andre Phillips and 1984 silver medalist Danny Harris did not show for the 400-meter hurdles. Jackie Joyner-Kersee, world-record holder and Olympic gold medalist in the heptathlon, was nowhere in sight. Butch Reynolds, world-record holder in the 400 and Olympic gold medalist in the 4 × 400-meter relay, pulled out. And there were others.

The no-shows had excuses: a sore leg, fatigue, busy schedule. But none of that mattered. The absences illustrated the sorry state of track and field in this country. If the national championships were all that they ought to be, the top athletes would have made it there.

A lot of people at the meet, including some reporters, wondered whether these other athletes were supporting my boycott. Not that I was aware of. And TAC president Frank Greenberg dismissed that idea. But his comments to reporters would not put fans in the stands. Fewer than two thousand people would show each day of the meet. Whatever Frank had to say would not be enough to derail some very negative stories.

"Suppose they gave a national track meet in Houston and nobody showed?" That was the first line of a *Houston Post* story on June 16. "Absence of star sprinters lamented," said a headline in the *Houston Chronicle*. And Dick Patrick of *USA Today* wrote, "No-shows are more prominent than entrants at the Mobil event."

This was not exactly the type of publicity TAC wanted. As the *Post* pointed out, "Athletes, officials and media representatives easily outnumbered the crowd . . . despite two of the most pleasant June days in Houston history."

The "boycott" was working. I figured that the press would finally have to address issues that TAC wanted to avoid.

The absence of so many top athletes would help in another way, too. It would provide some great opportunities for my Santa Monica and Houston training partners. Leroy Burrell, between his junior and senior years at Houston, Brian Cooper of the Houston Track Club, and Mike Marsh of Santa Monica would have a chance to run the 100 without me. Floyd Heard and Mark Witherspoon, competing for Santa Monica, would have a shot at the 200 without having to worry about beating Joe DeLoach. Cletus Clark of Santa Monica and Courtney Hawkins of the Houston club would have a good shot in the high hurdles. And Johnny Gray, a Santa Monica veteran and favorite at 800 meters, would probably get more attention than usual without me and Joe competing.

These guys would all be in positions to gain spots on the national team that normally would be filled by others. That would mean great exposure for them, Santa Monica, and the Houston program. So Joe Douglas, Joe DeLoach, and I, pulling for our family, were among the most excited fans in the stands.

The results were great.

Leroy ran the best race of his life, winning the 100 in 9.94 seconds, the fastest time ever for a collegian at low altitude and the sixth-fastest time ever for anyone, anywhere. Brian ran a fourth-place 10.12, still good enough to qualify for a U.S. relay team.

Floyd and Mark ran away with the 200, placing first and second in 20.09 seconds and 20.12 seconds, respectively. The 20.09 was the best 200 time of the year up to that point. Courtney made the national team for the first time, placing third in the high hurdles. And Johnny won the 800, as expected.

Courtney, Leroy, and Brian were directed by TAC officials to sign up for U.S. teams to compete in international meets, including the upcoming meet in Birmingham, England. One by one, they pulled me aside for guidance. Leroy told the TAC people he would run for Santa Monica, not the U.S. team. I sat with Courtney while he filled out forms, making sure he did not commit to anything he did not want to do. Brian had the most trouble deciding what to do, and I left before he made up his mind.

I was sitting way up in the stands with my mother, watching the final events of the meet, when Frank Greenberg, smiling, greeted us like old friends and joined us for what he hoped would be a cordial chat. For a few minutes, it was. My mother considered Frank a friend, so it was perfectly natural to exchange small talk with him. But then we got down to issues.

"I like you, Carl," Frank said, trying to start on a positive note.

"You know that. If you saw what I said in the paper the other day, I said, 'I like Carl.' But you have to understand where we're coming from."

"Fine, I do," I said. "But I'm tired of TAC telling us what to do. I'm tired of Ollan going behind our backs. We're trying to move the sport forward for all the athletes, and TAC doesn't want to do that. You can't even fill the stands at a national championship."

Frank said, "We should sit down sometime and have a meeting," which is one of his favorite things to say. All he and Ollan want to do is meet, meet, meet. But they accomplish only one thing by talking to me and Joe Douglas. That enables them to tell reporters, "We're trying. We've discussed the issues and we're all trying to work together." Big deal. That helps TAC's public relations efforts, but it doesn't do anything for the athletes.

It was probably a good thing that my mother was between me and Frank, providing a buffer zone. We were pretty far from most spectators, but still very much in view of anyone who wanted to see what was going on. A few kids, having no idea who Frank is or what we were talking about, came by to take pictures and get autographs, providing little breaks from the tension that was building. My mother didn't say much, but she tried to keep me calm, placing her hand on my leg and patting me, as if to say, "Easy, Carl. Don't make a scene."

But that would be hard to avoid once we started talking about the Birmingham meet.

"We spent $500,000 to put together a meet," Frank said, looking at my mother, as if she were going to side with him. "Then the promoter, Andy Norman, calls Joe Douglas and invites Santa Monica. That's not being fair." Turning back to me, Frank said, "You might disagree, Carl. Fine. But, at least, understand what I'm saying."

"First of all," I shot back, "if you're trying to help track in the United States, why are you spending $500,000 on a meet in Europe? And Andy Norman didn't just want us, he *needed* us. He called us because he wasn't selling any tickets. He needed a draw. And who does Ollan think he is? He's not going to tell us what to do. Tell him to flex his muscles with somebody else."

"But Carl . . ."

Now I was hot. Raising my voice without thinking about where we were, I had to give Frank a little lecture to take back to Ollan.

"Stop the bullcrap," I said. "You want to focus on this little issue, that little issue. Let's be realistic. We have to stop the amateur crap and move forward as professionals."

"This is not the place for this," Frank said, shaking his head and setting up his favorite line. "We should meet."

Before leaving, Frank leaned over my mother to get closer to me, softened his tone, and pleaded with me to keep all this stuff out of the newspapers. "Please be discreet with your mouth," he said. "We're still friends."

On June 20, 1989, the day before we were supposed to leave for the Birmingham meet, I got a call from Joe Douglas, who was already in Europe. The England meet was off—for our club, anyway. Ollan Cassell had called the promoter, Andy Norman, and told him that if he accepted the Santa Monica relay team, TAC would not allow any U.S. team members to compete. Once again, Ollan was fighting a personal war, not addressing issues. Ollan should have been excited about seeing the world's fastest people running against each other in England. The competition would be good for the sport. Instead, he had worked behind the scenes to avoid the possibility of Santa Monica embarrassing his team.

The threat was enough to make Andy back down. He really had no choice. But he was livid because he had been advertising that we would be in England, going for a world record. Andy made it clear that he would blame TAC—not us—for our absence.

It did not take long for word to spread that the Santa Monica club was out of the meet. Soon after Joe called me, a reporter friend called to read an Associated Press story that had just gone over the wires.

The story began:

Olympic champion Carl Lewis and three club teammates on an 800-meter relay team were barred from an international track meet this weekend by the sport's U.S. governing body, British officials said today.

The British Amateur Athletics Board said it had been told by The Athletics Congress, U.S. track's ruling federation, that Lewis and three other members of the Santa Monica Track Club had been refused permission to compete.

TAC denied, however, that it banned the athletes.

"We don't have the power to ban athletes at a meet on British soil,"
Pete Cava, a public information spokesman for TAC, said at the
organization's headquarters in Indianapolis.

The story then got into the background of our club's "feud" with
TAC. It reported that one of the four teams we would have run
against in Birmingham was a British squad led by Linford Christie,
who finished right behind me in the 100-meter finals the previous
summer at Seoul.

But the British board said it had been told by TAC executive di-
rector Ollan Cassell that U.S. club teams would not be allowed to run
against national teams in meets where a U.S. national squad was
competing.

Cassell said the move had the "full support" of U.S. team members
and coaches, the British board reported.

The British were blaming TAC for the cancellation, and TAC was
denying what we knew to be true. Once again, Ollan was losing
credibility. And his handling of the Birmingham situation definitely
undermined Frank Greenberg's attempt to quiet me down.

When word got out that we were not going to Birmingham, we
immediately received offers from the directors of three other meets,
and Joe Douglas chose one in St. Denis. The Santa Monica club, in
search of a world record, would go to France instead of England. Still,
I did not appreciate a bunch of bureaucrats telling me what I could do
and where I could do it. The war with TAC would escalate.

The next shot, in the form of a press release, was fired out of TAC's
Indianapolis headquarters on July 12, 1989. It said that the Japan
Amateur Athletic Federation would no longer invite me to compete
in Japan. The JAAF had notified Joe Douglas of this "through a letter
sent to The Athletics Congress," the release said. "The letter has
been forwarded by TAC to Douglas."

The JAAF was acting in response to "an incident" during a meet in
Tokyo on May 14. In a 100-meter heat, I had not worn one of my
number cards properly on the back of my uniform. Meet officials
were upset because the name of their sponsor, Mitsubishi, was not
visible—a violation of international rules, in the opinion of Hiroaki
Chosa, managing director of the Japanese federation.

Chosa said that I would be welcome to compete in Japan only as a member of the U.S. international team. But after skipping the TAC meet, that would not be an option.

I had altered the number card because it was too big—as number cards often are—causing the uniform to pull, which could affect my race. I often cut off some of a number card to make it smaller, and nobody complains. The Japanese were obviously playing politics, and—surprise, surprise—TAC was right in the middle of the game. Why would Chosa send a letter to Joe Douglas at TAC? Chosa knows where to find Joe without going through anybody else. TAC must have plotted with Chosa to embarrass me. The Japanese usually handle business privately and with class, not by issuing press releases.

And what about TAC opening a letter addressed to Joe Douglas, reading it, and releasing its contents for use in newspapers all over the world? As Ollan Cassell noted in a cover letter to Joe, the Japanese federation requested that its letter "be sent directly to you." There was no mention of sending it to anyone else.

The way TAC was acting, interfering with me all over the world, I had to wonder about the possibility of charging the organization and Ollan with restraint of trade. They were unfairly blocking me from conducting my business. The worst part was that now my problems with TAC had affected my relations with the Japanese, who had always treated me extremely well.

Still, I wanted to avoid the legal arena—if possible. My response to the Japanese situation would be limited. David Greifinger, the Santa Monica club attorney, would write Frank Greenberg to share some of our thoughts.

"The actions taken by the national office were at best, unethical, and possibly illegal," David wrote. "We can only guess at the motives behind the press release. Needless to say, we are not favorably impressed."

While he was at it, David also focused on the letter Ollan had written to Pierre Weiss of the French federation.

"The latter part of this letter can only be interpreted as a thinly veiled entreaty to Mr. Weiss to blackball the Santa Monica Track Club from meets in France," David began. "Once again, we are witness to behavior which falls somewhere in the range of unethical to illegal."

David was extremely disturbed about the timing of the letter to France. Ollan had written it at the same time (right before the national championships) that he and Frank Greenberg were telling us they wanted to make peace.

"I must tell you that this letter has greatly damaged the credibility of Ollan and of TAC in the eyes of our athletes," David concluded. "I still sincerely hope that some day, the Santa Monica Track Club and TAC will work out their differences. As we have both painfully learned, this will not be easy, and will not happen in the short term."

David was definitely right about that.

SIXTEEN

≡

A European Diary

THE BEST thing about competing outside the United States is that the meets are organized by people who know what they are doing, not TAC. That means big crowds, lots of publicity, large appearance fees, a crazy life-style of go, go, go for weeks at a time during the summer circuit in Europe. The differences between track in the United States and track overseas are the differences between minor league baseball and the major leagues, the Continental Basketball Association and the NBA, sandlot football and the NFL.

Most summers, I make two trips to Europe with the Santa Monica club. In June and July, we go for two to three weeks, which we treat like the first half of a season. After that, we go home and train until August. Then we return for the second half of the European circuit, which is usually a bit longer.

In 1989, St. Denis, France, was the first stop of the first half, which included five meets in two weeks. The club contingent was larger than ever, about twenty people including fifteen athletes, Joe Douglas, David Greifinger, and my brother Cleve, who was in charge of travel plans. My sister Carol, competing in the long jump, made it a family trio.

After the relay in St. Denis, I would run the 100 in Lille, France, long jump in Lausanne, Switzerland, run the 100 in Oslo, Norway, and finish with the long jump in Stockholm, Sweden.

I've always wanted to share the European circuit with Americans, to let readers and fans know what newspapers and television miss or ignore. To capture the circuit (not just the competitions, but also what happens between them) I kept a journal.

June 22
Houston, London, and Paris

Only one thing is certain about the European track circuit, and that is uncertainty. So many things change at the last minute. Can we get in the hotel we want? Do we have to appear at a press conference or can we rest? Who will be in what race? When will we go home? Should we compete in more races for more money or should we skip some meets so we can train and be in better shape for the races we are in? How will my sore back feel after being cramped up in a plane? Will the television in my hotel room get Cable News Network?

Today, there was an extra worry: Is it possible for a 137-pound suitcase to make it as far as I do? I had packed a huge suitcase with more than two hundred Santa Monica club T-shirts, dozens of uniforms for my teammates, and thousands of picture cards to autograph and give to children in Europe. This is the first time I've taken extra T-shirts to Europe. Some we will give away, some will be sold to raise money to pay for our uniforms. But first the heaviest suitcase in the history of international travel had to survive. Luckily, it did, thanks to a combination of luck and some serious tips for airport workers who lugged the thing around.

Before I got to Paris, Joe Douglas had been told by a promoter of the St. Denis meet that we could not stay in the hotel we wanted. No rooms left, Joe was told, so we would have to stay in a hotel that is not nearly as nice. But promoters, looking to save money, are not always straight with us. So David Greifinger called the hotel we wanted. Yes, we have rooms, he was told. How many do you need? David made reservations, then told the promoter we were able to get in. The promoter would be stuck with a bigger bill than he wanted. And we would have CNN. English-language TV is a must.

Soon after I settled into my room, the phone rang. The promoter wanted to make sure I would be ready for a press conference in about an hour, at 6:30 P.M. in St. Denis, a forty-five-minute drive in traffic.

"Let's do it here in the hotel," Joe said. "Carl just got here and he's very tired. It's not fair to ask him to go to St. Denis."

It has to be in St. Denis, Joe was told. All the reporters and photographers are on the way. Joe was upset. Nobody had told us where the press conference would be. He asked the guy to call back in a few minutes.

"I guess we should go," Joe said, knowing it would take some solid reasoning to convince me. "It's a sensitive time with the press. Everyone knows we're feuding with TAC, and the press appears to be behind us now. We can't get them mad over something like this. When you're taking on the establishment, you need to do everything right. We need the outside forces working for us, not against us."

So we went. We heard the same old questions, gave the same old answers, but we went. Nobody could complain.

I did pick up an interesting tidbit at the press conference. Posters and brochures for the meet listed the French Communist Party as a sponsor. You never know who is going to pop up on the circuit.

June 23
Paris and St. Denis

This morning, there was a knock on my door at 9:00. Figuring it was the maid, I went to the door in my robe. I would ask her to come back later. But, looking through the peephole, I saw it was not a maid. It was a man with a television camera and a woman with a microphone.

"We called this morning," the woman said through the door. "We want to take pictures of Mr. Carl Lewis."

Nobody had called about pictures. Nobody was even supposed to know what room I was in. I had already asked the front desk to stop putting calls through because I had been hearing from all sorts of people I did not know. Europeans are absolutely in love with track and field, and for some reason they all want to call me when I'm trying to rest.

Can we take a picture? We'd love to have you attend our reception. Can I have an autograph? Some children want to meet you. A local businessman has a great idea that you just have to hear about.

I enjoy meeting people and understand an athlete's obligations to the public. But there is a time for privacy, too, and the repetitive demands and expectations are sometimes tough to deal with. That is why most of my time in Europe is spent in a hotel room, not out shopping or sightseeing. One of the first things I do when I check into a hotel is ask for my calls to be forwarded to Joe Douglas.

I ignored the people outside my door, called the front desk, and asked for security to clear the hallway. Soon, Ms. Microphone and Mr. Camera were gone. But the phone kept ringing. I had to complain a few times to the front desk before they finally understood that I wanted NO CALLS.

It takes me longer to prepare for a meet in Europe than it does in the States because I have to be ready for the fans. There are so many more track and field fans in Europe than in the States. This afternoon, I spent a couple of hours signing piles of picture cards for fans at the stadium in St. Denis. There are two reasons why I do this. One, I appreciate the fans and enjoy giving them something. Two, it is the only way to get in and out of stadiums in Europe. Giving away pictures helps to keep people from surrounding me, grabbing me, and swallowing me in a pack. When I give them something—quickly— they are satisfied and I am safe. Back home, I don't need picture cards. Just give me car keys, and I can get in and out of a stadium all by myself.

In St. Denis, the crowd was great. With all the publicity about our last-minute decision to run here, our relay team was the center of attention. All the commotion was new to Leroy Burrell, who was traveling with our club for the first time. So I made a point of sticking with him, just the way I did last year with Joe DeLoach.

With the British sprinters and other top relay teams in Birmingham, we did not even recognize the other teams in our race. Breaking the world record would be the only real challenge.

We ran pretty well, but not great. Our handoffs were good, but not great. We ran away from the field. But we just missed the record. Our time was 1:20.33, seven-hundredths of a second off the mark.

The crowd still went wild. They loved us, and we put on a show for them, all four of us taking a victory lap. Then a meet official handed me a microphone and asked me to say a few words to the crowd.

"Do you want us to come back next year?" I asked.

Again, the crowd erupted, reminding me we were in Europe, not the States.

June 24
Paris and Lille

Before today, I thought I had heard all the excuses for running a bad race, failing to meet expectations or just missing a world record. But this morning I was introduced to a new explanation: The ground has a heart, and our relay team had not been in France long enough to feel that heart, to be comfortable with that heart, before our race.

The explanation came from Sri Chinmoy, who was in Paris for another road run to promote world peace. I was glad when I heard Sri Chinmoy was here because he wanted to meet my teammates, and this was a good opportunity for that. In our hotel lobby, Joe DeLoach, Floyd Heard, Leroy Burrell, and I visited with Sri Chinmoy. He was surprised when he heard we had arrived only a day before the meet.

"This explains why you did not win the world record," said Sri Chinmoy, his words coming slowly, his eyes opening and closing as he spoke, his head nodding gently as he focused on his thoughts. "The ground has a heart. Everything has a heart, a spirit and a heart. When you fly here you have to be on the ground long enough to feel the heart. Yes, that is important. And you missed the record by only a little bit. In a new place—you have to understand this—you have to be on the ground longer before you race."

I smiled and nodded, familiar with the way Sri Chinmoy explains things. But my teammates were a bit stunned. They did not say much to Sri Chinmoy. They just observed.

Sri Chinmoy gave me a birthday cake, a week early, but he wanted me to have it. Sri Chinmoy wished us good luck for the rest of our trip, and that was that.

Back in my room, Joe, Floyd, and Leroy agreed on a one-word summary of what they had just seen. "Interesting." Cleve teased me about the cake, knowing I was not real happy about another year being tacked on. While everybody was laughing at me, Joe Douglas entered the room and hounded us to pack our bags. We had to leave for Lille.

But not too fast. Our vans had disappeared, and it took almost half an hour for several hotel employees and our relay team to find them. Drivers for the rental company had left them on a side street instead of parking them in front of the hotel. Our departure was further delayed when Leroy Burrell accidentally slammed a van door shut on Joe Douglas's hand. This was only supposed to be a two-hour drive, but it was not going to be simple.

Halfway to Lille, we realized our van was running out of gas, and Carol asked Joe if he had enough French francs to fill the tank. "French fries?" Joe asked. "Why do we need French fries?" That slamming door must have affected Joe's ears, too.

A sign said ten kilometers to gas. "I can see it now," Carol said. "The track club pulls out of the meet because we have to push the van to Lille. Headlines everywhere: Santa Monica can't run. They're too busy pushing."

Later, Joe came up with enough francs to get through a tollbooth. But Cleve, driving the second van, had only American dollars. Realizing the other van was stuck, Joe Douglas stopped in the middle of traffic and sent Joe DeLoach—an Olympic champion on a mission— running down the highway with change.

Amazingly, we finally made it to Lille—only to sit around, killing time, with nothing planned until competition the next night. The road can be very boring, and I was already looking forward to going home.

Some of the guys on the team played Monopoly, some of us played cards. There was no CNN, only French channels. So the entertainment highlight of the night was watching Steve Lewis Live. Steve, who was only nineteen and still a student at UCLA when he won his two gold medals, is so much more than an Olympic champion. He is also one of the brightest and most hilarious guys on the track circuit, one of the rare few who can make a joke about your mother and get away with it. Tonight, as he often does, Steve chose Mike Marsh's mother as the target of his monologue—all in fun, of course. Doing a stand-up routine in front of the hotel, Steve had us crying, we were laughing so hard. This guy needs to be on TV—in English, not French.

June 25
Lille

For Santa Monica, finishing anything but first is a disappointment. Tonight was very disappointing. I was satisfied with my own race, winning the 100 in 10.05 seconds. But when I'm with the club, I'm just as concerned with everybody else's performances as I am with my own.

Leroy Burrell was third in the 100—acceptable, I guess, with a time of 10.11. Mike Marsh was fourth in 10.30. Brian Cooper was last.

Joe DeLoach ran a flat 200, finishing second in 20.41, and, making things worse, he hurt his leg in the process. Floyd Heard was third in 20.43, which is not good for him.

After the race, Joe decided he would return to Houston the next day. He would have to skip three meets—three of his best paydays of the year—so he could train and let his leg heal. "I'm going to miss the ching-ching," Joe said. "But I have to do the right thing."

Ching-ching is what Santa Monica calls money. The term came to our club courtesy of Danny Everett, an Olympic champion and quite a character. He was on the 4 × 400 relay team that won the gold in Seoul and he won the bronze medal in the individual 400. But Danny is best known for his personality, not his awards. He smiles and jokes all the time, except when he is suffering from allergies or complaining about being on the road. Danny must be allergic to everything in Europe, especially the service in hotels and restaurants, because every time we go there he sneezes all day. He is the only athlete on the track circuit who carries a box of Kleenex with his spikes and uniform. As soon as Danny stops sneezing, he starts complaining, usually about the lousy service. Sometimes he is joking, sometimes he is not. After a while, it's hard to tell. But we think he is usually joking, and we always laugh when he is around.

Danny is always trying to invent new terms or sayings. Ching-ching is one of his best, and it's become an important part of the official Santa Monica Track Club language. He came up with ching-ching while we were in Japan after the Seoul Games. A bunch of people from the club, including me and Danny, were making an appearance before a group of children, about a thousand kids at a show in an indoor arena. We were on the way to the airport, so this was going to be a quickie. One by one, we were introduced, we smiled and waved. Then we each got a thousand dollars for appearing and we left. That's when Danny started saying "ching-ching."

He remembers it well. "I was thinking of those old cash registers, the ones where you make a sale and they ring it up," Danny said.

"You know, they go, 'Ching-ching.' Well, certain appearances pay well. You have to go. Certain meets, same thing. You run, which is like making a sale, and you cash it in. *Ching-ching.* Once you get the ching-ching, it's time to go home."

When they made Danny they didn't throw away the mold, they smashed it. If too many people like him were around, we wouldn't be able to get anything done. We would always be laughing.

In the 400, Steve Lewis tried to save us, winning in 45.05 seconds. But Danny was a disaster in the same race, finishing fourth in 45.61. Danny is not even close to being in shape, and that's not right for an Olympic medalist with as much talent as he has.

"I should give the promoters their money back," Danny joked. "But I'm not *that* stupid." No, we were not about to return our appearance fees. If we were, Danny would not have been alone in the rebate line. Mark Luevano was last in the 1500. Cletus Clark was fourth in the 110-meter hurdles. And Kevin Young was upset in the 400-meter hurdles.

I don't think I could ever be a head coach because I hate it too much when my guys lose. Tonight, Joe Douglas hated it, too.

"Everybody was flat," Joe said at a quiet team dinner after the meet. "Everybody ran like a dog. As a team, it was our worst performance in a long time." Looking at his plate, talking to nobody in particular, Joe went on and on and on. "You guys better remember what got you where you are. Otherwise, you're going to get slapped in the face with reality. Some of you think you can go out late, chase girls, but it shows. You eat too much, and it shows. You better start thinking about what you're doing."

June 26
Lille and Lausanne

Despite our performances last night, we still got special treatment today. And other athletes on the circuit were jealous, as usual.

All the athletes and coaches going from Lille to Lausanne shared a charter plane provided by the meet promoters. But once we got to Switzerland, we went our separate ways. A bus waiting at the airport took our club to a beautiful hotel, with a huge lake and a breathtaking range of mountains right outside our front door. The rest of the athletes waited, frustrated, as we boarded our bus. They had to wait for a train, and they were staying at a small, crowded hotel in the middle of the city.

Our club gets what it wants because we have fought for years to improve conditions for athletes, we stick together, and the meet promoters need us. In return, we accept the responsibility to perform the best we can. That's why we are so upset with ourselves when we run the way we did in Lille.

A private bus and separate hotel are not the biggest things in the world. But they are indicative of the way our club demands and commands respect. There is no reason why world-class athletes should be treated like second-class sardines on the road. If we did not consistently stand up to the promoters, that's the way it would be.

A lot of athletes don't understand that. Or they do understand but they don't have the power of a group to make demands.

June 27
Lausanne

The international edition of *USA Today* is a hot commodity on the road. It is nice to read something in English. But not what I read today. A headline caught my attention: "Drug testing plan might be delayed."

The story says:

The year-round, short-notice drug testing plan The Athletics Congress hoped to implement by July 1 probably will be delayed for three months.

The executive committee of TAC, the national governing body for track and field, is expected to approve a suggestion to be presented this week by president Frank Greenberg to postpone the program until Oct. 1.

Typical TAC. Frank Greenberg and the other leaders are just playing public-relations games. By October, the season is over. So athletes can go the whole season without being tested.

The people at TAC have been running around screaming that they are against drugs, and they're finally going to do something about the problem. Well, they just lost any credibility they had. If random testing has been properly conducted since 1983 (which TAC claims), then why should it take so long to initiate the new, improved program?

"Oh, my God," Joe Douglas said when I showed him the article. "Everything with them is image, not reality. It's facade. A three-month delay is the same as a year. After September, nobody is training. Anybody can pee in a bottle then."

Joe quickly changed the subject, though, because he had come to my room with an entirely different problem. One of my best sponsors, a Swiss watch company called Tag Heuer, was unhappy.

"Dammit," Joe said, "we got nailed at St. Denis."

"What are you talking about?"

"The Tag Heuer people were there, and they're saying you didn't have a watch on at the press conference."

"Yes, I did. Not on the track when they interviewed me right after the race. They take my clothes away before the race, and the watch was in my pocket. But I had the watch on for the press conference inside."

"Okay," Joe said. "Let me call them back."

Keeping Tag Heuer happy is a priority. It is a company that I respect and one that I want to be with for a long time. But I was surprised to hear their people were upset because they had seen me on TV—once—without their watch on.

I had an idea for Joe: Tell them I can't do anything about being caught without my watch immediately after a race. But I know a way to guarantee publicity for them. Have them sew some Tag Heuer patches on my Santa Monica T-shirts. I always wear one until right before a race and can put one back on as soon as the race is over. When you have sponsors like Tag Heuer, you want to take care of them.

"Fine," Joe said. "Patches will be good." And off he went to call Tag Heuer.

After sitting around the hotel all day, I was happy to leave for the meet. I was ready to jump. But getting to the stadium—we had two vans—was not easy. The roads were narrow and the drivers around here are wild.

Halfway to the stadium, a Mercedes smacked into the second van, not the one I was in. Steve Lewis hopped out of the banged-up van, screaming and faking a leg injury.

"We'll sue for millions," said David Greifinger, safe in a seat behind me. "Definitely," Danny Everett said. "The mental anguish and emotional distress of watching my friends get hit is just too much for me." Kevin Young claimed he "pulled a hamstring just watching."

Leaving the second van right where it was hit, we piled sixteen people into the first van and arrived at the stadium looking like one of those circus cars with all the clowns in it.

I jumped pretty well, considering we had bad weather and it was my first outdoor long-jump competition of the year. My best jump was 8.43 meters (27 feet, 8 inches), enough to beat Larry Myricks and set a new meet record. Reporters were quick to remind me that my streak of long-jump victories now stood at fifty-nine. Reporters love streaks. Me, I'm just happy to beat Myricks again.

June 28
Lausanne, Geneva, Frankfurt, West Berlin, and Oslo

Today was car, airport, another airport, another airport, another car, hotel, another car, stadium, another car, another airport, another airport, a final airport, a final car, a final hotel—a lot of movement for little action, all because Joe Douglas had made a promise that helped us get what we wanted from European meet directors.

Late last year, some of the most influential European meet directors plotted to put a cap on my appearance fees. If they could stick together, they told each other, nobody would have to meet my demands. They had tried this once before, in 1985, and they failed. But now they really wanted to play hardball.

The directors, one by one, would offer me the same appearance fee, more than they wanted to pay, but thousands less than Joe and I expected. We had learned, over the years, what it means for the Santa Monica club to appear at a meet. It means ticket sales, and the meet directors are not the only ones who should profit. But if none of the directors gave in, we would be in a tough spot, unable to play them off against each other. We needed to crack what amounted to a meet directors' cartel. We would do something special to get the right money—tens of thousands of dollars—from one meet director. Then we could stick with our demands in negotiations to appear at other meets. Once we had one director, word would spread and the others would fall like dominoes, knowing they needed us if so-and-so at such-and-such a meet had us.

The first director to cave in was Rudi Thiel, for years the man in charge of an annual meet in West Berlin. The meet, traditionally one of the biggest and best in Europe, is scheduled for August 18 in the Olympic Stadium where Jesse Owens won his four gold medals in 1936.

As part of a deal to get Rudi to pay me what I wanted, Joe promised I would appear at a July press conference to promote the meet. That is why I had to get to West Berlin today between the meets in Lausanne and Oslo. Rudi joined me and Joe for the trip from Lausanne to Geneva to West Berlin.

At the Geneva airport, I happened to bump into Andy Norman, the director of the meet we missed in Birmingham, England.

"Sorry we couldn't make it," I told Andy.

"I am the one that is sorry," Andy said. "I lost a war with Ollan. I don't like losing to Ollan Cassell."

A few minutes later, Joe and I were surprised when Primo Nebiolo, head of the IAAF, approached us at the check-in line. What a day for coincidences.

Primo pleaded with me and Joe to compete in the World Cup, scheduled for September in Barcelona, Spain. This is a big IAAF event, and Primo said that my absence would hurt. But I am ineligible, having disqualified myself from the U.S. World Cup team by skipping the TAC championships. Trying to get into the World Cup representing Santa Monica would mean a fight with Ollan similar to the Birmingham battle.

"We'll go to Barcelona," Joe told Primo. "But first you have to do something about Ollan Cassell. Get rid of him, and we'll go."

"He is your problem," Primo said. "You voted for him. Well, your people voted for him. So there is nothing I can do."

Guess I won't make plans to be in Barcelona.

The West Berlin press conference was held in a fancy hotel. About thirty reporters and photographers showed. Most of the questions— How many times have you been to Berlin? When is your next competition in Europe? How old are you?—could have been easily answered without going all the way to West Germany. But Joe and I gave Rudi Thiel exactly what he wanted: smiles, patience, and publicity. We were not the only ones to benefit from our deal with Rudi.

He was a winner, too, because his willingness to negotiate put him a step ahead of other European promoters. Rudi deserves some credit for finding a way to have us in town weeks before his meet. Others would have us only a day before their events.

After the press conference, we were driven to the Olympic Stadium because Rudi wanted me to pose for pictures with a group of children. Then we were off, by car, plane, plane, car to meet the rest of the team in Oslo.

June 29
Oslo

Today was the first time this trip we had a chance to work out as a team. With a couple of days off before the next meet, we thought that would be a good idea.

Afterwards, I went to a museum because a television crew wanted to film me there for a profile piece. It was really the first "cultural" thing I've done since touching down in Paris, a nice break from the routine of being in my hotel room, resting, eating, or watching TV with my teammates.

When we returned from the museum, it was back to the room for me. But not before stopping in the hotel gift shop. With a couple of days to kill, I bought three automobile magazines, *USA Today,* and the *International Herald-Tribune.* With CNN showing the same news and feature segments over and over, I needed something else to do.

June 30
Oslo

This was one of those days when nothing is really going on but a lot is happening. There was no meet but plenty of action.

The first stir came courtesy of the hotel fax machine. When I'm on the road, Harold Sanco, my fan club coordinator in Houston, sends me messages and news clips by fax.

There was a knock on my door in the morning, and a clip from the *Houston Post* with the headline, "Canadian sprinter says Kersee unable to coach drug-free athletes." Finally, someone went public with what I had heard about Bob Kersee for so long. The story I got was incomplete, cut off by the fax machine. But what I read was enough.

TORONTO—*A Canadian sprinter said Wednesday she left UCLA Coach Bob Kersee in 1985 because he was unable to coach athletes who did not use drugs.*

The sprinter, Angela Bailey, was testifying at the government inquiry in Canada. Kersee is the husband and coach of Jackie Joyner-Kersee, who won gold medals in the heptathlon and long jump at the Seoul Games. Kersee also used to coach Florence Griffith Joyner.

"He didn't know how to coach me because I was drug-free," said Bailey, who left UCLA after six months. "And I didn't improve."

Bailey's coach, Bryan McKinnon, said the runner was tested after 80 percent of her European races. The coach testified she was repeatedly singled out for drug-testing to protect "dirty" athletes. . . . "She was a well-known clean runner and the results were always going to be the same—negative."

This was the second time in a week I had read an article with new allegations against Kersee or Chuck DeBus, another coach who was close to Kersee. The first article—which arrived by fax in France—quoted Mary Decker Slaney, the best-ever woman distance runner in the United States, as saying that DeBus had approached her years ago to encourage the use of drugs to help her perform.

Joe Douglas did not hide his excitement when I showed him the article about Kersee. "The dam is cracking," he said, pumping his fists in the air. "Get those druggies."

This was nothing compared to the way Joe reacted to the second big event of the day.

Hours later, in the hotel lobby, Joe was fuming.

"I don't give a shit what race Butch Reynolds runs," he was telling meet officials. "Steve Lewis is running the 400. You don't tell me which race my athlete runs."

This was early in the afternoon, and it was the beginning of quite a scene. Joe had just been told that meet director Svein Arne Hansen had put Steve in the 200-meter race instead of the 400, where he belonged. The change had been made because Butch, the world-record holder in the 400, did not want to face Steve, who had been on a tear since winning the 400 in Seoul.

The meet organizers would not budge for Joe.

"Fine, we're leaving," Joe said. He stared at one of the officials,

pointing a finger for emphasis. "Tell Svein to shove it straight up his
ass. We're leaving. All of us, the whole club. No discussion."

Joe does not often lose his temper, but now he was out of control.
He was not going to let a member of his club be bullied by a meet
director, even on foreign soil, and he knew we would all support his
decision, even if that meant we would miss a meet.

The best we could figure, Butch was not ready to run against Steve,
who had dominated the races in Lille and Lausanne. In Europe, the
game of top athletes dodging one another is not unusual. Athletes and
their managers sometimes deal with meet directors to keep certain
people out of their races.

But our club doesn't play that game. We're not scared of anybody,
and dodging is bad for the sport. We were not going to allow one of
our own to be victimized by it. Butch could have his race, but if the
directors' biggest concern was appeasing an insecure athlete, they
could do it without us. Then Svein could try to explain our absence to
thousands of fans in Oslo and to ABC, which was set to televise part
of the meet live to the States.

Joe came straight to my room to tell me what had happened, and
I started packing. Cleve started checking plane reservations out of
Oslo, as soon as possible, and Joe was ready to tell the rest of the team
to pack. But moments later, as Joe was about to leave, there was a
knock on my door.

It was Arne Hautwick, who works with Svein. Arne had come as
peacemaker. He looked very nervous. "I hear we have problems,"
Arne said.

"You bet we have problems," Joe shot back. "You can't kick the
Olympic champion out of the 400. You don't play these games with
me. We're leaving."

"But, Joe . . . There must have been a mistake. We want Steve in
the 400. We thought you wanted him in the 200."

"Of course not."

"Well, okay, then, he's in the 400."

I stopped packing.

Now Arne had someone else to see—Butch Reynolds. But that was
their problem.

We had a little team meeting in my room.

"Just so you know," Joe said, "the whole club just backed up Steve.
Carl didn't hesitate. Nobody hesitated. I kind of lost control. Sorry

about that. But we got what we wanted. They can't tell us what we do."

When Joe speaks, he does so with the support of us all. That is one of the biggest reasons our team is so successful.

July 1
Oslo

My twenty-eighth birthday, which I would have been happy to forget. But that would have been impossible, especially with all the nice things people did for me. Before I ran, I was given a huge barrel of fresh strawberries and more than twenty thousand people in the stadium sang Happy Birthday. That was a lot nicer than what happened next.

I lost in the 100, placing second behind Calvin Smith, who ran 10.05. I ran 10.11. I didn't run too bad a race, but I never felt as loose as I need to be. I felt terrible all the way down the track, and losing put me in a bit of a bad mood. If I have to lose, I would prefer to lose to another Santa Monica guy, not Calvin.

After the controversy over the 400, I was relieved to see Steve Lewis win. He just held on to first by a hundredth of a second, and to make things even better, Butch Reynolds finished second in the 200, which is the event he entered to end the controversy.

Reporters tried to make a big deal out of me losing, but it was not that big a deal. It is still early in the season, and we all have a long way to go before it is over. I repeated my goals for the season—9.9 in the 100, 29 feet in the long jump—and said that losing one race does not change them.

By focusing on one loss, the reporters missed a broader question. After the 1984 Games, I said I would probably retire by my twenty-eighth birthday. Well, here it is, and here I am. I have gotten here by taking one year at a time, never looking too far ahead. The crowds seem to get better every year, more and more reporters are being fair to me, and interest from meet promoters is stronger all the time. So any thoughts of hanging up the spikes have been outweighed by all the positive things that have happened.

The way I felt after losing to Calvin, I was perfectly happy that none of the reporters remembered what I had said years before about retiring. The last thing I needed on my birthday was another reminder that I was getting older.

July 2
Oslo and Stockholm

Fred Lebow, best known for creating the New York Marathon and making it a huge success, is everywhere in Europe. I have seen him at press conferences, hotels, airports, meets. He is here to promote his newest creation, an international track meet scheduled for July 22 in New York City. Fred is still recruiting athletes and struggling to sell tickets, having sold only about a thousand so far. But the New York meet could be the best thing to happen to our sport in the United States in a very long time.

Fred has seen American track stars mobbed in Europe, then ignored back home. At the U.S. Olympic trials last year, he was surprised to see how few fans showed. Fred considers road running a close cousin of track and field, and he does not like to see such a weak cousin. He decided to give track a try in New York, where any event needs big names and a lot of flair before it has a chance.

One of Fred's first moves was to call Joe Douglas. Fred could not pay me or the club our normal fees, he told Joe, but he needed us to try something that might help the sport grow. Joe knew that Fred is a serious promoter, much more professional than the people at TAC. So he wanted to give the New York meet a chance. It would be held at a good time, between halves of the European season. Most American meets are held during the collegiate season, which is really too early in the year for all the athletes but the collegians. The non-collegians are not in shape yet. So Fred's idea made sense.

Joe promised that Santa Monica would participate, and he said we would help promote the meet. Fred was excited and he convinced the board of his New York Road Runners Club to take a chance. At most, the club would lose two hundred thousand dollars on the meet, Lebow promised the board. Then, in private, he conceded that three hundred thousand dollars was a lot more realistic.

But Fred was looking down the road. He wants to help track and field grow and, eventually, he wants to help attract the Olympics to New York.

Not willing to settle for cable television coverage, Fred got a commitment and a hundred-thousand-dollar fee from CBS to broadcast ninety minutes of the meet. He had trouble landing corporate sponsors but ended up with a few, including the *New York Times*, American Airlines, and Mita, a Japanese copier company that pledged three hundred thousand dollars to be the lead sponsor.

Our club has been plugging the meet whenever possible because it is one of the few ideas that has a chance to improve the image of track as a *professional* sport in the States. Fred is talking about an impressive incentive plan, with payments of up to twenty-five thousand dollars for world records, ten thousand for American records, and one thousand for each first-place finisher.

But money is clearly not our only motivation for going to New York. As Steve Lewis told a reporter today, "It shows that Santa Monica is not purposely avoiding meets in the United States. And we don't have to rely on TAC."

"Maybe this will put fire into TAC," Danny Everett said. "The athletes will compete in the U.S. if they are treated right. TAC doesn't really understand that. They put together two-bit meets and expect the athletes to break down their doors to compete."

I'm hoping Fred Lebow will be the right person to help our sport grow. If not, he sure has wasted a lot of time being everywhere in Europe.

July 3
Stockholm

There were two interesting meetings at my hotel today. One was with Bill Shoemaker, the great jockey, who was scheduled to ride tonight in Stockholm at the same time I was scheduled to long-jump. Shoemaker, about to retire at the age of fifty-seven, was nearing the end of a European farewell tour. Promoters of the tour thought it would be nice to get some pictures of the Shoe with me. We spoke for a few minutes while a photographer for a local newspaper clicked away. Then Shoe, the winningest jockey of all time, pound for pound one of the best athletes in history, left in a huge limousine that made him look even smaller than he is, which is tiny.

There was much more substance to the second meeting. Sergei

Bubka, a Soviet who holds the world record in the pole vault, visited Joe Douglas in his hotel room. Sergei had always seemed to be more of an individual than other Soviet athletes, and now he was trying to accomplish the ultimate in independence. He wanted to sign a contract with a shoe company, and he was looking for an American to represent him in negotiations.

Joe could do a great job for Sergei, and Sergei and I could be great for each other. If Sergei were to sign with Joe, that would give Joe incredible leverage in negotiations for both of us. Imagine the media coverage if the best-known Soviet track-and-field athlete and the best-known American teamed up for a promotion or two. The Soviets could call it track-and-field Glasnost. And what if we put Sergei in a Santa Monica uniform? The meeting with Joe was only a beginning, and there certainly were no guarantees, but what an exciting prospect.

On another front, we noted a minor victory when a local newspaper was delivered. My picture was on the front page, and the newly stitched Tag Heuer patch on my shirt was well displayed, just as it was in a newspaper photo we saw at the airport on the way out of Oslo. I was thrilled with the publicity for Tag Heuer.

At the stadium, I felt fine, ready to compete, but my first few jumps were terrible. Larry Myricks took the lead with a jump of 8.39 meters (27 feet, 6¼ inches) on his second attempt. My first four jumps were so bad—the best was only 8.28 meters (27 feet, 1¾ inches)—that I took out a tape measure to make sure I had properly marked off a check point on my approach. I had. It was 34 feet from my check point to the board, precisely the distance I wanted. I was just jumping terribly.

The fifth jump was a little better, 8.32 meters (27 feet, 3½ inches), but still not enough to win. With one jump left, I was in danger of losing for the first time since 1981. Not since 1984 had I been trailing in an outdoor meet going into the last jump. All these people had come to see me—there were almost twenty-five thousand people in the stadium—and they were about to see me fail for the first time in sixty long-jump competitions.

I put my head down and told myself, I'm not going to let this happen. After all these years, all these jumps, I could not let myself lose to a jump of 8.39 meters. If Larry was going to beat me, he would have to *beat* me, not just make an average jump on a night when I was struggling.

The fans clapped in unison as I stood at the end of the runway before my last jump. My goal for the night had been 8.50 (27 feet, 10½ inches). Forget the lousy jumps, I told myself. Just jump the 8.50.

I landed in the sand with a jump of 8.53 meters (just under 28 feet), and the crowd exploded. I hurried out of the pit, smiled, and waved to the crowd, relieved even though Larry had one jump left. I knew he would choke. And he did. Larry fouled, stepping over the board, and it was time to celebrate.

"I have nine long-jump lives, and that was about my seventh," I told Cleve as I passed him at the end of my victory lap.

In the press conference, I stressed that this had been a great crowd and a great tour of Europe. The meets were a lot of fun because the fans everywhere had been so supportive of me and the club. After seeing such a small crowd at the TAC championships in Houston, it was so nice to compete again where people loved our sport.

July 4
Stockholm

At one o'clock in the morning I should have been one of two places: out with my teammates to celebrate the end of our last meet or in my hotel room packing for the trip home. Instead, I was in a photography studio, filling a glass with raw eggs, as if I were going to drink them like Sylvester Stallone did in the movie *Rocky*.

As part of my deal with promoters of the Stockholm meet, I had to film a commercial before leaving Sweden. This could have been done at a normal hour. But the sooner I finished, the sooner I could be home. So I said, "Let's go for it. We'll shoot all night if we need to, as long as I can make it to a plane in the morning."

The egg scene was part of a commercial for a new high-speed train that was going to be introduced in Sweden. In the commercial, I was supposed to be working out extra hard because I had heard about the new train and did not want it to be faster than me.

Just a couple of hours after winning the long jump, I was back in my Santa Monica warm-up suit, fake sweat from a makeup bottle spotting my chest and face, pulling eggs out of a refrigerator while cameras rolled. Luckily, I never actually had to drink the eggs, just make it look like I was going to.

Then we left the studio for a few scenes on the city streets. At this time of year, it is dark only about two hours a night in Stockholm, so we were able to shoot most of the night. I jogged up steps, down a sidewalk, up a hill, and I did push-ups on the concrete outside a subway station. The toughest part of the shoot was staying awake. Second toughest was chasing away pigeons and drunks who interfered with the shot outside the subway.

One of the crew members took me back to the hotel at 7:00 A.M. so I could sleep for an hour before another car came to take me to the airport. I was exhausted, but thrilled to be going home. As Joe Douglas says, once I can smell the airport, I'm like a horse heading for the barn. There is no stopping me.

SEVENTEEN

≡

The Professional Amateur

THERE ARE not many uses for a dictionary on the track circuit. But if people would look at one for a minute, just to check two words, we could quickly do away with the myth of amateurism.

My dictionary says an "amateur" is "a person who engages in some art, science, sport, etc. for the pleasure of it rather than for money . . . a person who does something without professional skill." A "professional" is "a person who engages in some art, sport, etc. for money, especially for his livelihood, rather than as a hobby . . . a person who does something with great skill."

Now, how would you define a track athlete who spends his or her entire year training and competing, is paid to appear in meets, paid bonuses for good performances, paid to wear certain shoes, paid to say good things about corporate sponsors? Unless you are totally naive and incredibly ignorant, or unless you have reason to twist the truth, "professional" would have to be your answer. Time after time, though, the people who run our sport call it "amateur," and they continue to do what they can to convince the public of that. What a sham—"trick or fraud . . . a hypocritical action, deceptive appearance"—and I get tired of hearing it.

Maybe Olympic athletes were really amateurs back in, say, the 1930s. An athlete would get up at five in the morning to train, then go to work, then train some more at the end of the day. The hard-working, driven amateur made for great Olympic stories. All you would hear about was dedication and sacrifice. The stories of the greatest Olympic champions would make you feel like crying. Well, those days were long gone before I was even born. Now, if you hear the real stories of Olympic champions, the reason you're crying is because you don't make near the money we do.

To consistently be the best in the world at almost anything, especially an athletic event, you have to be older than twenty-one or twenty-two. You need to train or study or practice or do whatever you do for long enough to reach your potential, or at least approach it. Of course, there are exceptions: the incredibly gifted athlete who bursts on the scene, breaking records before he even realizes the impact of what he is doing, the kid genius who shocks his teachers by knowing more than they do. But for the most part, to be the best in a track or field event, you have to compete once you've finished college, and you can't do that unless you can earn a living at it.

The people in charge of track and field, meet promoters and the leaders of national and international governing bodies or federations, have selfish reasons to perpetuate the myth of amateurism. Especially the leaders of governing bodies and federations. They want to make as much money as possible for themselves, and one way to do that is to keep what they can away from us. The longer they can hold on to the public perception of "amateurism," the longer they can keep negotiations secret, and as long as the system of payments remains secret, the more chance they have to keep the payments down. I'm not complaining about *my* payments, but for the vast majority of the athletes all this secrecy and hypocrisy results in exploitation.

With "amateurism," the governing bodies and meet promoters can continue to pretend that athletes don't have certain rights, like the right to wear a sponsor's logo on a uniform, the right to a written contract for each meet, the right to being treated like a person, not just another piece of meat moving from country to country, city to city, filling stadiums for the benefit of meet promoters.

What we have in track is a basic conflict between the way the leaders of the sport view athletes and the way athletes view athletes, or, at least, the way athletes ought to view athletes. Unfortunately, even the athletes don't all see things the same way, and that helps keep us down.

The leaders think of us as pawns in an amateur sport. They want to push us around in their game, fighting to maintain control every step of the way because—surprise, surprise—control equals money. The top athletes see our sport as entertainment, and we are the entertainers. We should be treated accordingly and should be paid our market value. The problem with this approach is that it divides the athletes. Market value of the stars is much greater than it is for people just filling lanes in a race. The stars are the ones drawing sponsors and crowds. People finishing seventh and eighth in a race don't appreciate being paid almost nothing when winners are getting big money, but they have to understand. Some athletes talk about forming a union and being treated as equals. But that will never work, not if we think of ourselves as individual entertainers out for our market value. That's how the best athletes think of themselves, and rightly so.

When Ben Johnson and I were battling on the track before the 1988 Olympics, we were definitely entertainers, not just athletes. Meet promoters treated us like entertainers, paid us like entertainers, and the other athletes didn't appreciate that. A bunch of them had a meeting in Zurich to complain to each other, but there wasn't much they could do. Nothing much ever came of the athletes' get-together in Zurich.

Maybe the best way to think of myself is as a "professional amateur," not that such a term exists, but it might be the most accurate description of what I have become in a sport that wants to keep fooling the public. *The Professional Amateur.* I like that. *Professional* because I am engaging in sport for money. Track is my livelihood, not a hobby. *Amateur* because the people in charge of our sport want you, the public, to think we compete only "for the pleasure of it," and so many of you still believe that. *The Professional Amateur* covers both the reality and the myth.

Sports fans don't know what to think of track anymore, so I get a lot of questions. Is it amateur or professional? Professional, I say. You're allowed to take money? Well, kind of. Doesn't someone else get your money? Don't you only get training expenses, or living expenses, or some kind of expenses? Actually, a system has been developed to make the public think that all our money is withheld in order to keep us "pure," but the system is a joke. It doesn't work because it doesn't make sense. A lot of athletes ignore it, others make it look like they are staying within the system but abuse it.

TAC requires its members to report all money they earn from track. That would include endorsement money, payments for special events, appearance fees and bonuses from meets—everything. We have piles of forms to fill out, asking for details and amounts, and where the money is going. It is supposed to go into a trust fund, where the money is to be held until the athlete retires. But the rules governing trust funds make the system laughable. In reality, the people at the Internal Revenue Service are the only ones to whom you have to report your income.

Once the money goes into a TAC trust, it is controlled by a trustee picked by the athlete. The trustee, usually a banker or broker, tries to follow TAC rules, but they are complicated enough to cause confusion and vague enough to allow a variety of loopholes. The trustee can put money in traditional investments (stocks, bonds, CDs, mutual funds) without consulting TAC. But if you want to make a more complicated investment, want to buy a house or car or something, you must get approval from TAC to take money from the trust fund. More often than not, TAC will approve a proposal if it is thoroughly presented and documented. In 1989, I bought an expensive Ferrari this way, as an investment.

The athlete can also take out "cost of living" expenses. That is where the rules are really loose. There is supposed to be a cap on these expenses, based on different formulas devised by TAC. But how do you determine what cost is a "cost of living" and what is not? In my case, the cost of living is pretty high. I have a big house in one of the nicest sections of Houston. I employ several people. I travel a lot. I have to maintain my cars (a jeep, a Porsche, and the Ferrari). I'm a professional amateur. Someone enters my house for the first time, he jokingly says, "What a shame, the way you poor amateurs are forced to live."

Athletes in the Santa Monica club have trust funds, and we're very careful about what we do with them. We have good reason to be careful. It doesn't take a genius to figure out that TAC doesn't like us. We've been very critical of the organization, so we don't want to take a chance on something that might get us in trouble. TAC would love to nail us, so we have to cover ourselves on any little thing that Ollan Cassell and his buddies might try to use against us.

But a lot of athletes don't even have trust funds. They completely ignore the rules. There are Olympic athletes who make good money and take it home without reporting it, and TAC doesn't really care. All TAC cares about is public image. Does John Q. Public still believe our athletes are amateurs? Yes? Then let's not cause a stir. If trust funds help the public think of the athletes as amateurs, that's all that matters. What actually happens with the trust funds is not all that important. Again, creating a myth is the important thing for TAC. Reality doesn't matter.

Some major loopholes in the system have never been addressed. What if an athlete retires, empties his trust fund and spends the money, then changes his mind and wants to compete again? That could happen very easily, and how could anybody stop it from happening? Nobody could, but that's fine. Loopholes don't damage the TAC myth.

There are plenty of other ways to get around the rules or ignore them. The simplest way is to keep TAC in the dark. A lot of athletes can get away with that, just pocketing cash without reporting it.

Last year, not long after I boycotted the national championships, causing media problems for TAC, Ollan sent one of his workers to see the banker who handles my trust fund. Alvin Chriss, Ollan's right-hand man, never told us exactly what he was trying to find. In fact, I didn't know until much later that he had looked at my records. Alvin and Ollan must not have found anything wrong with what they saw because Alvin told David Greifinger that there would be no follow-up.

Still, we didn't appreciate the way TAC went behind my back, inspecting my records in Houston while I was competing in Europe. David and Joe Douglas were furious when they heard about this, so David did what he often does when he is upset, especially when he is upset with TAC. He called to complain to Frank Greenberg, the TAC president, then wrote him a letter.

"First," David wrote, "Alvin grossly violated Carl's right to privacy, no matter what motivations or concerns he had for rummaging through Carl's financial records. . . . Secondly, I am told by people I can normally rely on that Ollan is going to great efforts to investigate Carl's financial affairs worldwide to establish possible [trust fund] violations. I know specifically that Ollan himself or through Alvin has contacted numerous meet promoters here and overseas to ask questions and gather information about Carl's finances. . . . I fear we may be witness to a heavy-handed response to Carl's numerous criticisms of Ollan and of TAC, and his failure to participate in the national championships. Carl and Joe share my concerns. I truly hope I am wrong, but I fear I am not."

The irony here was that TAC tried to use the trust fund—one of the weakest aspects of its amateur myth—against me. First, TAC distorts images for the public by holding up mirrors and talking about amateurism, then Ollan tries to use his creations against me. He must have been so disappointed when he looked at my records and discovered that, as hypocritical as his rules are, he could not find anything in the records to nail me.

The people who put on track meets, especially European promoters, profit more than anybody from the "amateur" label. It is a license to treat us like we're nothing, just cattle passing through town or kids on a summer tour. Don't worry about the athletes. Just give them some meal tickets, a small hotel room, a crowded bus. They'll show up at the track and run their hearts out for us. Thousands of fans will pay to see them, we'll collect as much money as we can and we'll give a little to the athletes—secretly, of course. Then we'll send them to the next stop on the circuit.

It is a system that leaves most athletes with little power. If a promoter decides to ignore a deal, that's the way it goes. It is a system that requires some creativity and boldness. Without either, you get screwed. With Joe Douglas and the Santa Monica Track Club, you have both. Joe has fought and fought and fought for his club, and as a result, we are treated like professionals, not amateurs. As Joe likes to say, all we have ever wanted is dignity and respect. For years, we had to demand it. Now, we command it. We have too many of the top athletes to be ignored, so promoters have to give us what we deserve.

We get the plane tickets we want. We travel by van or car, not crowded bus, and we stay in nice hotels. We don't wait in money lines because our fees are paid before we compete, not after. Only performance bonuses are paid after the meet, and even then we don't wait in line. Joe and David Greifinger make an appointment to see the money man, and they meet. And none of this is taken for granted;

it is guaranteed. We see to that by signing a contract before we agree to run in a meet. Otherwise, promoters will play games with you, and guess who ends up on the short end? We learned some hard lessons before we learned how to fight back.

We've had promoters try to weasel out of bonuses they promised to pay. We've had them offer certain fees to get us somewhere, then try to cut them once we're there. We've had them try to keep one of us out of a certain race, usually to protect another athlete who said he would compete only if so-and-so is not in the race. When any of these things happen, the Santa Monica athletes and coaches band together and do the best we can to come out of it without being ripped off. In the long run, things usually work out for us.

One of the classic cases started in 1987 with Andy Norman, the British promoter. After the World Championships in Rome, Andy wanted our whole club for a meet in London, and he was willing to pay our fees. But he would only let me run the 200, not the 100. This was during the period when Ben Johnson was dodging me, and Andy had promised Ben that he would not have to face me. I said, "No, I'm ready to run the 100." I was not going to let Ben dodge. If Andy wouldn't let me in the 100, I wouldn't run at all. He was offended, asking me who I thought I was, telling him what to do. But this was not a popularity contest. It was business, and I didn't appreciate Ben trying to dodge, or the promoter trying to make a deal on his behalf.

In protest, our entire club pulled out of the meet. Sticking together is the only way to survive. The next time Andy wanted us back for another meet, he had to pay more than usual—a "fine" is what we called it. Andy got the message, realizing it was not good business to push us around, and now we have a pretty good relationship.

There have been other bad experiences, other fines, but these days, things go pretty well for the Santa Monica club. Joe Douglas and David Greifinger make sure that we are treated like professional amateurs.

For years, agents and managers of track athletes have complained here and there about various financial aspects of our sport, but there has been little, if any, formal discussion about how to address the biggest problems. Part of the difficulty is that agents and managers have little in common. Each tries to make changes that will benefit his athlete or his country, but not necessarily the sport as a whole.

And it's easy to see why that happens. The problems of an agent representing Kenyan long-distance runners probably have nothing to do with problems faced by the manager of America's top sprinters. The problems of someone from a shoe company who is making deals for a college athlete have nothing to do with the problems a Soviet pole-vaulter faces when he tries to cash in on his talent and hard work.

Basically, the impact of agents and managers as a group has been limited by the diversity of interests they serve. As a result, some of the biggest issues in our sport are not properly addressed. When issues are raised, it is usually the result of an individual agent or manager complaining to an individual meet promoter or governing body, and that doesn't do much. No matter how badly an athlete is wanted by a meet promoter or a coach putting together a national team, the power of an individual is limited.

That goes a long way to explain why the myth of amateurism still exists, why we are not officially considered professional athletes, and why, as a result, many athletes are not treated properly. The best way to make changes is to band together. Unity is a requirement, as my parents learned during their days in Alabama and I learned from them as soon as I was old enough to understand the meaning of their experiences.

There are several reasons why a track-and-field athletes' union would not work the way unions work in some sports. First of all, track is truly an individual sport. It is impossible to get track athletes to agree on almost anything. Many are too selfish, some too stupid to understand the value of working together. Plus, the average track athlete comes and goes so quickly, how would you convince him that a union makes sense? By the time he realizes what is going on in our sport, he is out of it, looking for a real job.

Agents and managers might be the only people with enough clout to force true professionalism on the people who don't want it. In the short run, an agent or manager has only the power of his athlete or group of athletes. But the agents and managers are usually around longer than the athletes. Most survive generations of athletes, so they are older and wiser than most of their clients. Year after year, meet promoters and governing bodies rely on them to deliver athletes, so agents and managers are able to maintain some stability. Also, they represent a mixture of athletes: old and young, stars and newcomers, people competing in a variety of events. Their voices must be heard. Their views can be ignored for only so long.

That is why I think one of the most positive steps ever toward professionalism came during the 1989 Grand Prix circuit in Europe. In a series of meetings—one in Germany, one in Belgium, one in Monte Carlo—the top agents and managers discussed problems and plans. They established a new group, calling themselves the International Association of Athlete Representatives, or IAAR, and on the day of the Grand Prix finals, they released a list of purposes and goals that would overhaul our sport. The ultimate goal would be "a free and open market" for athletes. In other words, no more myth of amateurism.

In comparison to what they ended up doing, the motivation for agents and managers getting together when they did was pretty small-scale. Some of them were pissed off at a meet in Zurich when they were told at the last minute that certain athletes would not be able to participate. Sorry, meet promoters said, but there's nothing we can do about it. There simply isn't enough room for everybody in certain events.

Zurich is one of the biggest stops on the summer circuit—biggest in the number of fans, biggest in budget, and, therefore, in money available for appearance fees and bonuses. But some athletes who had gone all the way to Switzerland for the meet would leave empty-handed. They didn't appreciate that, and neither did their agents and managers.

This was not an unusual problem. Stuff like this happens all the time to athletes who are good enough to make it to Europe, but not good enough to be wanted at every stop on the circuit. Politics often comes into play when a meet promoter is cutting down his fields, and some athletes get screwed. The difference this time was that agents and managers were going to do something about it. Some were upset about what happened in Zurich, others had their own horror stories and were ready to share their frustrations. The time seemed to be right for change.

The first meeting was at a hotel in Cologne, West Germany, just before a Grand Prix meet there. Half a dozen agents were involved, including a few who represent some of the best-known American track athletes. David Greifinger was there for the Santa Monica club. Brad Hunt, a Washington-based agent for Butch Reynolds and others, was there. A couple of shoe-company representatives attended. And Tony Campbell was there for Olympic sprinters Calvin Smith and Dennis Mitchell, among others. (After the 1988 Olympics, Dennis had switched back from Russ Rogers to Tony.)

Initial talk was about lane assignments and seedings at the Zurich meet, and how similar problems could be avoided. But before long, the discussion moved into broader issues and the agents were talking about the need for "A Declaration of Independence."

David made a list of demands to be considered. Written contracts for every athlete. No more waiting in line outside hotel rooms to be paid. All fees paid in advance. Minimum standards for travel and hotels. No pestering from federations. We represent athletes, not federations, the agents agreed. Technical meetings at all meets, so lane assignments and seedings can be challenged. Appearance money at all Grand Prix events.

The agents decided to meet again in Brussels, about a week later. Meanwhile, David and a few others would talk to other agents and come up with a list of things they might agree on. Then David would write a document, they would vote to approve it, and it would be released to the press and the various track federations. Getting these agents to agree would not be simple, but there would be enough common ground for the plan to work. Personal feelings had to be put aside. For example, people who didn't like our club, people who resented the special treatment we get, would have to overlook those feelings for now.

As David told the others in Cologne, "Forget petty jealousy toward a group that is doing better. We all need to rise, not lower ourselves to the lowest common denominator."

After their initial, secret meeting, the agents were ready to be a little more open about what they wanted to do. Athletes, coaches, agents, reporters, and others connected to the track circuit were staying at the Brussels Sheraton Hotel. A huge ballroom was being used as a dining room for everyone on the circuit, and outside the dining area a bulletin board was set up to post the current Grand Prix point standings. Each meet in the Grand Prix awards points based on the order of finish, and the leading point-getters are invited to the finals, which were now a week away. So everyone was checking the board, where seventeen pages of standings were neatly tacked.

At the bottom of the board, handwritten in purple marking pen, was a sign that said, "Managers Meeting, 10:00 A.M., Second Floor." Word got around quickly that something big was going to happen, and more than twenty managers, agents, representatives, whatever you want to call them, showed up. A sheet of paper was passed around, so everyone could sign in, list his address and phone number for future contact. Now the group was a lot more diverse, much more complete than the small gathering in Cologne.

There was a lot of power in the room now, definitely enough to make an international stand that would get some attention. Twenty-two people signed the list. There were more Americans than any other nationality. There were several British agents, some from Nigeria, Holland, Spain, Italy, Germany, and a few other places. Very international. David Greifinger strengthened his position as one of the leaders, and he was joined this time by Joe Douglas, which gave Santa Monica a strong presence. John Nubani, a lawyer who lives in Pittsburgh and represents Roger Kingdom, also emerged as a leader of the group. Roger is an Olympic champion, and in Zurich he had set a world record, running the 110-meter high hurdles in 12.92 seconds, so Nubani's stock was higher than ever before.

There was only one American college coach in the room—Russ Rogers, the former Fairleigh Dickinson coach and former Olympic coach who was now at Ohio State. I was a little surprised when I heard that Russ was there, and that he had signed the list, because college coaches are not allowed to act as agents for athletes. NCAA rules prohibit them from collecting money for athletes. But I guess Russ wasn't concerned about the NCAA. He had been acting as an agent for years without being bothered, so why should he worry? Plus, he is tight with Ollan Cassell, the executive director of TAC. Maybe that puts him in a position to play above the rules.

After two hours, there was enough agreement on enough points for David to start drafting a document. None of the agents said much to reporters waiting outside the closed-door meeting. The message was clear, though. Something is going to happen. Stay tuned. See you in Monte Carlo.

When we got there a week later, on September 1, David borrowed a hotel typewriter and went to work. He spoke to Joe Douglas, Nubani, and a few more of the most prominent agents as he went along, trying to make sure nothing he was writing would cause any division.

In a hallway off the lobby of the Loew's hotel in Monte Carlo, about twenty-five agents pulled chairs into a circle. It was the afternoon of the Grand Prix finals, one of the biggest days of the year for the top officials in international track and field, people like Primo Nebiolo and Ollan Cassell. But the agents were working hard to steal some of the show. David presented his draft, most points were voted up, a few were voted down, and the document was approved. The IAAR was born, and people started talking.

"We're the only professional sport that is not officially recognized as a professional sport," David told a reporter. "Track and field is where tennis was 20 years ago. It's time for the rules of the sport to catch up with the reality."

The IAAR's "Declaration of Formation" listed eleven purposes. Some were broad enough to allow future interpretation, some were bold enough to cause an instant stir. One of the most-talked about purposes was the elimination of trust funds. "If you eliminate that restriction on the athlete, you'd have more cooperation," Nubani said. "Trust funds are not necessary anymore. They give the public a false impression that the athletes somehow are still amateur."

The agents said they wanted to protect the rights of athletes to compete and to earn compensation in a free and open market. No restrictions on what logos can be worn on a uniform. No restrictions on sponsorship deals. No outside interference.

The agents also called for "acceptable standards of treatment for athletes and athlete representatives," which would cover a lot of things David wrote down at that first meeting in Cologne. Acceptable food and lodging. Transportation to and from meets. A technical meeting. The elimination of money lines. Payment of guarantees in advance of all meets. Written agreements for the participation of all athletes in all meets. Basically, all the things that our club had been demanding and getting while other athletes, coaches, and agents complained about us getting special treatment. As David had said, we were looking to improve the situations of as many athletes as possible, not striving for the lowest common denominator.

Of course, IAAF officials did not like any of this, especially when agents circulated their declaration to reporters at the stadium in Monte Carlo.

"Any group of private individuals has the right to express an opinion," said Jon Wigley, IAAF director of competitions. "But I don't know with what authority this group is speaking. The declaration runs against the principle of the IAAF and leaves no room for discussion."

Typical IAAF reaction. The IAAF wanted to focus on the track, where some big races were taking place. But some people were distracted. They were more interested in talking about the future of our sport, and they were saying it is now. It was time to acknowledge the Professional Amateur, but time to start calling him simply a professional.

EIGHTEEN

≡

Ben Again

IN LATE September 1989, on the way back from a meet in India, I heard that another drug scandal was breaking. First, I heard bits and pieces from a reporter at the hotel in New Delhi. Then I heard more at the airport. Then I called Cleve in Houston, and he had heard a few things, but we weren't sure exactly what was going on. Something about a German magazine. Something about steroids. Something that might include me. That's all I knew.

It was just short of a year since Ben Johnson had tested positive in Seoul. The Dubin Inquiry in Canada was winding down, TAC was supposedly about to announce the beginning of its random drug-testing program—finally—and now there was a new bomb coming, as if track and field needed more controversy. It seemed like steroids would be in the news forever. There was always going to be something else.

When I landed in New York, I called Cleve to see if he had heard anything more, and he had. A television reporter had faxed him an English translation of what had appeared in a German magazine called *Stern*. I had been accused of using drugs back in 1982. *What?!* I said. *Cleve, what are you talking about?*

The entire story was based on a former sprinter named Darrell Robinson. Darrell had been at the University of Houston for a few weeks in 1982, but I didn't know much about him. All I knew was that Darrell never went to class, didn't get along with Coach Tellez, and left school before most people even knew he was there.

Florence Griffith Joyner was also named as a drug user by Robinson. In a debate on NBC's "Today" show, she pointed out that Robinson had been well paid for his opinions, and the two of them went at it on national television. My favorite part of the show (which I later saw on tape) was when Florence called Darrell "a compulsive, crazy, lying lunatic." Darrell was stunned, looked ridiculous, and didn't know what to say.

The magazine story was the long tale—a fairy tale, as far as I was concerned—of an admitted drug-user who wanted everyone to believe that a lot of other people were also into drugs. Darrell claimed that he had been to my apartment in 1982, and had seen me with another athlete, Kermit Bowers, just after Kermit had injected me with a "whitish liquid." Darrell said he thought that the liquid was testosterone, a steroid.

I wasn't the only one at Houston fingered by Darrell. He also said he was in a meeting with Coach Tellez, me, and other members of the track team when Coach T handed out blue pills—again, steroids, Darrell claimed.

None of this was true. I have never been injected with a steroid, or injected with anything, by Kermit Bowers. I have never been injected with a steroid by anybody. I have never tried steroids—not the type you inject, not the type you take in pills, none, period. And Coach Tellez is totally against steroids. He never gave his athletes pills, and never would.

This whole story reminded me of the time in 1983 when the newspaper in Oslo reported that I had tested positive for drugs. It was a ridiculous rumor then, and it was a ridiculous story now. But how should I respond? Or should I? Everybody knew who I was and what I stood for. For years I had been the number one anti-drug spokesman in my sport, and now I was being accused of using a drug.

The allegations against Florence and the people around her were even more sensational than the stuff about me and Houston. Darrell said that in 1988, the same year she had won three gold medals in Seoul and broken all sorts of records, Florence had given him two thousand dollars to get her some human growth hormone. HGH, as it's called, is meant for children with growth problems, but has been used by some athletes as a performance-enhancing drug. Darrell also said that UCLA track coach Bob Kersee had told him how to use steroids and gave him two kinds of steroid tablets, Anavar and Dianabol.

I don't know about the truth of what Darrell said about Florence and Kersee, but given the fact that he was lying about me, Coach Tellez, and others at Houston, it is impossible for me to give Darrell much credibility. Kersee, Coach Tellez, and everyone else mentioned in the story were just as quick as me and Florence in saying that it was nothing but a pack of lies. A few of us talked about the possibility of a lawsuit, but we weren't sure if that would be worth the time and effort. Who would we sue, Darrell? He's in Canada. *Stern* magazine? We don't know anything about libel laws in Germany. Our attorneys would have to look into all this.

Meanwhile, I discussed the situation with Joe Douglas, and I decided to issue a brief statement. First I said that Darrell needed psychiatric help. Then I stressed that this would not affect my views about steroids and my fight against drugs. I would continue to speak out whenever possible against drugs, and I would continue to push for an independent agency to test for drugs and conduct hearings when necessary.

A lot of reporters used my quote about Darrell's need for psychiatric help, but that was all they used from me. Most of the stories focused more on Florence than me, maybe because she had appeared on television with Darrell, but I think there was another reason. This was the chance reporters had been waiting for. They had been waiting to go after Florence.

For more than a year now, a lot of people in our sport had been saying that Florence used drugs. A lot of people on the track circuit considered that to be common knowledge, and a lot of reporters had been told that Florence used drugs. In fact, at one time or another most of the reporters who regularly cover track had told me that they had information implicating Florence. They just couldn't get the story past their editors and lawyers and into print.

Still, no matter what people thought about Florence, there were some major problems with the *Stern* article. I wasn't really surprised by that, considering that this was the same magazine that had paid huge money for the rights to "Hitler's diaries," then published them only to learn that they were fakes. The magazine had been fooled. This steroids story could turn out to be equally embarrassing.

Stern could not have done much digging into what Darrell told them. Nobody from the magazine even called me to ask about what Darrell was saying. If someone had, I would have told him that Darrell was lying, and would have offered some details to impeach his credibility. First on my list would have been Darrell's claim about what he supposedly saw in my apartment. He could not have seen anything happen in my apartment because he never visited there during his short stay at the University of Houston.

Next, I would have discussed Darrell's claim that Coach Tellez handed out steroid pills in a team meeting. Again, Darrell's desire to sell a story led to some major distortion of facts. Darrell said that he was with a bunch of us—Kirk Baptiste, Anthony Ketchum, Cletus Clark, Mark McNeil, and me—in Coach T's office for a meeting before the season. Coach Tellez supposedly talked about plans for the season and discussed proper nutrition. Then, according to Darrell's fairy tale, Coach T took a plastic bag containing small, blue pills from his filing cabinet and handed them out, telling us each to take two pills every night after dinner. Darrell said there must have been fifty to seventy-five pills in the bag. Well, I was never even in a team meeting with Darrell. I was finished competing for Houston by the time he arrived.

Sports Illustrated, in its coverage of the Stern article, delivered another blow to Darrell's credibility. According to Darrell, Florence Griffith Joyner had paid $2,000 for a 10-cc vial of HGH. But manufacturers of HGH told Sports Illustrated that they sell the drug in 5-cc vials, not 10-cc vials. Looked like Darrell hadn't done his homework, and Stern hadn't either. Sports Illustrated also said that two 5-cc vials of HGH sell for about $350. Darrell would have been doing some serious marking up if he had gotten $2,000 from Florence.

It would have been so simple for Stern to examine Darrell's story before printing it, and if the magazine had bothered to check the story (or had wanted to check it), it would have uncovered plenty of these little inconsistencies in Darrell's story. All the reporters had to do was make a few phone calls, and think a little. But they didn't do either. The goal was to publish the story, not find a way to check it out.

I've had my problems with American reporters, but this reached a new low for journalistic standards. At least an American reporter would have called to hear my side before printing the story. Well, I think *most* American reporters would have called. I couldn't believe that *Stern* wrote an entire story like this based on one source without calling any of the people implicated.

Another interesting tidbit popped up soon after the story came out: Charlie Francis, who had coached Ben Johnson and other drug-users and had been one of the key witnesses at the Dubin Inquiry, was somehow involved with Robinson. They were friends. Francis had called reporters in Canada and the United States to make sure they had the *Stern* story, and he had driven Darrell to the Toronto television studio for his "Today" show interview.

Hearing that Charlie was involved didn't surprise me at all. For years, Charlie had been very open about the fact that he didn't like me, didn't like Joe Douglas, didn't like Coach Tellez—and he would do just about anything to hurt us, anything to make us look bad.

Charlie had been using a machine-gun approach to talking about steroids, spraying the whole sport with assorted accusations. He wanted the public to believe that the whole sport was dirty, especially the best-known athletes. That was his way of saving face. If the whole sport looked bad, he and Ben would not look so bad.

There was no way for me to know just how involved Charlie had been in Darrell's story. But I was definitely suspicious.

The *Stern* story led to some interesting conversations behind the scenes, and one of the leaders of The Athletics Congress slipped, saying a lot more than he should have. The week after the *Stern* story, Alvin Chriss, the attorney who had inspected my trust fund records for Ollan Cassell, had a few drinks and ended up on the telephone, telling David Greifinger what he really thought. Alvin started by saying he was calling in response to David's complaint about his inspection of my bank records. But Alvin didn't wait long to change the subject to drugs. He admitted that certain people, including some at TAC, were out to get me and the Santa Monica club. The Darrell Robinson article would be a good start, and he said that there would be more. There is "big trouble" ahead for Carl, Alvin told David. Alvin cussed out David, coming up with some pretty creative combinations of words, and made several threats during this long phone call.

Alvin went on and on, and David took notes the whole time. David filled me in right after the first phone call, and after several more phone calls with Alvin that week, David sent me a long, detailed memo describing what had been said. Alvin's language and tone were just as important as the message he delivered. TAC's leaders couldn't stand me and would say or do almost anything to get rid of me.

Here are some excerpts from David's thirteen-page memo about the Alvin Chriss phone calls.

On September 26, 1989, I sent a fax to Frank Greenberg to register my objections to Alvin Chriss' visit earlier this summer to Carl Lewis' bank to inspect records. . . . That evening, at about 8:00, I got a call from Alvin. He gave me his views—and a whole lot more.

Alvin exuded hostility from the outset. I told him I needed to turn off my television; he told me to turn off my tape recorder as well. I told him I didn't have one; he responded by telling me that he didn't believe me and called me a "fuck."

The initial purpose of Alvin's call was for him to voice his extreme displeasure with my letter. Alvin's position was that he only inspected Carl's TACTRUST records, and that he had every right—even an obligation—to do so under Carl's signed TACTRUST agreement. Alvin gave his views while using a barrage of expletives, the like and scope of which I have never heard in my 32 years of existence, in describing me, my family, Carl, Joe Douglas and the Santa Monica Track Club. . . . Among the names Alvin would call me were "Cunt," "Fucking Miserable Prick," "Dumbfuck," and "Bastard."

Alvin's demeanor was a level of craziness above the controlled rage that he usually applies in confrontations. Alvin mentioned that he had had a couple of drinks. . . . The words flowed, and Alvin repeated most of his lines several times.

I expressed my views on Alvin's bank visit. . . . Whether or not we have rules of amateurism, people have a right to privacy in their financial affairs.

Alvin then dropped this bomb:

"Make sure your man's clean because I'm going to nail him."

I reacted with absolute outrage, and told Alvin I would quote him on that. Alvin dared me to, but then after about a minute of further obscenities, Alvin hesitated, and demanded I read the quote back to make sure I got it just right. I did, and Alvin told me that was not what he said. Rather, he claimed his words were, "Make sure your man's clean, because if he's not, I'm going to nail him," and "If he ain't clean, he ain't clean."

Amidst a fresh volley of expletives, I told Alvin that I would hold him to his first statement. What ensued was an escalating barrage of obscenity-laced threats against me, Joe Douglas, the Santa Monica Track Club, and especially Carl Lewis.

Alvin told me he would deny making the first statement and that I got it wrong. I told Alvin I wasn't deaf and that I had heard him loud and clear. He also challenged me to take our differences before the TAC Board of Directors . . . and that the worst thing I could do to him would be to get him fired. He pointed out that he could do a lot worse to me, and especially to Carl.

Alvin accused me of opposing TAC's fight against drugs. I responded with utter incredulity. As usual, I asked for specifics, and was treated to the standard round of expletives.

Alvin then indicated to me that the Darrell Robinson story . . . was only the start of things for Carl. I tried to get specifics from Alvin, but this was like pulling teeth. I achieved only marginal success.

Alvin repeated that big trouble lay ahead for Carl in the drug scandals soon to play across the United States. When I asked him to be specific and tell me what allegations and troubles he knew of, Alvin obstinately told me he would not tell me, adding, "Don't ask me to identify your fucking troubles, you cunt."

I did not respond to the insult, except to make a note of it.

Alvin indicated to me that TAC, and he in particular, could still save Carl from this drug mess. (I still didn't have any idea what he was talking about!) Alvin added that if something weren't done, Carl would be ruined, "would suffer the same fate as FloJo," and, also, my way of life would be ruined. In retrospect, Alvin's reference to FloJo is most intriguing; I wish I had had the presence of mind to ask him what he meant.

Again, when I expressed my doubts and asked for specifics, Alvin called me a "fucking miserable prick." Alvin repeated this several times for emphasis, and told me to write it down. I did.

Alvin constantly vacillated between stating that TAC would simply stand by and let Carl go down the toilet and halfway inviting me to get down on my knees and ask for deliverance. Alvin said specifically that in the near future I would be calling him for his help. He would not call me again. When I called, it would be on HIS terms, not mine.

I continued constantly to ask Alvin to tell me what he knew or what allegations he had heard, but he cursed at me for asking and refused to divulge information. He challenged me not to believe him and let Carl take his fall. If this were a course in salesmanship, Alvin would have graduated at the top of his class, save the cursing.

Alvin added that even if we killed him, the bad news about Carl would still get out. "Kill you?" I responded. "Now that's real paranoia."

Alvin asserted that if the members of TAC's Athletes Advisory Committee were presented with the right evidence, they'd "love to cut Carl's balls off." He added that this group would "love to see Carl take a big fall."

I told Alvin that I would let him have the last word.

At 7:00 the next morning, September 27, David got another call from Alvin.

Alvin wanted to clarify the last night's conversation. He told me that he had heard lots of things about Carl, but the information he had didn't rise to the level of proof. He told me he had been drinking last night.

That afternoon, Alvin called again. He apparently couldn't get enough of David.

Alvin averred that I was "courting disaster for myself and my clients."

I mentioned to Alvin that I had told Joe and Carl all about our conversations, and that they were quite offended. He acted as if he were surprised and told me that last night's call was "a loving phone call."

Alvin inevitably got back to the drug thing. He asked, "Do you think you'll escape the barracudas by yourself?" This time, when I asked for specifics, Alvin cited the Stern *article and the tidbits he said he got all the time from reporters who call him. He said he had nothing in his file himself. The barracudas would get Carl. We needed his help. . . . If I didn't realize this, he added, "Carl Lewis needs a new lawyer."*

No, I would stick with David. And I was sick of hearing about threats from Alvin and TAC.

"If those bastards think they're going to run me out of the sport, they're mistaken," I told David and Joe. "They've got three or four more years of me. I'll never give up my career or my fight against drugs. They're up against a fighter, not some lackey athlete who will do what they say."

Just when I thought the steroid issue would go away for a while, I heard that it was about to make headlines again. A week after my press conference to discuss the *Stern* article, Ben Johnson was coming to Washington to talk about steroids. A congressman from California, Mel Levine, had invited Ben to help introduce legislation that would place new restrictions on performance-enhancing drugs.

Levine wanted a federal law to classify steroids as controlled substances, like cocaine and other illegal, recreational drugs. That way, police and the courts could treat people who use and sell steroids the same way they treat regular drug criminals—harshly. And that's how they should be treated. Someone who distributes steroids could get twenty years in prison, and possession alone could lead to a year in prison. Levine's bill also called for programs to educate youngsters about the dangers of steroids.

The congressman's program sounded good to me, but why Ben? Why would Levine use Ben—an admitted drug-user and a Canadian—for publicity? That bothered me a little. There are plenty of clean athletes he could have used, and plenty of Americans. In fact, all Levine had to do was look in his own backyard. His congressional district includes Santa Monica.

But this was Levine's show. Obviously, he would do whatever he thought was best. So would I, and I thought I should go to the press conference. Not to crash the party, as some reporters would say, in their typical negative way. I had two reasons for wanting to go: First, I was right in the middle of writing this book, and I wanted to continue following the steroid issue, as I had been doing all year. I would have gone to see the introduction of a steroid bill with or without Ben being there. Second, I wanted the congressmen there to know that I supported their efforts. Half a year had passed since I testified before Congressman Stark's subcommittee, and I wanted to let Congress know I was still committed to helping in the fight against steroids.

The press conference was in a hearing room in the Rayburn House Office Building, the same place I had testified in March, and it was packed, reporters and photographers everywhere, just as Levine had planned. The only thing he hadn't planned was having me there. On the way into the building, a security guard asked me if I was Ben Johnson. I enjoyed that one.

The reporters went nuts when I arrived.

"What are you doing here?"

"I'm working on my book."

"No, really, Carl, what are you doing?"

"I'm writing my autobiography, and there's going to be a chapter on steroids."

The reporters didn't want to believe this. They wanted drama. They wanted to write about a showdown between Carl and Ben, about how this was the first time we had seen each other since the race in Seoul.

"Does Ben know you're coming?"

"I don't know. I don't think so."

"Are you going to talk to him?"

"I don't think so."

"What's your relationship with Ben like?"

"Off the track?"

"Yes."

"There is none."

By the time Levine arrived with Ben, walking through a door in the back of the hearing room, most of the reporters had settled back down in their seats. Levine must have been as surprised as Ben was when he spotted me, seated a few rows back near the middle of the room. Ben's attorney, Ed Futerman, was the first to notice me, I think. He kind of nodded, and I just looked at him. I took out my notebook and acted like the reporters, taking notes and looking through press releases that had been sitting on a table outside the hearing room.

Levine, a Democrat, started the press conference with a prepared statement, saying all the things a politician says, thanking this colleague and that colleague, defining a problem and offering his solution. He introduced a few guests—a man who represents bodybuilders, a doctor who had written about drugs and athletics, a high school football player—and waited until the end to introduce Ben. He said he was "very, very honored" to have Ben there.

When Levine was done, two other congressmen spoke, then each of the guests gave a statement. Everyone seemed kind of bored until it was Ben's turn. That's who all the reporters wanted to hear. As Levine said, all the television cameras wouldn't have been there if it weren't for Ben.

Ben had a little trouble getting started. He was very nervous, stuttering a few times, and I felt bad for him. So much was expected of him, and he didn't have a whole lot to offer.

"I got caught in Seoul, lost my gold medal, and I'm here to try to tell people in this country it's wrong to cheat, not to take it, and it's bad for your health," Ben said. He was still struggling, talking slowly and quietly. "I started taking steroids when I was nineteen years old because most of the world-class athletes were taking drugs."

That was what Ben had been saying for months, that for him to compete against the best athletes in the world, he had to use steroids. He had to use them because most of the other athletes were using them.

I don't buy that. I don't agree that most other athletes were using them, and I wish Ben would stop saying that. It's a worn-out excuse, and a bad one. People who choose to take drugs are choosing to cheat. It's as simple as that. You don't get away with taking cocaine by saying everyone else is taking it. You don't fool your body, don't reduce the health risks of steroids by saying everyone else is taking it.

But this was Ben's script. Once he was done with it, which took only a minute or two, Levine jumped in front of Ben. It was time to protect him. Only questions pertaining to the legislation, Levine said. There will be no questions about "detailed biographical material." In other words, be nice to my guest. You don't have a choice.

A few reporters still asked Ben questions that Levine didn't consider to be nice, and each time, Levine or Futerman jumped in before anything came out of Ben's mouth.

"We're not going to get into personal details," Levine said. He looked almost as uncomfortable as Ben. Levine must have been scared that I was going to blast him for having Ben there, or do something to make a scene, because right in the middle of all this, one of Levine's aides came over to me. He said that Levine had wanted me to speak at the press conference but didn't know how to reach me. I wasn't buying that for a second. Reaching me would have been as easy for Congressman Levine as it had been earlier in the year for Congressman Stark. People from all over the world reach me all the time.

The aide kept saying the congressman is sorry, and he hopes to work with you in the future. Of course, I said. This sounds like a great bill, great ideas, and I'll do anything I can to help. The aide went away happy. Actually, he was probably more relieved than happy. A few minutes later he was whispering to Levine, who was still standing at the podium, blocking Ben from reporters.

Then Ben was saved by the bell. A bell sounded, indicating that the congressmen had to leave for a vote. Levine said that they would return in a few minutes, and Ben was rushed off to a back room to wait for the congressmen.

That's when the reporters tried to make this into a crazy scene, a big confrontation between me and Ben. They circled me, probably about fifty of them, and tried to bait me into saying something bad about Ben. I didn't give them much, though, just praised the legislation and again said I was there to do research for the book. They were so frustrated.

Then a reporter tried to draw Futerman into a controversy.

"Do you feel like Carl tried to upstage you?"

"No, because we're just a guest here. The main event is the legislation."

Another reporter tried but also left without what he wanted.

"This country is a free country," Futerman said, "and Carl Lewis or anyone else has any right to be here."

When the congressmen returned, a few more questions were asked, Ben kept avoiding them and Levine kept protecting him, talking about how courageous it was of Ben to appear, what an honor it was to have him. "Now, if there are any questions pertaining to the legislation . . ."

Futerman deflected a question by saying that Ben had not read the legislation, as if that had anything to do with the questions reporters wanted to ask. "He hasn't read it, but he understands what it stands for, and what it stands for is stopping the spread of steroid use, illegal steroid use, in this country. That's why he's here."

On my way out of the building, another aide of Levine's stopped me. Would I mind waiting a minute to talk to the congressman in a back room? No, that would be fine. Before I got out of the hall, a photographer asked me if I would go back into the hearing room to pose for a picture with Ben. No, I wasn't going to do that. This was not a freak show, and I didn't have any reason to speak to Ben, so I didn't.

In the back room, Levine apologized to me, as his aide had. He said he knew that I competed for Santa Monica and that he had jogged in the area. He apologized again. But I'd like to meet with you soon, Carl. Maybe you would testify for our committee. We might have a hearing in California.

Yes, Congressman, anything I can do to help. Anything I can do to fight the problem of steroids.

We shook hands and left, and again I thought of Ben. I couldn't help but think about the way Ben had been used. Levine and the other congressmen were totally using him for publicity. For years, Ben had been used, pushed around by coaches, agents, people who wanted to ride him to the big time, and this was another example of it. Then again, Ben and Futerman were using the congressmen, too. They were doing what they could to rehabilitate Ben's image. I guess I shouldn't have been surprised.

A year had passed now since the 100-meter final in Seoul. I had gone through different ways of thinking about Ben. I had cussed him for taking drugs. I had tried to understand him. I had spoken for him and against him at different times, and I wasn't sure which way was best for the sport, for Ben, for me.

I don't know if I'll ever face Ben on the track again. But that's not what I focus on. Sometimes I find myself drifting back to Seoul, to the moments when I thought that Ben had gotten away with using steroids and that I had let down my Dad. But I catch myself, and then I start looking forward again. That's what my religious beliefs and sense of family are all about, looking forward. That's how I got past being the nonathlete in the family, the little loser. That's how I got past the reporters who wanted to crush me, the rumors that wanted to follow me. That's how I deal with the backward people who run our "amateur" sport. That's how I have made it through the roadblocks, by looking forward, and that's why I will always be comfortable with who I am.

NINETEEN

≡

Leroy Burrell and the World Records

By THE middle of 1990, with Ben Johnson's two-year suspension winding down, there was an overload of speculation about when and where Ben and I would race again. The so-called match race was still a year away. But promoters were already making some interesting offers. There was talk about a match race for millions in Las Vegas. One-on-one down the Strip, bright lights and gambling for all, a made-for-television gig with the glitz and hype of a heavyweight championship bout. But Joe Douglas and I quickly put an end to that. If Ben and I were going to race, we would do it as part of a track meet, not a circus. A high-profile 100 in a regular meet would be a plus for the sport; a sideshow in the streets of Vegas would not.

Some of the other offers—from Japan and Europe—made more sense. But then there was a new twist. Leroy Burrell, my teammate and training partner, went on a tear, winning everything in sight. In 1989, his first year on the international circuit, Leroy had been very impressive but a little inconsistent. His 9.94 had been the fastest 100 of the year, but he was not able to beat me head-to-head and never was able to snatch my number-one ranking. In 1990 Leroy wanted to do something about that, and while I took a little break from competition, he was unbeatable. I came back for the 1990 U.S. championships and won the 100, which surprised a lot of people, but that was without Leroy in the field. In need of a break from the 100, he had competed only in the long jump.

Without me around—I was busy promoting the first edition of this book—Leroy then went off and won all his races in Europe. All you could read or hear about was Leroy Burrell, the young star, the future of the sport. That was great for Leroy and the Santa Monica Track Club, and I was happy for both.

But I was not finished yet. Yes, I was twenty-nine years old, not exactly young for a sprinter. True, I had not run a really fast race since the 1988 Seoul Olympics. But I got a little tired of people writing me off. I was not ready to curl up in a retirement home. And I certainly was not going to roll over and play dead for the biggest competition of the year, the Goodwill Games in Seattle.

In addition to being training partners and teammates, Leroy and I were also close friends, just as Joe DeLoach and I had been before the 1988 Olympics. As a teenager in Lansdowne, Pennsylvania, Leroy had watched me on television in the 1984 Olympics, and he told friends that I was his idol. I later helped Coach Tellez recruit him to the University of Houston. After Leroy overcame a serious knee injury, I encouraged him to compete for Santa Monica, just as I had encouraged Joe. So, here we were again, another one of the young-sters trying to take away one of my titles. These guys show no respect!

The 100-meter showdown was the talk of Seattle, and it was great to see Leroy get so much attention. It was the biggest international meet of his young career, and, as always, I wanted to help him take another step toward stardom. Not that I wanted him to win. I wanted the victory for myself; second would be fine for my friend. More than anything, though, I wanted Leroy to enjoy himself, run a good race, and gain some valuable experience. His time to win the big races would come, but not now.

At the press conference a day before our race, Leroy was seated behind a placard that identified him as "Larry Burrell." Everywhere in the world, sports fans knew all about American Leroy Burrell, the new sprint sensation. But in his own country, he was "Larry" for a day. We were asked about the return of Ben Johnson, who would be eligible to compete in two months, on September 24, 1990. But we deflected those questions. When I was grilled on the supposed par-allel between a rivalry with Ben and a rivalry with Leroy, I said, "I don't really see the parallel, regardless of what might happen here.

To me, Ben hasn't run any races. I go to meets to find the best competition for me, and Leroy has the same feeling."

Some of the reporters went fishing for nasty comments they could use to build up a Carl/Leroy rivalry. But there would be no war of words between friends, and if the reporters wanted to create something like that, they would have to do it on their own, without our help. They would have to get used to that. The best they would get from Leroy was: "We're not competing against each other, but *with* each other. Maybe it's a better race because we like each other."

When it was finally time to race, Leroy achieved his first victory over me after five defeats. He did not start very well and fell behind the field, but he used the second half of the race to reel everyone in. He caught me with about fifteen meters to go, and, after that, it was all over. Leroy leaned for the tape and crossed the finish line with a time of 10.05 seconds. I was second in 10.08, and Mark Witherspoon, with a 10.17, made it a sweep not only for the U.S., but also for Santa Monica. Joe Douglas had the top three sprinters in the world—at least for the moment—and that was very exciting for all of us, especially Leroy, who was thrilled. Leroy had proven that he was for real, and, without saying a word about it, he had ended his short-lived identity crisis. We had seen the last of "Larry Burrell."

There would finally be more talk about Leroy than Ben. And that was the way it should have been all along.

Leroy continued rolling in early 1991. Ben was trying a comeback indoors, and he had a few good paydays, courtesy of promoters who wanted to cash in on Ben's notoriety. But his times were nothing special, and the promoters quickly lost interest. Meanwhile, Leroy got bigger and bigger. In a worldwide survey of forty-five sports editors for a sportsman of the year award, he was one of only two Americans in the top ten, placing third. Michael Jordan was number nine.

And that was before February 1991, when Leroy became the fastest indoor sprinter of all time, setting a new world record for 60 meters. He ran a 6.48 in Madrid, two-hundredths of a second faster than the previous record held by American Lee McRae. What a way to start the year. The world championships would not be until late August in Tokyo, but Leroy was already flying. And now there was an additional way to build up the Carl vs. Leroy rivalry. He held the world record indoors, I held it outdoors. But not for long.

On June 14, at the national championships in New York, Leroy shot out of the blocks and ran away with a new world record, 9.90, in the 100. After a terrible start, I had been able to gain a good bit of ground, probably running faster than I ever had, but not quite fast enough. It was a dramatic finish. We were in adjacent lanes, and, according to what I later heard, Leroy was less than a foot ahead of me down the stretch. In fact, when we hit the tape, nobody was quite sure who had won. But it was definitely Leroy's race. I was second in 9.93 seconds, as close as I could come to my old record, 9.92, without reaching it. A week earlier, Ben Johnson had run a 10.41, his best time since returning, but more than half a second slower than the new world record. In the 100, that is light years away.

"It's hard to explain how I feel," Leroy said. "I'm so overwhelmed by the whole thing. When you dream about setting a world record, you imagine feeling very happy, but that's not exactly what it is. There are so many emotions flowing through me right now that I just can't describe the feeling. I never thought it would feel this way. It's very humbling."

It had been my best race—by far—since the Seoul Olympics. That would give me a lot of confidence for the rest of the year. And if the record had to go, I was glad that it had gone to Leroy, a friend and a clean champion. Clean was very important to me. Plenty of talent and a lot of hard work, but no drugs. That night at dinner, I told Leroy we could not have planned anything better than what had happened. "I got my confidence back, you got the record," I said. "It's gonna be a great summer."

The next day did even more for my confidence. Or maybe it was my confidence that carried me through the next day. Either way, I ended up in an incredible long-jump battle with Mike Powell, who had worked hard to become a much more consistent jumper since winning the silver medal in Seoul. Mike had finished only an inch and a half behind me in the Goodwill Games. Now, before my last attempt in New York, he was ahead of me, and the stadium announcer was telling the crowd that my sixty-four-meet, ten-year winning streak was on the line. I didn't appreciate that, but maybe it was just what I needed to hear. There was no way I was going to let some announcer get the last word. I was going to win this thing. And I did, jumping 8.64 meters (or 28 feet, 4¼ inches), just one centimeter ahead of Mike's best jump. Mike still had one jump left, but he came up short, and I escaped with the national championship. Once again, I was the cat with nine lives. But I was not sure how many were left.

I had not spent a whole lot of time thinking about the long-jump streak, and at the end of the meet, answering a reporter's question, I said, "I don't think Mike thinks about it either."

"Yes, I do," Mike corrected me. "The streak is important to me. I'm looking for respect as the best long jumper in the world. I plan to beat him sometime this year. I took it to the sixth jump. He beat me, but by one centimeter. Next time, it could be different."

Regardless, the whole weekend had been very rewarding for me. I was about to turn thirty—as everyone kept reminding me—but I was still ticking, and felt like I was entering a whole new career. After the 1984 Olympics, I was supposed to be dead and gone, and I got to 1991 with people asking how I'd feel if I didn't qualify for the world championship team. Well, now I had made it in three events—the 100, the 4 × 100 relay and the long jump—and my training sessions were going better than ever.

There was still plenty of interest in a match between Ben Johnson and me, but now the importance of a showdown without Leroy in the field was being questioned. Some promoters went even further, saying we should forget about Ben altogether. He was running 10.4s. Why should they pay him big money to appear when they knew he did not have a chance to win? But it was too late for second-guessing. We had signed a contract with promoters in France, and the race would go on, July 1—my 30th birthday—in Lille, a French manufacturing town by the Belgian border. Leroy would be in the meet, but only running the 200, not the 100. He had made his schedule for the season long before breaking the record, and he wanted to stick with his plan. He would run a few 100s between the New York TAC meet and the Tokyo world championships, but Lille would not be one of them.

At the Stadium Nord, I prepared for the race with Ben the same way I get ready for any race, including the traditional good-luck handshakes before getting in the blocks. But when I extended my hand to Ben, he waved me off, still trying to play head games, as if that was going to make a difference. I went about my business, thinking about the mechanics of my start, staying focused, staying relaxed. This was not Seoul, and I was not going to be distracted.

I was in lane four, next to Ben, who was in five. We were close for about fifty meters, but then Ben could not keep up. Running clean, without steroids, he was without his usual burst out of the blocks and did not have the same strength for the second half of a race. He was not a factor. But Ben was not the only one out there. Dennis Mitchell ran away from all of us, winning in 10.09 seconds. I was second in 10.20, not a very good time, especially considering the kind of shape I was in. Ben was seventh and said he was satisfied with his 10.46, which was hard to believe. But at least we could now put the Carl-vs.-Ben stuff behind us and move on to more important issues.

Before the world championships, there was supposed to be one other race with Ben, August 5 in Sweden, and this time Leroy was also going to be in the 100. It would be my first race with Leroy since New York. But the promoters in Malmo lost interest in Ben. He would run in a "B" race with the second-teamers. Leroy won the real race in 10.06 seconds. After another bad start, I was second in 10.13, just beating Dennis Mitchell, who was third in 10.14.

In Monte Carlo, Ben ran first leg on a Canadian team that got drilled—a distant fourth place—while Mike Marsh, Floyd Heard, Leroy, and I set a world record—37.79 seconds—in the 4 × 100 relay. It was the first time I knew of that a club team, not a national team, had set the mark. Then in Zurich, an American team—the same Santa Monica runners except for Dennis Mitchell replacing Floyd—again lowered the world mark, this time to 37.67 seconds.

Leroy and I were now focusing on the world championships, August 24 through September 1 in Tokyo.

The morning of the 100-meter final, Sri Chinmoy called from New York to tell me that my father's soul would be with me for one of the biggest races of my life. It was such an uplifting conversation just hours before I would settle into the blocks. After the phone call, I got a fax from another friend, Sam Mings of Lay Witnesses for Christ, who wrote, "I know God is allowing your dad to rejoice in your success." Two messages within an hour, and both had focused on my father. This was not so unusual; I am often inspired by thoughts of my father. But the timing was a bit strange.

At the same time, in another hotel room down the hall, Leroy was also drawing energy from his father, Leroy Brown. Mr. Brown was in a hospital back in the United States, recovering from major heart surgery. For several days, Mr. Brown had been in the intensive care unit, and Leroy, so far away at a track meet, had been unable to speak with him. Now, for the first time since arriving in Tokyo, Leroy was able to reach his father by telephone. That meant so much to both of them.

There had been so much hype about Leroy and me challenging each other for the title of World's Fastest Human, so many words written and spoken about us competing to be world champion a year before the Barcelona Olympics. But now, as we prepared to leave for the stadium, we could do so with the proper perspective of what was truly important in our lives. Both of our mothers were with us in Tokyo to watch us compete, which was great. And both of our fathers would be there, too—not physically, but spiritually.

Leroy and I could be the best of friends without that hurting our performances. In fact, more than anything, our friendship had made us both better athletes. But some people still were not willing to accept that. In Tokyo, for example, an American television producer wanted to tape Leroy and me face to face, staring at each other like heavyweights before a title bout, as mean as we could look, preceding the 100. Leroy told him to forget it, and walked away before the guy had a chance to suggest the idea to me. Because of all the attention, people finally started to understand that Leroy and I were really friends. On top of everything else, we were even in business together. Along with six other members of the Santa Monica club, we had started a clothing company. And when we travel, which seems like always, we spend a lot of time together.

Leroy always stops by my hotel room to slice up apples and carrots and all sorts of stuff to put through a food processor. We make some pretty wild juice combinations. Or we're in his room, chasing down one of his CDs to play on a portable stereo system. We leave the hotel to go shopping, or in search of a good sushi bar. We visit with Joe Douglas or David Greifinger, our club lawyer, to talk business. We play Monopoly with other members of the club, and the games get hilarious, with Joe playing all the angles, and creating new ones, the same way he does when he's negotiating with meet promoters. Basically, we do whatever we can to make long road trips bearable, and to be ready when it is time to compete.

Of course, there are times I like to be with Leroy, having fun, and there are times I'm off on my own. The hour before the 100-meter final in Tokyo was one of those times to be on my own. At the warm-up track, we went our separate ways.

In the past, at the Olympics and world championships, I have felt I ran better in the semifinals than in the finals, even if the times didn't always show it. This time I wanted to do everything possible to make the final my best race, because I felt strongly that a world record would be set. Someone was going to do it, and I wanted that someone to be me.

At the track, Leroy and I were separated by a lane; he was in three, I was in five, with Linford Christie of Great Britain between us. Out of the starting blocks, I felt pretty good, even though I was behind just about everybody. Dennis Mitchell got the start of his life, and Leroy got a good one. But what mattered most to me was that, technically, I had a good start. I was up and driving better than I had been doing most of the summer. Still, everybody else was flying. I'd bet four people broke the world record for fifty meters. I felt great at sixty, and I was still about fifth. I knew I had a shot at winning, but I would really have to come on. At eighty meters, I had a great shot. With ten meters left, I had cleared everyone but Leroy—and he was in trouble. He had used up most of his energy to get where he was, and was probably pressing a little too hard. With five meters left, the race was mine. Leroy would soon be telling people I had passed him and the others "like we were standing still."

But that was definitely not the case. When I turned to look at the stadium scoreboard, the first thing I saw was my time, a new world record, 9.86 seconds. And that blew me away. I was overwhelmed. Then I saw the other times. 9.88 for Leroy, 9.91 for Dennis Mitchell—an American sweep. And the other times were equally amazing. It is hard to believe that Christie could run a 9.92—a new European record for the 100—and not even get a medal. And what about six guys running under 10 seconds in the same race? Unbelievable. Easily the greatest race of all time.

But taking my victory lap, none of that was on my mind. I was hit again with thoughts about my father, and filled with incredible joy for my entire family, my coaches, teammates, and friends. Never before have I been so overcome by the importance of the people closest to me and the strength I am able to draw from them. It would have been impossible to hide my emotions. I cried. And several times before the night was out, I cried again.

This was already one of the most emotional meets ever for me, and the long jump and the 4 × 100 relay remained. The biggest challenge of all would be putting the joy of the 100 behind me and moving forward, staying focused.

Mike Powell could not forget what had happened in New York, seeing his victory slip away on my last jump, and he was definitely ready to go at me in Tokyo. Twenty-three years after Bob Beamon's record-setting jump of 29 feet, 2½ inches, everybody was still waiting for me to break the longest-standing world mark in the sport. But Mike had some ideas of his own. He was tired of hearing about my chances of breaking the record. He wanted to do it himself. And he was sick of my winning streak. He wanted finally to put an end to that.

Mike was so pumped up for the competition, he started hyperventilating before his first jump, and actually felt faint. He jumped less than 26 feet. On my first jump, I broke the meet record, going 28 feet, 5¾ inches, and I felt I could go farther. If Mike—or anyone else—was going to beat me, he would need to do something spectacular. Mike was much better on his second jump, just passing 28 feet, and his confidence was building. But my third jump had to jolt him a little. It was 28 feet, 11¾ inches, the longest of my career. It was wind-aided, but so what? It counted just the same, and to beat it, Mike would have to go 29 feet. Next jump, I made his task even more difficult, going 29 feet, 2¾ inches, better than Beamon, but again wind-aided. It would not count as a world record, but I certainly thought it would win the world championship. And I still had two jumps left. I felt like I could go 29 feet and beyond even without the wind. Resting between jumps, I started thinking about the possibility of this being my last long-jump competition. I couldn't help but think about setting the world record, then walking off into the sunset, announcing right after we were done that I would jump no more. What a thought. No more painful landings in the pit. No more backaches the next day. No more questions about the streak. Just happy memories, and total concentration on the sprints, maybe even a return to the 200.

But these thoughts did not last long. On his fifth jump, Mike hit the board hard, and landed in the sand 29 feet, 4½ inches away. It was a legal jump—better than my wind-aided mark, better than Beamon's leap at high-altitude—and Mike started dancing. He had achieved the dream of a lifetime. But it was not over. The momentum had definitely shifted, but I had two more tries. My fifth jump was 29 feet, 1¼ inches, the best legal jump of my career—and it was *against* the wind. So close, yet so frustrating that the wind had turned on me.

While I prepared for my last jump, Mike folded his hands in prayer. He could not handle seeing another last-jump defeat as had happened in New York. I went 29 feet, which had long been my goal, but now it was not enough. Three 29-footers in a meet, the best series of my career, but not enough. The streak was over. Mike was the new world champion, the new world-record holder, and he deserved it. Now, I would have to keep jumping. With the 29-foot mark a thing of the past, I would have to start thinking about 9 meters, which is 29 feet, 6½ inches. I accepted the fact that there would be plenty more backaches, and I starting looking forward to another shot at the long-jump gold, hopefully at the 1992 Olympics.

There was one more world record to come. In the 4×100 relay on the last night of the Tokyo meet, Andre Cason, Dennis Mitchell, Leroy, and I ran 37.50, improving on what we had run the month before. That was the clincher. It had to have been the best meet of my career, better than the 1984 Olympics.

Everybody kept reminding me that I was thirty years old and my career was supposed to be winding down, but it was definitely not time for the old man to give up. One night at the stadium in Toyko, one of the meet officials told me, "Save some for '96 in Atlanta," a reference to the Olympics four years after Barcelona. "No," Leroy said, cracking a smile, "Retire. Retire." We had a good laugh together. For me, there will be no Atlanta in '96. Maybe as a fan, not as a competitor. But there are still plenty of big events to come, and none will be bigger than the 1992 Olympics in Barcelona.

INDEX

241